THOSE WHO CAME BEFORE

To the Superintendents of National Park Service installations in the Southwest, who diligently carry out the dictate to protect, preserve, and interpret their cultural resources for the understanding and enjoyment of the public.

SOUTHWESTERN ARCHEOLOGY IN THE NATIONAL PARK SYSTEM

THOSE WHO CAME BEFORE

SECOND EDITION

Robert H. Lister and Florence C. Lister

Foreword by Emil W. Haury

*Featuring photographs from the George A. Grant Collection
and a portfolio by David Muench*

THE UNIVERSITY OF NEW MEXICO PRESS
Albuquerque, New Mexico

SOUTHWEST PARKS & MONUMENTS ASSOCIATION
Tucson, Arizona

Editorial: T. J. Priehs, Sandra Scott
Design: Christina Watkins
Lithographed by Lorraine Press; vegetable ink on acid-free, recycled paper
Photography from the George Grant Collection courtesy
of the National Park Service

The Preservation of Our Cultural Heritage

Each year hundreds of archeological sites in the Southwest are vandalized to the detriment of our cultural heritage; to the detriment of what we might still learn. All prehistoric artifacts are irreplaceable and protected by Federal law. It is also important to understand that potsherds, arrowpoints and other artifacts can only add to our understanding of the past if left completely undisturbed in their original context.

If you discover artifacts, leave them in place and notify National Park Service personnel.

Cover photograph: White House Ruin, Canyon de Chelly National Monument.
DAVID MUENCH.

CONTENTS

Betatakin, Navajo National Monument. GEORGE A. GRANT, NATIONAL PARK SERVICE, 1935.

ILLUSTRATIONS

FOREWORD

The arid American Southwest rightfully boasts of more natural and man-made attractions than any comparable part of the New World. High among its many wondrous features is the treasury of ruins, mute testimony that many people before us found a bountiful haven in the land's embraces.

The spirits lingering in the abandoned hunting camps, and in the villages and towns of the more developed agricultural people, have an eloquence of their own—if we will only listen. How does one recapture the excitement permeating a hunting band that had just succeeded in bringing a mammoth to earth eleven thousand years ago, a feat accomplished with stone-tipped spears and the cunning and bravery of the hunters? That success could only be followed by gorging a hungry gut as long as the protein lasted and by giving thanks to the spirit of the animal whose life had been sacrificed. What of the ceremonied and joyful celebrations at summer's end among town dwellers giving thanks to the ruling spirits for a bountiful harvest and the assurance that hunger will be stayed through the winter? Who those people were, when they were here, and the kinds of lives they led are questions for the archeologist to decipher.

The value of these traces of the past as a part of our national heritage was recognized almost as early as were the incomparable natural wonders of Yellowstone's thermal displays and the glacially sculptured landscape of Yosemite, the former set aside as the world's first national park in 1872, and the latter in 1880. Casa Grande—the Big House—a four-story adobe building erected in the fourteenth century and today rising starkly above the desert brush, was first set aside in 1889, and the notable cliff dwellings of Mesa Verde were brought into the federal system in 1906. That year also saw the passage of the Federal Antiquities Act signaling the concern of Congress for the nation's archeological riches. Soon after, other units were chosen for protection. As a result of these actions, the Southwest boasts more archeological national parks and monuments than the rest of the country. In addition, each of the places set aside for its natural wonders, such as Grand Canyon National Park, has its own wealth of ruins and a human story to tell.

Collectively these places are silent reminders of how Native Americans developed from camp to village to town dwellers, how the arid lands were tamed and made to produce by applying various irrigation and ingenious water-control techniques. Those were largely inspired by the possession of maize, a precious grain that truly "built a hemisphere." All of this spanned many millennia. In the sixteenth century came the *conquistadores* who opened to the western world what had been until then the isolated homeland of the American Indian.

This saga, magnificently preserved in a great variety of ruins, has captivated the popular and the scientific mind for a hundred years. It has been told and retold in fragments and, all too often, in the bewildering and technical prose of the archeologist deemed essential to satisfy the critical eyes of peers.

I have long contended that unless professional archeologists are willing to share the excitement of their findings popularly, they are not fulfilling their potential as discoverers of new truths. The rewards of doing that—or not doing that—are reflected by the often unreceptive or even antagonistic attitudes expressed by laymen or by elected officials. This broader responsibility of the investigator was admirably expressed by nineteenth-century naturalist Elliot Coues (*Elliot Coues: Naturalist and Frontier Historian* by Paul Russell Cutright and Michael Broadhead) when he stated that the popularizer is ". . . an office of not less dignity than that of the systematist or the monographer . . . and one not so easy to fill creditably as those who have never tried to do so might imagine. The increase in knowledge is one thing, and its diffusion another; but the latter is the real measure of the usefulness of the former."

Sensing the need for a book broadly covering the story of Southwest archeology, the Southwest Parks and Monuments Association approached Robert and Florence Lister. One has difficulty imagining a more eminently qualified team to undertake this work. Dr. Robert H. Lister held some of the most prestigious positions in Southwest archeology, including chairman of the Department of Anthropology at the University of Colorado, director of the Archaeological Research Center at Mesa Verde National Park, participant in the University of Utah Glen Canyon Archeological Project, and president of the Society for American Archaeology. His tenures as chief archeologist for the National Park Service and director of the Chaco Center speak to his qualifications for addressing our cultural heritage as preserved in the national parks.

Florence C. Lister has been involved in extensive ceramic research in the Southwest and North Africa, but most recently has specialized in Spanish colonial period maiolica pottery.

Their joint contribution is impressive not only because it has greatly increased our scientific knowledge, but also because they have accepted the responsibility of making that knowledge available to a wide audience. Books such as *Chaco Canyon: Archaeology* and *Archaeologists and Earl Morris & Southwestern Archaeology*, along with this volume, recognize that commitment.

This broad experience has allowed them to expand on the traditional approach of discussing the differences between southwestern prehistoric cultures. Rather, the emphasis is on the similarities of these traditions, on how they interacted and influenced each other. This "pan-southwest interpretation" invites a holistic view of the story.

The old houses and the lands they were built on, the pots and pans, and the myriad tools used by prehistoric peoples are the grist the archeologist must start with in restructuring the life of past societies. Little wonder that the material side of cultures, the artifacts, receive so much attention. They are, after all, the tangible measures of levels of achievements and the substance for working out chronologies and relationships with neighbors. But translating the hardware of culture to the essence of life, the economic, political, and social natures of people, has always confronted the archeologist with a need which has been met with varying degrees of success. I think it is fair to say that this book goes a long way toward breathing life into the dusty record of the past.

It is fitting that this book should address those priceless ruins now protected and interpreted by the National Park Service, steward of the most impressive archeological resources in the Southwest. Lest the reader gain the idea that the inventory of places mentioned encompasses most of the Southwest's ruins, it should be said that for every major site under National Park Service protection, many others exist that are worthy of that care as well. And hundreds more large and significant sites merit state, county, and city protection. Surprisingly, beyond those, there are thousands of vestiges of human activity that together echo the rich, long story of the past here.

It is little wonder then that the Southwest for so long has attracted the world's attention and has become the proving ground for budding archeologists. It was the most fertile and accessible place to go. Whether hired as shovel hands in early expeditions or later as students in numerous university-sponsored field schools, people who have trained here and gone on to gain professional prominence comprise a long list. Their contributions and those of others is the story the Listers have excerpted and condensed for us. It is a story of those who came before, seeking knowledge about man's relationship to this awesome landscape.

This volume is evidence of Bob and Florence Lister's skills in bringing the people and places of the past alive. They favor us by having made a profession of archeology and, in their own way, by making an art out of their profession.

Emil W. Haury, 1904–1992
November 1982

Hohokam pottery plate, Colonial Period. HELGA TEIWES, ARIZONA STATE MUSEUM, UNIVERSITY OF ARIZONA.

PREFACE

Thousands of clues of ancient human activity in the southwestern United States have survived to the present because of a combination of factors. Often left in localities uninviting to modern development, covered deeply by soil and rocks, and residing in a dry climate, the remains have had nature itself as a prime preserver. Also, since President Theodore Roosevelt's administration, credit for the preservation of many of these unique areas goes to a farsighted federal government. Since 1916 the National Park Service has been given this specific responsibility.

Thirty-seven existing or proposed federal areas in Arizona, New Mexico, Utah, and Colorado were devoted to various facets of the archeological record. Where necessary, stabilization programs and continuous maintenance have halted further collapse of the ruins. In addition to making these resources more accessible, continued research has been encouraged in many government parks and monuments to assure an accurate, complete interpretive background for visitors.

Equally, or in some instances more important in documenting the annals of man in prehistoric and early historic times, are the thousands of ruins not included within the national parks. Most of these have been reconnoitered, some have been excavated, and findings from them are as significant as those made within federal preserves. Fortunately, some of the more valuable of these have come under the care and protection of state and local entities and may be examined by the public. This account, however, focuses upon the National Park areas because in them most facets of southwestern archeology are represented in readily accessible localities complete with interpretive personnel, explanatory visitor-center exhibits, and facilities to further the enjoyment and education of hundreds of thousands of people who annually visit the parks.

Circumstances arising from the nature of the archeological remains and their state of preservation, their suitability for exhibition to the public, and events related to their discovery, investigation, and inclusion in the national park system have resulted in an uneven representation of the total spectrum of southwestern prehistory in the parks and monuments. Twenty areas on the Colorado Plateau feature ruins of the Anasazi. Remains of the Hohokam of the Arizona deserts are present in three monuments. Fremont antiquities are found primarily in six facilities. Mogollon materials may be seen in only three facilities in the mountainous region along the south-central Arizona–New Mexico border. Blendings of several cultures are included in twelve installations. A few areas display ruins of two or more cultural developments. Known Paleo-Indian remains are in or near two monuments.

This book is a review of southwestern prehistory, as it is interpreted by archeologists, and a correlation of the regionally designated cultural variants into an interrelated whole. The latter emphasizes the similarities and affinity of all ancient southwestern peoples, shows their dependence upon advanced cultures in Mesoamerica for many basic ingredients, and notes environmentally conditioned regional differences. The account focuses on historical events leading to the exploration, excavation, and interpretation of the antiquities of the public areas. Highlighted are their significance in prehistoric cultural achievement and their particular contributions to a rich panorama of life still partially observable among the modern Tohono O'odham, Mohave, Maricopa, Yavapai, Hualapai, Havasupai, and Pueblo Indians of Arizona and New Mexico. Relations are noted between these southwestern old-timers and the Navajo and Apache newcomers.

In gathering the data for this presentation we have relied upon firsthand knowledge of the Southwest and each of the areas considered. Also, we have drawn upon the works of many scholars who have contributed to our understanding of the archeology of the greater Southwest and particularly their reports upon investigations in National Park Service areas. To those individuals we owe a great deal and acknowledge to them our gratitude and sincere appreciation.

For our brief review of southwestern archeology and our formulation of an integrated scheme of the events of prehistory, we have basically followed the terminology and cultural sequences employed in the Southwest volume of the *Handbook of North American Indians* published by the Smithsonian Institution.

Many of our former associates in the National Park Service made our task easier and enjoyable. The regional directors of the Southwest, Western, and Rocky Mountain regions, and the general superintendents of the Navajo Lands and Southern Arizona groups facilitated our visits to the parks, and members of their staffs assisted us in many ways. We profited from discussions with many Park superintendents and their interpretive personnel. Especially helpful in providing information, unpublished data, or logistical support were Adrienne Anderson, regional archeologist, Rocky Mountain Region; Bruce Anderson, archeologist, Southwest Region; Superintendent Robert Heyder and Archeologist Jack Smith of Mesa Verde National Park; James Truesdale, archeologist, Dinosaur National Monument; Matthew Schmader, archeologist, Rio Grande Consultants; and Archeologists Keith Anderson, George Cattanach, Don Morris, Trinkle Jones, and Adrianne G. Rankin of the Western Archeological and Conservation Center. To all of the above we express our thanks.

Finally, we acknowledge that the concept of this volume was conceived by Earl Jackson, former executive director of the Southwest Parks and Monuments Association, who encouraged us to undertake its preparation. His successor, T. J. Priehs, has provided us stimulation, advice, and constructive criticism throughout our writing, and his staff and consultants have furnished secretarial and editorial assistance and designed the book. The Board of Directors of Southwest Parks and Monuments Association made the book a reality by approving its publication.

The suggested readings following each national park area discussed in no way reflect the many items consulted by the authors but are a list of some accessible works to which inquiring readers may turn for additional discussions and more detailed accounts.

My late husband and senior author of the original text of this book felt a revision was in order because of further research, the addition to the National Park Service system of southwestern monuments containing archeological resources, and the need to include additional facilities in order to expand the prehistoric story. An ardent supporter of the park service goals of preserving, protecting, and interpreting antiquities on federal lands for the benefit of the American public, Robert H. Lister was an occasional member of the team as an employee, collaborator, or advisor. He joined the National Park Service ranks as a ranger-archeologist just out of college in 1938 and retired forty years later after having served as chief archeologist. During that time, he personally was involved with work in seven of the monuments included in this book, in several instances for many years. He was especially proud of receiving the Emil W. Haury Award by Southwest Parks and Monuments Association, given in recognition of his contributions to scientific research in the national parks and monuments of the Southwest.

My efforts to meet Bob's desire for this revision are a small tribute to his enthusiasm, energy, and insight.

To Robert H. Lister, 1915–1990

Florence C. Lister
Mancos, Colorado
October 1992

Robert Lister in the field at Chaco Culture National Historical Park, New Mexico, 1972.

THE SETTING

The American Southwest incorporates notable extremes in contour, climate, and natural resources that have led to its division into four main geographical entities. The Southwest's variable geography inevitably placed limits on human use of each area which necessitated different cultural adaptations.

The northernmost province, the southern Rocky Mountains of central Colorado and north-central New Mexico, was of least importance to the southwestern Indians because of long, frigid winters and lack of arable soil. Only occasional hunting parties roamed through the region in search of game.

South of the Rockies is the Colorado Plateau, encompassing western Colorado, southeast Utah, northern Arizona, and northwest New Mexico. In its lower elevations it is a formidable, though beautiful, landscape of canyons sliced deeply through colorful sandstone, flat mesas rising abruptly above broad valleys, little fertile soil, and only one perennial river system—the Colorado and its northern tributaries. There are cool, moist mountains with pine and fir forests, and uplands with mixed stands of juniper and pinyon. Patches of grass and scrub brush dot the lower mesas. Most of the province has a long, dry, warm summer broken by localized thunderstorms that tear at the thin soil. Winters are cold with considerable snow. Even with so many apparent drawbacks, the Plateau offered a suitable habitat for a dense, aboriginal farming population. In some parts of the region these folk adapted and survived in greater numbers than anywhere else in the Southwest. In others, thoughtless destruction of timber and other resources caused disastrous erosion, stream entrenchment, and their own ultimate downfall.

The Basin and Range province within the United States includes southern Arizona and New Mexico. Here are basins interrupted by steep, jagged mountains of igneous and metamorphic rocks whose higher reaches are temperate and forested. Most streams are intermittent, but the Rio Grande usually flows year-round. The Gila and Salt and some of their tributaries were permanent rivers in the past. Interior drainage basins are common. The extensive desert lands have protracted, withering summers, though punctuated by violent downpours. These slowly yield to mild winters with little rain. Thorny shrubs, cacti, and drought-resistant trees, such as mesquite, are abundant. Surprisingly, man learned to cope with this hostile environment so successfully that he stayed in impressive numbers for centuries.

The southwestern corner of the High Plains province penetrates into eastern New Mexico and west Texas and is bisected by the Pecos River valley. Its broad grasslands once attracted herds of large mammals which, in turn, brought ancient hunters. When the animals disappeared, the hunters left the High Plains, and the region became a buffer zone between the farmers of the Colorado Plateau and the nomads and later villagers of the Plains.

Extremely significant to the prehistoric cultural development of the American Southwest was northern Mexico. The Sierra Madre Occidental, rising from the central

Mexican plateau and the narrow littoral along the Sea of Cortez, includes some of the most rugged terrain in North America. Though potentially a barrier, it has natural north-south corridors through which repeated cultural impulses were transmitted from Mesoamerica north to the distant borderland societies. Had the topography in this intermediate area between central Mexico and the American Southwest been different, cultural attainments of the northerners would surely have been fewer.

THE PREHISTORY

The Paleo-Indian Period

Between about 9500 and 9000 B.C. the Southwest experienced slightly greater moisture and lower temperatures than at present. These environmental factors favored the spread of lush grasslands, which attracted herds of large grazing animals such as mammoths, camels, horses, and bison. In turn, they lured Paleo-Indian hunters, who apparently drifted westward from the mid-continent prairies. Because they roamed over terrain that is now eastern New Mexico, these first southwestern big-game hunters have been named Clovis, after remains found near the town of Clovis.

Clovis culture appeared during a brief time when the mammoth, an extinct elephant, was the preferred prey of the Paleo-Indian. Consistently in archeological finds the remains of one or more mammoths are associated with a group of implements that invariably includes a characteristic fluted point and several kinds of knives fashioned from flakes of stone. The long, leaf-shaped Clovis points, with rudimentary flakes struck from their sides, once tipped spears that were used in dispatching the huge beasts. The knives were then used to butcher them. The inequalities in size and strength between the men and their quarry were partially compensated for by use of a notched throwing stick, known as an atlatl, that provided extra leverage in propelling the spear. Sites yielding Clovis artifacts reveal additional human ingenuity. Generally, they are on formerly boggy pond or lake shores or stream banks where a heavy animal would have been inescapably mired. Skinning the animal, dismembering the carcass, and cutting the flesh from the bones took place at the kill spot. After disposing of the meat, the Clovis drifted on to encounters with other game. Apparently, they gradually established themselves in certain territories to which they returned seasonally year after year. Other than their basic quest for food, their tools, and a presumed informal small band organization, nothing is known about the Clovis people. By approximately 8500 B.C. unfavorable environmental conditions in the western Southwest had doomed the grazing animals, except the bison. Consequently, their pursuers slowly retreated eastward to happier hunting grounds.

As the scope of Pleistocene research widens, it is possible that a pre-Clovis complex of Paleo-Indian hunters may be identified. If so, the arrival of humans in the Southwest will be pushed back thousands of years. A number of suggestive finds of this sort have been made, such as one in a cave near El Paso, Texas. Thus far, lingering questions about stratigraphy, artifact associations, and dating have made cautious researchers slow to accept their authenticity.

Clovis hunters were succeeded by others following the same general mobile life, stalking the surviving bison. These now are identified as Folsom because in 1926 a site near Folsom, New Mexico, was found to have their distinctive fluted points and other stone tools in direct association with bones of bison that had become extinct some time between about 6000 and 5000 B.C. Subsequently, Folsom hunters appear to have specialized

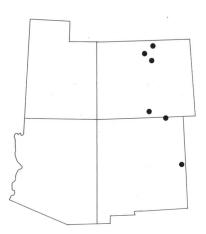

Paleo-Indian sites

in maiming or dispatching the bison in cul-de-sacs or stampeding them over precipices.

After Folsom times, the final era of Paleo-Indian hunters on the southwestern plains is marked by a limited initial occupation by a group called Cody, which substantially expanded in New Mexico and southern Colorado between 6500 and 6000 B.C. Perhaps this was because herds of buffalo and those who hunted them had moved back into the area from the eastern plains in response to a temporary increase in moisture. Most diagnostic of the Cody tools were finely chipped, parallel-edged or lanceolate points. Frequently these had an indented stem.

Triangular knives usually stemmed on one side occur along with other large stone knives, choppers, scrapers, hammerstones, drills, engraving tools, grooved abrading stones, and antler flaking implements. Cody sites usually were located near water and land suitable for the grazing bison. Three kinds of areas have been identified: base camps, where one or more bands gathered periodically; work areas, where groups of hunters apparently flaked projectile points while waiting for game; and processing stations, where slain animals were butchered and hides were processed. The diversity of sites and even greater variety of tools suggest technological advancements to meet the needs of more specialized activities.

The Archaic Period

Beginning about 7000 B.C., perhaps earlier, foraging people that archeologists call Archaic filtered into the Southwest from the west, north, and south to occupy territories abandoned by the hunters. They first appeared in western Arizona and gradually drifted eastward. Although in some areas the foragers and hunters may have been contemporaneous, no evidence exists at present for any direct relationship between them.

The new arrivals exploited such a wide variety of local resources that they were able to utilize regions ranging from broken canyonlands to deserts that had been unimportant to the Paleo-Indians. Although they moved with the seasons to take full advantage of water and certain foods, in some cases the Archaic people sustained themselves long enough in one locality to erect rudimentary shelters. At first these were merely stone-walled "sleeping circles" in work camps. Later, huts or windbreaks may have been erected, and are suggested by shallow circular depressions outlined with postholes. Storage pits for excess foods and cooking pits with fire-cracked rocks occur at a few late Archaic locations.

While stone projectile points had to be continuously manufactured to take small game, fiber snares and nets served to capture birds and rodents. Most important to Archaic survival, however, was an emphasis on simple stone chopping, scraping, cutting, and milling implements used to process fibers, roots, tubers, and seeds. As time passed, the inventory of material goods expanded to include stone, bone, shell, baskets, textiles, cords, and sandals.

The first identified complex of Archaic traits in the Southwest was termed the Cochise by archeologists because of its concentration in and about Cochise County in southeastern Arizona. Its earliest occurrence seems to have centered there, but later

Clovis and Folsom points. TOM MASAMORI, COURTESY OF THE COLORADO HISTORICAL SOCIETY.

followers of this long-lived tradition spread as far afield as northeast Arizona and the Glen Canyon area of the Colorado River, central New Mexico, and southern Chihuahua. Recently, a distinct Archaic pattern called the Oshara has been recognized in parts of the northern Southwest. Still farther north and toward the Great Basin the Archaic horizon is identified as the Desert Culture.

So successful was their adjustment to the varied and often inhospitable environment that the Archaic population swelled over the centuries until hundreds of sites were littered extensively with debris from long occupation. The similarity of cultural remains from different parts of the Southwest testifies to some sort of social intercourse between Archaic bands, likely composed of small groups of related individuals.

Thus, with these beginning steps, by about 2000 B.C. the cultural complexity that was to underlie later developments in the Southwest essentially had been achieved.

Agricultural Beginnings

In the Southwest excavated archeological sites dating between 2000 B.C. and A.D. 500 are spread from northern Chihuahua, Mexico, to southern Colorado and Utah. The small, widely dispersed family groups of nomadic hunters and gatherers were, almost imperceptibly, undergoing a significant modification to an infinitely more complex, sedentary village existence. Such fundamental re-orientation was made possible by the slow diffusing of agriculture, social attitudes, and certain technologies from Mexico. Of these, agriculture was of the most immediate consequence.

The plant that was to become a staple was corn. Corn, or maize, is believed to have evolved from teosinte, a wild grass found in many parts of Mexico. Tiny cobs of an early variety of corn dated approximately 5000 B.C. have been unearthed from dry caves in the Tehuacán valley of central Mexico. But another fifteen hundred years passed before this corn was being purposefully cultivated there. By that time squash, beans, gourds, chili peppers, avocados, and amaranth were to be found in gardens. Through steadily improved growing methods, selective planting, and cross breeding, larger, more nutritional corn was grown at Tehuacán by 1500 B.C. It probably grew in similar, as yet unstudied, ecological pockets tucked away in Mexico's highlands. Corn's importance soon was so great that a mystical regard for its life-sustaining properties made it an object of worship.

Even before improvement of the strain, the vital plant and knowledge of its propagation gradually passed from tribe to tribe up the Mexican northern cordillera into the Southwest. Squash seems to have spread to the north along with early corn. Beans, the third of the domesticated plants that were to become the foundation of southwestern Indian agriculture, did not appear there for many centuries.

Although primitive corn and squash may have reached some parts of the Southwest as early as late Archaic times, they did not appear in any important quantities until after 2000 B.C. Even then and for the next fifteen hundred years, when Mexican cultures began to flourish, these humble domesticated plants had little impact. The possibilities of agriculture were lost upon foragers still in tune with Archaic ways. The introduced plants were casually grown in irregular patches, given little attention while the group engaged in summer hunting and gathering activities; in autumn they were harvested like native crops. Their survival and naturalization were minor miracles. Yields from stunted plants must have been minimal, variable from year to year, and surely insufficient for surplus. As years, even centuries, progressed, the basic diet of wild products remained unaltered though occasionally supplemented by small quantities of homegrown corn, squash, and beans. Nevertheless, the notion of planting and reaping nature's bounty became a fixed, though unexploited, aspect of regional life. Tending the crops would surely follow as agriculture eventually came into its own.

The soil-based revolution occurred in the Southwest after 500 B.C. And revolution it was, because a new cultural intricacy had arrived through converging influences from Mesoamerica, the Great Basin, the California coast, and the Plains. Increased dependence upon agriculture entailed more permanent residences. Pole, brush, and mud habitations soon nestled, partially concealed, in the earth. Communities of such structures arose for distinct purposes such as working, worshipping, sleeping, and hoarding. All the inherent social controls that came with such togetherness were instituted. Leisure time that could be devoted to tasks unrelated to food production or preparation promoted the adoption and perfection of new technologies. Some offered opportunity for aesthetic expression. Pottery making was one of these. Hunting was done by the bow and arrow, which replaced the cumbersome atlatl and spear. There was a heightened appreciation for cooperative, organized labor to increase chances of success. The overriding power of supernatural forces, which seemingly determined the fate of a farmer's crop, was magnified and dramatized. Tomorrow became equally important as today, as times of fallow fields, inclement weather, or natural disaster required stockpiled surpluses. The population expanded or diminished in direct relation to the size of such stores.

What caused the shift from exploitation of environmental diversity to the concentration on a few crop plants? One reason could have been Mexican colonists who had made the transition to village-dwelling irrigation farming farther to the south and had attained an elaborate material and social life. They may have pushed into the Gila and Salt river valleys, absorbing or replacing the local Archaic peoples and influencing others beyond their occupied territory. The hunter-gatherers could have been more gradually transformed by adaptation of southern domestic plants to local environments. Continued introduction of more nutritious strains of corn would have encouraged their greater use. Also, expanding population or a period of deteriorating climate could have pushed some groups into places with such limited wild resources that farming was the only alternative. Whatever the cause, or combination of causes, by A.D. 500 the distinctive Southwest Tradition had emerged in rudimentary form.

The Southwest Tradition

A century of research in what is now regarded as the Southwest Tradition has involved surface examination of thousands of ruins and excavation of hundreds. Material and human residue have been painstakingly identified, diagnosed, measured, compared, and subjected to innumerable physical tests. Living native peoples have been consulted to learn answers about probable social, economic, and religious attributes of their possible ancestors. From all this effort has come the realization that the ancient cultures which arose in the Southwest slightly before or at the beginning of the Christian Era were as varied as their physical settings, even though they shared common Archaic roots. However, the recognition of such dissimilarity and the varying degree of Mexican stimulus partly responsible for it was slow in coming.

Because of their proximity to regions where the earliest, most intense Spanish, Mexican, and American penetration occurred, the large abandoned structures slowly crumbling on the crests and in the faces of the northern mesas were, predictably, the first focus of major archeological interest. The San Juan drainage is the lodestone, and it has thus followed that, for many years, southwestern prehistory was thought to be exclusively the ancient history of Pueblo Indians who lived there. As late as 1927, when a master taxonomic chronology known as the Pecos Classification was accepted by all researchers working in the area, it was rationalized that, despite some puzzling regional differences, what had happened in the northern half of the Southwest also had taken place in the south. To most scholars of the time, ancient southwesterners were ancestral Pueblo Indians regardless of whether they had lived their lives amid the cacti or the pinyons. According to the nomenclature adopted by archeologists meeting at Pecos, New Mexico, in 1927, one could be part of culture stages Basket Maker I through III or Pueblo I through V, depending upon time of existence and level of cultural attainment. Later, one was simply called Anasazi rather than Basket Maker or Pueblo. To the Navajos, the Anasazi were the Old People who had preceded them into the nooks and crannies of the Four Corners region.

Physiographic features divide the Colorado Plateau into four natural provinces to which resident Anasazi made some distinctive adaptations. Archeologically, the San Juan basin is known as the Chaco district. Lands north of the San Juan River from its headwaters westward to the Colorado River comprise the Mesa Verde district. The area south of the San Juan River and west of the present New Mexico–Arizona border to the Colorado River is the Kayenta district. The Arizona Strip north of the Colorado River and southern Utah to Nevada is the Virgin River district, regarded by some researchers as a sub-branch of the Kayenta. While regionalizations of some cultural elements evolved among each of these entities, a basic Anasazi homogeneity remained.

As the ranks of Southwest prehistorians grew and more remains were exposed, it became clear that the Anasazi had had neighbors, some of whom probably could claim to be older. Foremost among the newly recognized people were the desert dwellers of southern Arizona called the Hohokam after a Tohono O'odham word meaning "all used up." Scientists separated this continuum of culture into Pioneer, Colonial, Sedentary, and Classic periods. Within a few years, another grouping was suggested, distinct from the Anasazi and the Hohokam. This complex was named Mogollon, after the rugged highlands along the Continental Divide extending down the New Mexico–Arizona borderlands and into northern Mexico where these antiquities were found. Once the validity of the Mogollon as a distinguishable entity was confirmed, its growth was expressed through a sequence of named or numbered periods.

The Anasazi, Hohokam, and Mogollon retained their identities, though they did not exist in total isolation from each other; some cultural fusion occurred at various times and places. Nor for long were they regarded as the three, sole components of the Southwest Tradition. Following World War II, accelerated research revealed many local deviations. Especially in the zone where the Colorado Plateau breaks down into the Colorado River valley and its adjacent low deserts did the variations become most complex. Among newly recognized groups were Sinagua, around Flagstaff, Arizona, and the upper Verde River; Cohonina, who lived south of the Grand Canyon; Cerbat, who resided along the Colorado River as it emerged from the confines of the Grand Canyon; Prescott, of the verdant elevations west of central Arizona; and Laquish, the riverine dwellers of the lower Colorado. Further studies indicated not only the interdependence and interrelationship of these westernmost peoples, but their coherence as a recognizable unit compatible with, but distinct from, the rest of their southwestern contemporaries. This cluster of regional variations became the Hakataya, a Yuman word for the Colorado River along which they spread. The Hakataya exhibited an unusual blending of traits liberally borrowed from all surrounding contributors.

Another localized development along the modern Arizona-Mexico border has been proposed by some archeologists. They interpret the evidence there as supporting the notion that the indigenous sedentary farmers who shared the simple agriculture and pithouse homes of the arid lowlanders were gradually metamorphosed into a separate group about A.D. 900. This distinction came through an infusion of Mesoamerican traits from the neighboring Hohokam, meagerly reinforced through time by sporadic trade with the south. The name O'otam was bestowed upon this marginal development in the belief that it represented the remote background of the modern Tohono O'odham (Pima-Papago) Indians, whose traditional range this region is.

Another enigmatic group was the Salado. They followed a basically Anasazi lifestyle, but somewhere along the way from the Little Colorado River area, where they may have originated, to the Salt River basin where they settled, the Salado had picked up some Mogollon cultural baggage. In Spanish *salado* means salty, a reference to their place of settlement. Through face-to-face trade, invasion, or more subtle diffusion, the Salado in turn appear to have influenced the nearby Hohokam during their Classic Period, from about A.D. 1300 to 1450.

At the opposite extremity of the Southwest, another regional variant was called the Fremont Culture because of its appearance on the Fremont River drainage of east-central Utah. Its lifeway was seen as another mixture of ideas and traits stemming from an Archaic base, superimposed with elements absorbed from Anasazi, Great Basin, or Plains people.

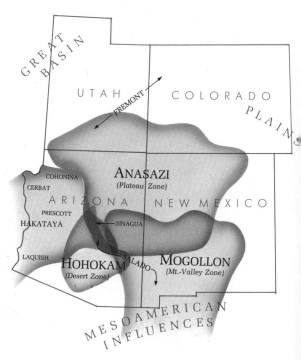

Southwest Tradition:
The overlapping of cultures in central Arizona resulted in various blendings.

THE HOHOKAM

The origins of the Hohokam culture in southern Arizona remain controversial. Perhaps as early as 300 B.C. the original stock from somewhere in the Mexican interior was tempted to migrate northward by the streams that then existed in the deserts and the flat, broad lands suitable for farming. Or over many centuries local Archaic peoples may gradually have adopted certain southern traits, such as farming, communal villages, and hand technologies, which ultimately changed their society completely.

In either case, the Hohokam responded to the challenge of their chosen homeland by evolving into the most skillful desert agriculturalists the aboriginal Southwest ever knew. Through stone implements, organized labor, and sheer human will, the Hohokam created an efficient, lengthy irrigation network from the Salt and Gila river systems to their farmlands that allowed them to survive in an extreme, arid environment against overwhelming odds. Before modern developments obliterated it, the system was so commonly encountered that white settlers in the region dubbed their predecessors the Canal Builders.

As craftsmen, the Hohokam demonstrated an engaging flair. Aided by the simplest tools, their facile hands artistically fashioned utilitarian, religious, and ornamental objects. Their talents were most uniquely revealed in the use of shell obtained by trade from the Gulf of California and the Pacific coast. The Hohokam created an impressive repertory of beads, pendants, rings, and bracelets. Forms were made from blanks by cutting and grinding that demanded a delicate touch because of the fragility of the shell. Geometric or animal shapes were etched or applied as mosaics to their jewelry. The resourceful Hohokam then became entrepreneurs in a thriving trade with their neighbors, the Mogollon and Anasazi.

Hohokam artistry was also displayed in two other, very different materials. Bowls and palettes, rectangular tablets on which paints were prepared, were carefully shaped from hard stone and then decorated with carved replicas of snakes, toads, lizards, birds, and even human stick figures. In clay, comparable skill and uniqueness were apparent. Their coiled pots were finished by use of a paddle to smooth and refine exteriors while an anvil held inside the vessel supported flexible walls. Lively Hohokam creativity expanded into buff utensils decorated with painted red designs, a style that remained characteristic throughout their culture. Figurines of clay, mostly of human females and likely derived from Mexico, probably functioned in fertility rites.

The precise fate of Hohokam culture remains obscure. Quite possibly the present-day Tohono O'odham are linked to that past. An apparent break in the cultural records occurs between the first half of the fifteenth century, when the Hohokam disappear as an archeologically identifiable unit, and the time bridging the sixteenth and seventeenth centuries, when the Spaniards arrived to find a native group of Pima-speaking irrigation farmers.

An idealized Hohokam chronology is divided into four periods. They are not uniform over the entire geographic area inhabited by the Hohokam, and numerous local variations existed.

Pioneer Period (300 B.C. to A.D. 550)

Previously unknown cultural traits appear to have been introduced by the rapid northern extension of a Mexican group that settled along the Salt and Gila rivers. Few, if any, conflicts arose with the native Archaic people because they exploited different zones of the arid landscape. Near their farmlands the newcomers built small, scattered settlements of pole, brush, and mud houses over shallow pits. Corn, beans, squash, and cotton were planted in the fields. Undoubtedly, the extensive canal system helped provide domestic water for the villagers, but wells were dug primarily for that purpose. Despite their expert farming abilities, the Hohokam continued to gather saguaro cactus fruit and mesquite beans that grew wild. They also hunted many desert animals to supplement their domestic foods.

Plain, but well-crafted, early pottery bowls and jars gradually were replaced by buff-colored vessels decorated with red designs. Crude human figurines were produced, along with ground and polished stone bowls, palettes, axes, and several kinds of shell ornaments. Metates and manos for pulverizing corn and beans were the basic tools. Troughed metates were neatly shaped by pecking on porous rock. A mano, or handstone, was pushed back and forth in the trough to grind dry plant foods. Small, chipped projectile points suggest use of the bow and arrow.

To the dismay of those interested in skeletal studies, Hohokam dead were cremated. Their ashes, unconsumed pieces of bone, and the damaged or destroyed funerary offerings of pottery or stone were buried in pits or trenches.

By the end of the Pioneer Period, the Hohokam had spread over a triangular area marked at its corners by present-day Phoenix and Tucson, and the junction of the Verde and Salt rivers.

Colonial Period (A.D. 550 to 900)

Consistent with its name, the Colonial Period was one of expansion. The Hohokam moved into tributaries of the Salt and Gila, up the Verde River valley to the vicinity of Flagstaff, west along the Agua Fria toward Prescott, into the San Pedro and Santa Cruz valleys of southeast Arizona, and east along the Gila to the vicinity of Safford. Many new traits and elaboration of existing artifacts, especially luxury items, suggest strong continuing contact with Mexico. In most respects, the Colonial Period was the climax of Hohokam culture.

Expansion probably was stimulated by improved farming methods, population growth, and increased ties with Mexico and other regions. Villages were larger and settlements more numerous. Among the new traits were notable architectural additions including the platform mound, a hard-surfaced, flat-topped elevation upon which ceremonial structures could be erected or rites performed. Ballcourts, elongated unroofed arenas excavated into the soil, were sites for ritualistic games. Both these constructions were obviously borrowed from Mesoamerica.

Irrigation canal systems were greatly extended, allowing more acres to be cultivated. Canals were cut narrower and deeper so that more water could be accommodated with less surface evaporation.

The designs of the typical red-on-buff pottery were repeated in bands encircling large plates and jars. Especially intriguing were lines of top-knotted quail, rows of dancers holding hands, and figures carrying burden baskets. Ceramic figurines were more lifelike, usually depicting the human female and often emphasizing sexual attributes. Bits of clay or paint representing clothing, headdresses, ornaments, and body tattoos were applied to the figurines.

During the Colonial Period a great deal of attention was paid to carving nonutilitarian objects. Sculptured stone bowls and effigies were decorated with a wide assortment of animal motifs. Archeologists have found buried caches of these objects, deliberately destroyed as if part of some ritual. The appearance of the mosaic plaque or mirror, made of thin, reflective iron pyrites, is further evidence of intercourse with Mesoamerica, where they were manufactured.

Sedentary Period (A.D. 900 to 1100)

During these two hundred years the Hohokam reduced their experimentation and elaboration in arts and crafts. It seems to have been a time of mass production rather than individual craftsmanship. The culture's territorial borders remained fairly stable, with one exception: an extension north and east of Flagstaff occurred about the time of the eruption of Sunset Crater in the A.D. 1060s, believed to have been due to soil improved by volcanic ash and cinders.

The most impressive architectural innovations involved ceremonial structures. Platform mounds were better constructed, and some underwent periodic refurbishing. Generally, settlement patterns changed little, although some houses were arranged around a plaza. Cremations continued, but some burials began during this period.

Large storage jars with the Gila shoulder, a sharp angle formed by the top and bottom parts of the vessel, prevailed. Small, thick-walled vessels, animal effigies, and footed forms also were made. Painted patterns on red-on-buff ceramics displayed complicated geometric panels with fringed lines and interlocking scrolls. Realistically modeled clay heads, with bodies presumably fashioned from perishable materials, represented the only humanlike forms.

Bowls and palettes of stone were less ornate, while mosaic plaques became more elaborate. Most of the Hohokam's creative energy went into working shell. Etching, a technique confined to this period, was introduced. Large concave shells were coated with pitch in geometric or animal designs and then immersed in a mild acid solution probably produced from the fermented fruits of the saguaro cactus. The acid dissolved the uncoated surfaces of the shell, leaving the areas protected by the pitch standing out in relief. Often the shell was then painted. The Hohokam also made trumpets by cutting off the spires of large conch shells.

Hohokam pottery effigy jar, Sedentary Period. HELGA TEIWES, ARIZONA STATE MUSEUM, UNIVERSITY OF ARIZONA.

Small copper bells, perhaps made along the west coast of Mexico, are first found in the Sedentary Period.

Classic Period (A.D. 1100 to 1450)

Once thought to represent the apex of Hohokam culture, researchers now view the Classic Period as one flooded with such great change that its cultural integrity was weakened. The archeological record reveals one major difference from the past: steady territorial contraction. The core area in the middle Gila-Salt valleys remained intact, but most frontier extensions were abandoned.

During this period some Hohokam tended to construct villages farther from rivers, necessitating more and longer canals. In a few areas it appears that dry lands, hillside terraces, and floodwater plains were also being farmed.

Classic communities were larger than Sedentary villages, but fewer sites were occupied. Although the Hohokam continued building houses of wood, brush, and mud over pits, a totally new architectural form appeared. This was a surface structure of contiguous clay-walled rooms, sometimes placed on top of a dirt mound contained by massive walls. Frequently, the walls were surrounded by a stockadelike clay or stone wall up to twenty feet high. Often the enclosures had no entry, so ladders must have been used to climb over the walls. Other compounds had a single portal for access. Within a compound, the randomly scattered houses in pits and the new clay-walled houses created a compact, crowded appearance. Early surface structures were of single stories, but later in the period multistoried buildings, such as the Casa Grande, came into vogue.

The purpose of the compound wall is not known, but defense is certainly suggested. The idea may have been adopted to segregate different segments of the population. It is unknown whether the Great Houses, resembling northern pueblos, represented a fourteenth-century intrusion of Anasazi or Mesoamerican architecture into Hohokam territory. They may have served as priestly houses, ceremonial edifices, observatories, communal storage facilities, or dwellings. Ballcourts continued to be associated with the villages.

In ceramics, the red-on-buff tradition still was followed, but, significantly, white-and-black-on-red wares began to appear. They may have been trade pieces or locally made copies of a ware more typically northern.

The presence of the adz and hoe may indicate some modified agricultural techniques. Luxury items of stone were fewer and less excellent, but those of shell, especially mosaics, increased. Mosaic plaques, stone palettes, and etched shell were no longer used.

Whenever so many innovations—surface houses of adjoining rooms, platform foundations, walled enclosures, burials, polychrome pottery, and farming hillside terraces far from water—surface in cultural waters in such a relatively short time, they generally can be linked to unusual circumstances. These elements may have been dormant for a long time and only developed sufficiently to be recognized during this period. Perhaps this constellation of traits, previously unknown to the Hohokam, resulted from either the generalized Mesoamerican influence or from a meeting with the Anasazi or Anasazi-influenced cultures.

If the first is true, the selective cultural seeding from Mexico at last flowered through increased trade with commercial centers such as Casas Grandes in Chihuahua, Mexico. If the latter is correct, the most likely candidates would be the Salado. This Anasazi group, evolving under Mogollon influence, possibly moved into Hohokam communities from the Tonto basin northeast of Phoenix, bringing their blended lifeway with them.

Meanwhile, the native Hohokam in the low deserts did not experience these dramatic changes but instead clung to their traditional ways by cremating the dead, living in single-room houses just below ground, and finishing their duochrome ceramics with the customary paddle and anvil. This would help explain the fact that two distinct modes seemed to be operating during the Classic Period.

According to this scenario, after a time the restless Salado moved on to the southeast, leaving the Hohokam culture to ultimately disappear or to become so simplified as to be unrecognizable.

Another northerly group possibly responsible for some of the alien elements appearing among the Hohokam was the Sinagua, who lived in the Verde valley. Having absorbed attributes of the Colorado Plateau Anasazi and of the desert Hohokam, they could have served as intermediaries between the two.

Culturally drained by about A.D. 1450, the Hohokam faced obliteration as a viable entity from a probable barrage of troubles. Their irrigation system, parts of which had been in service almost fifteen hundred years, may have fallen into disrepair, its canals silted and in dire need of extensive maintenance that disheartened farmers were not prepared to undertake. Idle farmlands became sterile and choked with salts leached from soils long tilled but not drained or fertilized. Other causes may also have been responsible—disease, skirmishes with neighbors or invading nomads, interruption of contact with Mesoamerica and loss of cultural rejuvenation, or possibly natural disasters. Whatever the reasons, the deserts once again became brown and quiet.

THE MOGOLLON

The group occupying the broken highlands that separate New Mexico and Arizona and the elevated Basin and Range province straddling the Mexican border was the least advanced of the major groups of the Southwest Tradition. Known as the Mogollon, for centuries these people eked out a simple existence. Such limited cultural growth may have been the outcome of a dearth of southern inspiration, surprising considering their juxtaposition to central Mexico. Environmental demands perhaps were too weak to call up those latent human reserves that underlay great achievement elsewhere under less propitious circumstances.

Onto an Archaic hunting and gathering root, successive cultural additions were grafted. These included corn agriculture by about 2000 B.C., bean and squash cultivation somewhat later, use of elementary pithouses around 500 B.C., and pottery making in the centuries between then and A.D. 300. With these traits, several aspects of which had diffused north from Mesoamerica, the Mogollon had sufficiently evolved out of the common background to be reckoned with as a distinct group. But even though they learned to farm the steep slopes and cool valleys and to slightly modify the terrain to bring rain and river waters to their tiny plots, they never abandoned considerable dependence upon their homeland's abundant wild plants and animals. It was this retention of an ageless subsistence pattern that distinguished the Mogollon from their fellow southwesterners.

Between A.D. 900 and 1100 Anasazi cultural dominance virtually swamped the Mogollon. Either their lifestyle was completely submerged by their northern contemporaries, or a merger of Mogollon and Anasazi traits resulted in the formation of a new regional variant called the Western Pueblo. Hohokam ideas also were likely included in this combination. The resultant mixed culture may have contributed heavily to the background out of which the historic Hopi, Zuni, Acoma, and possibly some of the Rio Grande pueblos eventually arose.

Mogollon 1 (200 B.C. to A.D. 650)

Mogollon culture in its formative period was a tenuous transition from nomadism to settled village life made possible by rudimentary farming. Fearful of raids by other foragers, the Mogollon selected easily defensible home sites on promontories near their fields with approaches that could be blocked by rudely constructed walls. Those villages consisted of four to fifty small, identical pithouses, a special chamber now called a Great Kiva, and numerous granary cists.

The tools conceived for this unelaborated life reflect an expectable low standard of manual competence. Ground or pecked stone mortars, pestles, bowls, manos, and metates served as grinding implements. Stone axes, mauls, and hammerstones were construction gear. From chipped or flaked stone there were projectile points, knives, scrapers, and choppers. Small animal and bird bones left from the hunt provided raw material for awls, needles, fleshers, and flakers to be used for making baskets, sandals, and clothing. For the lighter side of life, there were large, stone tubular pipes to which bone or wooden mouthpieces were attached; beads, bracelets, and shell pendants; and bone whistles. Pottery was formed by a coiling technique from a clay heavily impregnated with iron. These vessels fit the term earthenware because they remained a deep earthy brown or reddish color after firing. The moist surfaces of red pots often were compacted and smoothed before firing so that a low sheen was achieved. Brown pots occasionally were gouged, scored, incised, or pinched on the outside.

Mogollon 2 (A.D. 650 to 850)

For the next two centuries the Mogollon remained content with the status quo. Their numbers increased, and they grew complacent enough to forsake the heights and build their larger villages in the valleys near their expanding fields. Modifications in the artifact complex were few. In addition to the usual red and brown types of pottery, Mogollon artisans became sufficiently creative to experiment with banding jar necks with overlapping coils or smudging and polishing bowl interiors to create a two-color, two-texture ware. Most important, they sometimes painted red designs over brown vessel walls. Later they dressed up their customary dark pots with a slip coat of white clay and a poorly executed array of red zigzags, spirals, and serrate lines.

Mogollon 3 (A.D. 850 to 1000)

The population, villages, and cultural complexity continued to grow in direct ratio to the Mogollon farming abilities, although nondomesticated plants and animals augmented their diet. To hold or accumulate tillable soil in their mountainous terrain, the Mogollon erected stone terraces along hillsides or across normally dry stream beds. They laid out lines of stones on slopes to halt erosion and distribute runoff.

Pithouses occasionally were lined with masonry for extra stability. Great Kivas became even greater. Some were up to thirty-five or forty feet on longer sides of a rectangular plan. In pottery, neck bands were pinched into piecrust relief, smudging remained in vogue, and the red-on-white palette was giving way to black-on-white. This color scheme and the introduction of some masonry liners for pithouses are possible evidence for the mounting impact of the northern Anasazi upon their culturally weaker southern neighbors.

Mogollon 4, Anasazi, Western Pueblo (A.D. 1000 to 1450)

The world as the Mogollon had known it came to an end in this period. Perhaps the local people merely resigned themselves quietly to cultural pressures from the north. Perhaps the vigorous Anasazi actually established colonies in traditional Mogollon territory. Or the two groups may have merged to produce a hybrid culture. What is obvious is that the takeover was peaceful.

The most striking change was a great increase in population. Also, an architectural style new to the Mogollon but typical of the Anasazi was adopted. Surface pueblos composed of unworked stones set in mud mortar became common. Early, small units were built in a linear or square plan. Later, larger pueblos, some with several hundred rooms and two stories, were arranged around open courts. In southern New Mexico and northern Chihuahua, small cliff dwellings were placed beneath rock shelters and in caves in canyon walls. A few rectangular and round Great Kivas were in locations suggesting their joint use by several small pueblos. Modest-size kivas in Anasazi style also were included in some communities.

Farming expanded to meet new demands of greater numbers, helped along by the introduction of ditch irrigation.

Burial in pits beneath house floors was practiced. Bodies often were extended and were accompanied by more elaborate offerings, consisting primarily of pottery receptacles that had holes poked in their bases to allow the spirits trapped inside the vessel to accompany that of the deceased.

Common goods were virtually indistinguishable from comparable tools used at the beginning of the Mogollon culture, although ornaments became more commonplace. Imported copper bells from Mexico were popular.

Pottery mirrored the dramatic cultural mixing that had occurred. In addition to the typical Mogollon types, a colorful red-and-black-on-white polychrome was traded into the region and occasionally copied by local potters. Most amazing was the sudden appearance of a stunning, superbly crafted black-on-white ware based on Anasazi methods and artistic leanings but nevertheless distinctive. It came from a restricted area along the Mimbres River of southwestern New Mexico where a throng of settlers poured from all the surrounding regions between A.D. 1050 to 1200. Apparently, in the resulting cultural crosscurrents, an aesthetic spark was ignited. Skillfully controlled brushes precisely executed a typical Anasazi geometric style whose individual elements were bold solids played off against fine line hatchure and parallel lines. But it was a totally original gamut of naturalistic designs depicting humans, animals, and mythical composite figures that made Mimbres earthenware unique. No other southwesterners could claim this fanciful repertory.

The same cloud of defeat that darkened the sky over the Hohokam lengthened over the Mogollon realm at about the same time. Circumstances differed, but the outcome was the same. Depopulation of most of the eastern portion of Mogollon territory, begun in the A.D. 1100s, was complete by A.D. 1250. In the late 1300s in the northwest highlands, people in a few large towns started to leave, but total abandonment did not occur until about A.D. 1450.

THE ANASAZI

The Anasazi, the third major component of prehistoric life in the Southwest, have been the subject of more romanticized, as well as scientific, attention than any other ancient Indian group in the United States. They not only dwelt in the most topographically unusual and starkly beautiful part of North America, but they also left behind thousands of stone houses and piles of discarded goods.

The Anasazi emerged from the same Archaic milieu as the other regional groups, and throughout their history have remained one facet of a larger human mosaic that is the Southwest Tradition. Before the opening of the Christian Era, they had progressed from a hunting-gathering stage to increasing dependence on domesticated corn, squash, and beans. They were, however, more reluctant than the Hohokam or Mogollon to become fully committed to sedentary agricultural life, probably because of their greater distance from Mexican sources of cultural stimulation. However, once certain Mesoamerican elements reached them about A.D. 500, Anasazi culture evolved rapidly.

Anasazi dry farming relied on direct rainfall or manipulation of that moisture.

Anasazi, Basket Maker III, black-on-white bowl. ROBERT H. LISTER, EARL MORRIS MEMORIAL COLLECTION, UNIVERSITY OF COLORADO MUSEUM.

Frequently, garden plots were placed in spots where runoff from summer showers supplemented normal precipitation. Successive lines of stones laid across slopes and terraced arroyos spread surface flows and controlled erosion. In some areas more extensive arrangements were made for funneling runoff water into canals and ditches that led to planted fields. This was not irrigation in the usual sense, but a judicious means for capturing unpredictable rainfall.

A noteworthy Anasazi contribution to prehistoric southwestern culture was their architecture style. Stone masonry, or more rarely adobe, was employed for communal structures of cellular, contiguous, flat-roofed rooms. The edifices ranged in size from several small units sufficient to shelter a few families to immense, many-storied apartment buildings with staggered elevations whose hundreds of living and storage rooms accommodated a swarm of people. Subterranean or semi-subterranean ceremonial rooms, called kivas, were family or clan religious and social centers. Community Great Kivas probably were adopted from the Mogollon.

The craft of pottery making also was borrowed from the Mogollon. Following the introduction of coil and scrape methods of construction, the Anasazi developed a gray ware made into distinctive shapes and often painted with black decorations. As expertise grew, a white slip was applied to the pots over which were drawn geometric motifs. These steadily became more intricate and skillfully executed. Some Anasazi also learned the art of making black-on-red, black-on-orange, red-on-orange, and several combinations of these colors to produce a polychrome product. Likewise, many utility pots were unique. Their interior surfaces were scraped smooth, but exteriors retained the corrugated pattern of unsmoothed, pinched construction coils.

The Anasazi showed a preference for particular styles of axes, milling stones, and tools for cutting, scraping, pounding, piercing, and cultivating. Their individual taste can also be seen in certain kinds of shell, bone, and stone ornaments, particularly those made of turquoise.

Customarily, bodies were flexed when buried in abandoned storage pits, beneath floors of houses, in outside graves, or quite often in a village refuse mound. Funerary offerings were usual.

Trails, roads, and established points from which signals could be sent comprised means of communication. Local and distant trade in utilitarian and luxury goods was extensive. At the cultural climax, a few centers existed where commodities were collected and redistributed. Some had connections to commercial establishments in northern Mexico. Annual ceremonial cycles probably were geared to agricultural activities, and may have been timed by astronomical observations and led by religious specialists.

After about A.D. 1000, when their culture began to peak, Anasazi dominance expanded southward to the Salado and Mogollon regions. Less obvious movements in other directions reached peripheral peoples.

Six hundred years later several reversals had brought severe shrinkage of Anasazi territory. By the early 1600s remaining enclaves existed only around the Hopi mesas in northeastern Arizona; in a scattering around Zuni, Acoma, and Laguna to the southeast;

and along the upper Rio Grande of northern New Mexico. Behind these demographic readjustments may have been climatic changes which affected water supplies and productivity of farmlands and caused erosion and lowering of the water table. Increasing numbers of people in some areas depleted limited resources. Failure in controlling water supply and breakdown in economic, social, or religious customs invited internal conflicts and perhaps raiding by enemies.

Basket Maker II (1500 B.C. to A.D. 400)

Those archeologists who strictly adhere to the Pecos Classification of the initiation of the Anasazi continuum with the partial adoption of maize horticulture place the opening phases of this cultural horizon within the second millennium B.C. Their conclusion is based upon radiocarbon dating of scattered plant remains recovered from a variety of sites with some evidence of early sedentism. While recognizing a prolonged transitional period from nomadic Archaic to more sedentary Anasazi lifestyle, others prefer to begin the sequence closer to the Christian Era, when supporting evidence is greater.

Most known sites of this period of changing subsistence strategies are sparsely scattered in caves and rock shelters throughout the Four Corners region. Because of optimum conditions for preservation, many normally perishable artifacts have been retrieved from dry deposits there. The most important of these are beautifully woven baskets for which this and the succeeding period are named.

Basket Maker II camps or small villages were located where water and soil were adequate for farming but collecting and hunting were also still possible. Corn and squash were cultivated, but wild plants, grass seeds, and pinyon nuts remained important. Also significant was meat from rabbits and other rodents, elk, deer, mountain sheep, and turkeys. Storage pits in the floors of shelters, and surface cists of stone slabs and mud protected stored food supplies from the voracious rodents who claimed the same habitat. Though they are rare, crude dwellings in the open were built of a domelike covering of short logs, poles, brush, and mud over a saucer-shaped depression or circular pit. Most burials were in rock shelters or crevices. The air was so dry that some remains became mummified. Baskets, clothing, and tools frequently accompanied the dead.

Milling stones verify the importance of plant foods. Heavy, rough choppers and hammerstones, large projectile points for spears, knives, and drills, and many simple flake cutting and scraping tools completed the assortment of stone artifacts. Bone awls, fleshers, flakers, and notched scapulas and ribs for combing fibers were used. Gaming pieces and several kinds of ornaments also were crafted from bone. Dried juniper berries and shells were worked into beads and pendants. Tubular pipes were made of stone.

Baskets were made in various forms for specific jobs. Large conical ones held loads carried on the back. Globular containers served for storage, while trays were used for winnowing and parching seeds. Bags, sandals, bands, and bikini-size aprons were finger woven of fibers, particularly yucca. Blankets were prepared from strips of rabbit fur or deerskins.

Hunters used the atlatl for hurling spears, curved sticks to throw at game, large nets into which rabbits were driven, and snares for taking small game and fowl.

Pottery was seldom present. Where found, it resembles Mogollon brown ware and probably was not locally made.

Basket Maker III (A.D. 400 to 700)

The numerous villages with abundant storage facilities and the widespread occurrence of ceramics indicate a full-fledged, settled life in Basket Maker III times. The population increased and moved to valleys and highlands where conditions were suitable for farming. Domesticated plants included beans. Turkeys appear to have been tamed and kept within villages.

Settlements contained two to fifty pithouses, generally deep and circular to rectangular in plan, with pole, brush, and mud above-ground structures. Storage pits were placed within or near dwellings. Many communities had outdoor work areas and Great Kivas. Most frequently the dead were buried with offerings in the communal trash dump.

The abundance of small projectile points suitable for hafting to arrows suggests that the bow and arrow had become popular. Use of turquoise for jewelry increased, and locally made pottery replaced basketry for many uses. Small amounts of Mogollon browns still were imported or copied, but the first gray Anasazi pottery became widespread. Both undecorated bowls and others with geometric black designs were typical. A few crudely modeled female clay figurines, generally unbaked, probably were used in fertility rites.

Pueblo I (A.D. 700 to 900)

Pueblo I villages typically were in localities similar to those of Basket Maker III. Village size varied. Small complexes were common, but a few known ruins had more than one hundred individual dwellings. Rectangular surface structures built in a linear plan were separate or attached. Made of *jacal*, or mud plastered over a pole framework, they may have evolved from the earlier, small surface storage unit. By the end of the period, masonry was substituted for mud and brush in some areas.

Another Pueblo I innovation was the kiva, a subterranean religious or social structure resembling a pithouse. Among its specialized features were an encircling bench, roof support posts, a central firepit, a ventilator shaft for fresh air, and a *sipapu*, a small hole in the floor symbolizing the entrance to the spirit world below. A roof opening allowed smoke to escape and, with the aid of a ladder, it also served as entrance to the kiva. The larger, earlier Great Kiva occurred in some villages.

A typical Pueblo I village often had several dozen jacal living and storage rooms, several old-style pithouses, a few small kivas, perhaps a Great Kiva, and some outside areas for food preparation, cooking, or tool making.

Anasazi, Pueblo I, gourd-shaped, black-on-white vessel. ROBERT H. LISTER, EARL MORRIS MEMORIAL COLLECTION, UNIVERSITY OF COLORADO MUSEUM.

Cotton was added to the list of domesticated plants, presaging the appearance of the true loom. Finger-woven bags and sandals and large carrying baskets and winnowing trays were disappearing. The practice of binding infants to hard cradle boards was instituted. These boards artificially flattened the back of the babies' skulls.

The Pueblo I ceramic assemblage continued to include a few brown wares, some gray wares—including a new utility jar with neck banding—a number of black-on-whites, and regionally important red-on-oranges and black-on-reds. Jars, bowls, and ladles were favorite forms.

Pueblo II (A.D. 900 to 1100)

By the beginning of the Pueblo II period practically all material ingredients of Anasazi culture had been introduced. Thereafter, even though some local differences in agriculture, architecture, and pottery were found, the peoples' movements and trading activities helped preserve a widespread cultural uniformity.

During this period the Anasazi reached their maximum geographic distribution and probably their greatest numbers. Both the dispersed occupation and climate records indicate generally more favorable conditions for elementary agriculture. Also, the refinement of water-control structures was coupled with the introduction of a more productive strain of corn.

Small, compact masonry pueblos of twelve to twenty living and storage rooms, one or more kivas, and a communal trash deposit became ubiquitous. Often they were clustered in larger villages. Kivas normally were circular and masonry-lined. Great Kivas became larger and more elaborate, and they began to exhibit typical features, including stone linings and benches, masonry fireboxes and vaults, ponderous posts or columns to support the heavy, flat roof, and a side entrance. Occasional small rooms, possibly for storing ceremonial paraphernalia or other materials, were built on the surface around the outside of the Great Kivas.

Ornaments of all sorts became more prevalent. Burials and offerings were placed in the refuse and in abandoned houses and storage chambers.

Much experimentation is evident in pottery. Typical products include characteristic gray corrugated jars and numerous types of black-on-whites that are regionally distinct in form, design, clay, pigment, and firing method. Red, black-on-red, and brown with smudged black interiors also were produced. Jars, bowls, pitchers, canteens, ladles, and some effigies were customary objects.

In Chaco Canyon, located in the San Juan basin of northwestern New Mexico, a cultural flowering known as the Chaco Phenomenon occurred. About A.D. 1000 the Chaco Anasazi advanced culturally beyond their contemporaries in numbers, in harnessing runoff waters, and in establishing a sophisticated network of several hundred small- to medium-sized villages and a dozen large towns. Roads and signaling outposts afforded rapid communication within the Chaco territory and with other Anasazi. Contact with the Mexicans brought certain new ideas and materials into Chaco life.

Pueblo III (A.D. 1100 to 1300)

The Anasazi reached their apogee in Pueblo III. At the same time, they occupied fewer but more densely settled localities, many of which were on ledges and in shallow caves in canyons.

Archeological evidence suggests a group of Pueblo III provinces, including Chaco Canyon in the northeast, which was of major importance. Distinct units also were found in Mesa Verde in southwestern Colorado, in the vicinity of Zuni in west-central New Mexico, in the upper Rio Grande in north-central New Mexico, and about Kayenta, the Hopi mesas, and south to the Little Colorado drainage in northern Arizona. Indians in intervening and borderland areas drew on the ideas and products of those principal centers. Thorough Anasazi dominance of former Mogollon territory was achieved.

The Chaco Phenomenon prospered for the first half of Pueblo III, then suffered a rapid decline and final dissolution by about A.D. 1200, if not earlier. To the north, the many spectacular cliff dwellings and large mesa-top and valley towns on or near the Mesa Verde continued to flourish for another century, then were abandoned. Total depopulation of the northern Anasazi provinces saw most people shifting to the south and southeast. Complicated, intertwined reasons were behind the final exodus from most of the San Juan basin. Among them were adverse climate; overpopulation of some of the more favorable places; breakdown of organized agricultural, commercial, social, and religious patterns; and severe competition for lands and resources that ended in internecine raiding.

Architectural achievement was characterized by large, well-planned, multistoried pueblos embracing many plazas. Masonry construction predominated, but techniques varied from province to province. Kivas, by then universal, usually were circular, but some were square. Both circular and square Great Kivas were common, located either within villages or at intermediate spots where they could serve several communities.

There was much local and foreign trading in ceramics, in materials for artifacts and ornaments, and possibly in foodstuffs. Luxury goods, such as raw and worked turquoise, were exchanged with Mexican trading partners for macaws and special objects of shell, stone, and metals.

Water and soil erosion controls were present to some degree in the more populous centers. Artifacts and jewelry did not differ much from Pueblo II. Burials in refuse heaps and in abandoned units of pueblos were the vogue, but puzzlingly few burials are known from such heavily occupied areas as Chaco Canyon.

Regionally distinct black-on-white pottery that was exchanged widely is useful in identifying the important centers of influence. Other black-on-whites of restricted distribution were produced in the outlying zones. Those of the Mimbres region reached an artistic excellence unmatched elsewhere in the Southwest. In several places reds, black-on-reds, black-on-oranges, red-on-browns, and polychromes were of local significance.

Pueblo IV (A.D. 1300 to 1600)

More people continued to concentrate in fewer localities during Pueblo IV, especially around the Hopi mesas, the land of Cíbola around Zuni, and the upper Rio Grande. Cliff dwellings became rare as the canyons were forsaken. While some small settlements existed, large towns of several hundred to more than a thousand rooms were more characteristic.

By A.D. 1450 most of the sites on the Colorado Plateau and in the Mogollon highlands had been deserted. During the next century big urban centers in the settled zones also were vacated. Added to the same factors that prompted earlier Pueblo III withdrawals were the presumed threats from newly arrived nomadic Indians, such as the Ute, Paiute, Apache, and Navajo.

Despite this decline, a lively, colorful pottery industry persisted. Cooking and storage jars had plain or tooled surfaces. Black-on-yellow or -orange and polychromes of red and white added to the designs were favored in Hopi districts. Polychromes in pigments that vitrified upon firing produced a number of wares with glazed decorations in the Zuni and Rio Grande vicinities. Several kinds of black-on-whites and pots with specks of shiny mica also were made by Rio Grande potters.

The ritual side of Anasazi life is strongly substantiated by extensive murals painted on the walls of kivas depicting deities, mythical creatures, masked dancers, and ceremonial objects.

Pueblo V (A.D. 1600 to present)

Pueblo V was the historic period for the Pueblo Indians, the direct descendants of the prehistoric Anasazi. Following the conquest by the Coronado expedition in 1540 and 1541, and the arrival of Spanish settlers, soldiers, and priests, these Indians were subjected to successive, often demoralizing, European influences.

In 1680 the Pueblos, in an unusual alliance, staged a coordinated revolt. Most of the Catholic priests were killed, buildings were sacked, and colonists and soldiers were expelled from New Mexico. Twelve years later Diego de Vargas reconquered the Indians.

Then new troubles descended upon the embattled Pueblos; this time it was other Indians. These were nomads who had converted quickly into raiders after they acquired horses from the Spanish. The Navajos were especially troublesome.

Early in the American era, administrators established some degree of law and order, broke the hold of Hispanic communities on Pueblo lands, reduced the power of the Catholic church, and finally brought an end to Navajo depredations.

The first three hundred years of contact with Europeans meant dramatic changes for the Pueblos. Some groups became extinct; others scattered and disorganized. Still others abandoned and reoccupied their villages or went to live with relatives.

Today there are eighteen pueblos along the Rio Grande. Acoma, Laguna, and Zuni thrive in western New Mexico, as do the Hopi villages in northeastern Arizona. They remain distinct from neighboring Native Americans. However, despite general cultural unity among the Pueblos, differences do exist in language, social institutions, ritual or ceremonial organizations, environments, and resource uses.

THE IN-BETWEENS AND OUTLIERS

Aside from the Mogollon, Hohokam, and Anasazi, local cultures existed in areas where the dominant entities overlapped (the in-betweens) or in border zones where southwesterners met and mingled with non-southwesterners (the outliers). They were variable prehistorically and remain comparatively ill-defined today.

Archeologists do not agree on the names, characteristics, importance, or even existence of all of these groups. The following is one way of identifying these units and outlining their attributes and relationships.

Hakataya

A fourth ingredient of the Southwest Tradition was a loosely knit, heterogeneous grouping called Hakataya. Unlike its contemporaries, it was a composite rather than a clearly defined individual group. The Hakataya assumed an early course of receiving, rather than giving, cultural stimulation.

Two essential factors bound the Hakataya together: their territorial range on the western flanks of the Southwest province and a mutual hunting-gathering background. However, the setting was so varied, extending from the snow-capped San Francisco Peaks to the torrid Colorado Desert, that five regional variants of the Hakataya have been identified. They resulted from contacts with other southwesterners or with people west of the province. Certain cultural hot spots were successively enriched at various times and in different ways, while more isolated peoples languished in a mode of life scarcely advanced beyond the Archaic.

The earliest Hakataya were part-time farmers who, because they relied on limited foraging, needed a certain degree of mobility. Most of them lived in small, transitory camps of jacal or low-walled rock shelters with bedrock milling stones for grinding foods and pits for roasting. None of them erected structures which can be assigned ceremonial usage. They made a few crude stone chopping tools and projectile points and some plain ornaments of stone or shell. Their pottery was a simple brown ware finished by a paddle and anvil technique.

To this shared background, the Laquish of the lower Colorado River valley added a red-on-buff pottery whose methods of manufacture they borrowed from the Hohokam. Meanwhile, in the uplands the Cerbat, Cohonina, and Prescott dipped into a cultural grab bag proffered by the Hohokam, Mogollon, and Anasazi along their borders. From these mixed sources at different times they selected pithouses, surface masonry pueblos, and red- or black-on-gray pottery to augment their usual traits.

The Sinagua are the best known Hakataya regional group. For five hundred years, beginning about the A.D. 500s, these people carved a meager existence from the jagged volcanic field that fanned out east from the San Francisco Mountains near Flagstaff. Pockets of fertile soil and sources of water were so restricted that only a small population could be sustained. The Sinagua followed a usual Hakataya simple life based on corn farming supplemented by whatever nature provided in the way of wild edibles. Some elaboration in lifestyle came with the adoption of pithouse architecture and acquisition of a few items through trade with the Hohokam, Anasazi, and Cohonina.

Contacts with the Hohokam to their south increased as the Sinagua colonized the middle Verde valley. Their influence may have been felt in some modifications to the pit dwelling, but a local sequence of changes on the traditional form was unique. First, the subterranean part of the buildings was lined with timbers, perhaps to seal the living quarters from ground moisture and pervading cold. Then, the same shape structure was erected above ground, with the addition of a side alcove. Apparently reversing older practices, the alcoved surface structure occasionally was placed over a pit. Rarely it was built on a low earthen platform. Examples of these timber-lined and alcove houses have been excavated at Sunset Crater Volcano National Monument.

In the middle of the eleventh century the Sinagua bore the brunt of one of the major physical disturbances of the ancient southwestern world. New, violent volcanic activity fiercely remodeled their homeland with the birth of Sunset Crater. There is no evidence that any of the people were annihilated, but lava flows, ash, and cinders buried their fields and homes and drove them away.

As the earth cooled, astute observers witnessed a rejuvenated soil and a greater volume of both running and retained water. Farming in the area became a more attractive possibility than it had ever been. Shortly, an aboriginal land rush was on, led by returning Sinagua. Other farming peoples quickly followed. Within a century groups of Cohonina and Anasazi from the north, Mogollon from the east, and Hohokam from the south had converged on the Flagstaff area and settled down together. Inevitably, a significant cultural cross-fertilization occurred.

As a direct result, the Sinagua assimilated a bank of alien elements into their traditional mode to reach a peak development between A.D. 1125 and 1215. From the Hohokam they accepted village life and the use of ballcourts. From the Anasazi they adopted masonry communal dwellings in the open, on canyon ledges and in overhangs, as well as certain soil and water conservation practices. And from the Mogollon they learned the manufacture of plain and smudged red wares.

It was at this time that the Sinagua occupied Walnut Canyon, where they erected tiny cliff houses and storage rooms. In the area of Wupatki they came together in pueblos. Some were small, but others were three stories high with one hundred rooms. Crowded out of the Flagstaff environs, other Sinagua moved south into the middle Verde valley where they established large centers such as those at Tuzigoot, Montezuma Castle, and Montezuma Well. Some aspects of their culture may have spread even farther south down the Verde River to the desert country around Phoenix at the beginning of the A.D. 1200s.

Perhaps their most significant role in these times was as strategically placed middlemen in a surging trade between the motley peoples who found themselves thrust together on this western frontier.

By the late thirteenth century the same natural and human dilemmas that brought down the other prehistoric southwesterners confronted the Sinagua. The results were similar: abandonment of settlements and dissolution of a worn cultural pattern.

Some Sinagua may have migrated north to join the ancestral Hopi. According to tradition, others may have trekked southward and mingled with the Tohono O'odham of the desert lowlands. Or perhaps some remained in the vicinity of the San Francisco Mountains, where they reverted to a predominantly hunting and gathering way of life, gradually to evolve into a culture reminiscent of the Yavapai in early historic times.

Salado

The Salado people were first identified as a distinct group living in the Tonto basin of south-central Arizona. They appear to have originated in the upper reaches of the Gila, Salt, and Little Colorado river drainages along the borders between the Anasazi and Mogollon, generally a mountainous evergreen area. For unknown reasons, about A.D. 900 they spread down into the warm arid basin of the middle Salt River. There for the next three centuries they exploited a frost-free climate, fertile soil, and perennial waters to become highly competent farmers. They dug miles of irrigation canals controlled from a series of settlements placed on top of spaced earthen platform mounds, both features perhaps adopted as a result of influence from their Hohokam neighbors further downriver. Numerous granaries and huge earthenware storage jars within house blocks attest to substantial farm yields. At least one recently explored structure suggests a temple where celebrations of the cycles of the sun's movements—so basic to the rhythms of agriculture— could have been part of calendric formulations by a priestly class.

Successful adaptations to a demanding environment afforded the Salado a comfortable life. Their artisans created outstanding polychrome pottery, shell jewelry, and cotton textiles, which were traded for turquoise, obsidian, sea shells, and bird feathers from distant regions. However, around A.D. 1200 trouble seems to have been brewing because the Salado began moving their villages. The selection of isolated, defensible locations suggests pressures from other peoples. The cliff dwellings at Tonto National Monument represent this stage of Salado culture. Finally, after briefly occupying the arid uplands, the Salado again moved. This time they went farther south into the lowlands of the Gila and Salt river valleys where they took up residence among the Hohokam. Most authorities consider them responsible for the appearance among the Hohokam of such foreign elements as multistoried pueblolike structures or Great Houses, compound walls for encircling villages, black-and-white-on-red polychrome pottery, several new types of stone tools, and inhumations. After a brief residency with the Hohokam, the Salado dispersed into southeastern Arizona and southwestern New Mexico, where their presence is traceable through diagnostic pottery types and some ruins dating between A.D. 1300 and

1450. In those are found large, several-storied pueblos that roughly resemble the Great House at Casa Grande. What ultimately became of the Salado is unknown.

Fremont

On its northwestern edge, in southern and eastern Utah and northwestern Colorado, the Southwest Tradition met the cultures of the Great Basin. There, several medleys of the two ways of life evolved. The best known of them is the Fremont Culture, a highly variable response by small groups of people adapting to some of the most diverse ecosystems on the continent. Five regional Fremont variants are recognized, those on the Colorado Plateau exhibiting enough similarities in cultural traits to originally be considered a peripheral branch of the Southwest Tradition. Now all Fremont variants are treated as a development distinct from that of the Anasazi but perhaps influenced in some respects by it. The Fremont remained more rooted in an Archaic-style hunting and gathering subsistence base than the Anasazi, but in favorable microenvironments they practiced some agriculture and enjoyed sedentism. Although many occupations are thought to have been seasonal or short-term, small Fremont villages featured pit dwellings. Houses and granaries of jacal, adobe, or masonry sometimes were included. Kivas were absent. Gray pottery, constructed by coil and scrape method and sometimes embellished with corrugation, incision, applique, or painted decoration, shows some Anasazi influence, as do certain stone implements. Elaborate, well-executed rock art was a typical Fremont attribute. Certain Plains traits, for example bison hunting and use of tipis, moccasins, and shields, also appear in the Fremont complex. Between A.D. 1300 and 1400 the Fremont vanished. Whether the people emerged as the historic Shoshoni, Ute, and Southern Paiute, or straggled south into Pueblo country or east into the High Plains, is uncertain.

Plains Relations

Where southwestern and Plains village farmers met along the east and northeast edges of the Southwest, trading relationships were established and intermediate cultural patterns appeared. The Antelope Creek development of the Texas Panhandle, which drew on Plains agricultural practices and Pueblo architecture, is one such hybrid. Also, within certain Anasazi districts in northern New Mexico the occurrence of pointed bottom pots, effigy vessels, and stockaded settlements suggests some Plains affiliation.

Mesoamerican Relations

Although the Southwest Tradition is distinct, in broad perspective it can be considered a provincial, watered-down version of Mesoamerican cultures. From the south came its first domestic crops and farming methods, its pottery making tradition, and certain architectural details. Ceremonial mounds and ballcourts, intensive irrigation projects, clay figurines, a number of exotic trade goods, and many of its ceremonies,

Yucca sandal from Montezuma Castle. SOUTHWEST PARKS AND MONUMENTS ASSOCIATION.

religious beliefs, and rituals also came from Mexico. Objects, as well as ideas, spread by different routes to the Southwest through diffusion and, in later times, through long-distance traders. Highly important in this Mexican-southwestern association was the establishment of a series of trading centers in northern Mexico by diverse Mesoamerican merchants. Casas Grandes in Chihuahua was one such thriving commercial entrepôt between the late eleventh and the mid-fourteenth centuries. Its merchants and craftsmen assembled raw materials and finished products from distant sources, produced quantities of pottery and luxury items, and distributed many commodities south into central Mexico and north as far as the upper reaches of the Southwest. From the Southwest the Mexican middlemen probably obtained turquoise, peyote, salt, selenite, and perhaps slaves by setting up formal trading channels to various places, including Chaco Canyon. One must credit the Mesoamericans with providing the seeds from which a Southwest Tradition bloomed and for diffusing northward repeated material and spiritual stimulation to keep it thriving. A rippling aftermath of the collapse of the Mesoamerican supportive system may in actuality have hastened the withering of certain southwestern complexes. ▲

Fourteenth-century polychrome olla, Salado culture, Tonto National Monument. GEORGE H. H. HUEY.

Traditional Interpretation

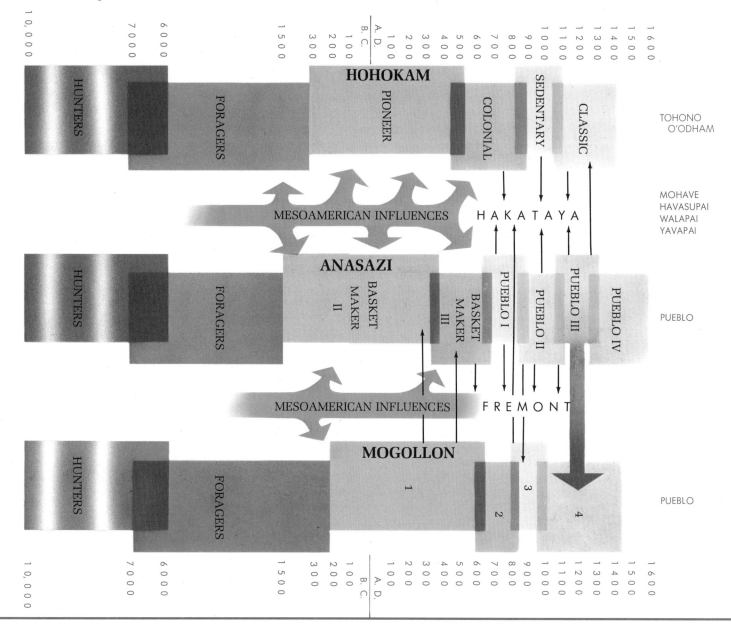

AN ALL-SOUTHWEST INTERPRETATION

Traditionally, the archeological definition of Southwest prehistory tends to emphasize the differences between cultures. It may foster the impression that the Southwest was so fragmented that each group evolved independently and in isolation.

While this is the conventional approach, an alternate way of explaining the archeological record is to partially attribute regional deviations from the cultural norm to peoples' adjustments to environmental limitations in the Southwest. This interpretation seeks similarities throughout the entire area, shared achievements, and those vital, mutually experienced exchanges that encouraged advancement. In essence, prehistoric human groups appear more as a subtle collage than a distinct mosaic of identifiable pieces. This view paints a picture of interrelated parts that fuse into an orderly whole, given perspective within a time frame.

For the first ten thousand years of human presence in the Southwest, man was a hunter and forager, totally at the mercy of his wits in recognizing and securing life's necessities. First came those who stalked the mammoth and bison, about whom little is known except that they participated in a simple lifestyle that seems to have been centered in the High Plains. When climatic change caused game animals to migrate eastward, those who subsisted upon them trekked out of the Southwest in their wake. They were replaced by others who in distant, less favorable, surroundings already had learned to survive on an astonishing variety of native plants and smaller animals. Both hunters and collectors moved periodically to take advantage of seasonally available foods. Tool kits were meager and portable, containing specialized weapons and tools, including the atlatl and spear. They also made cutting and scraping implements for taking and processing large game. Gatherers created a more general set of milling stones, choppers, baskets and bags for accumulating and preparing plants and small animals. Minimal clothing was made, mainly from skins. The people lived in shelters of brush windbreaks in the open or camps under protective rock overhangs. Small social units, such as extended families, probably ranged together, each member contributing to the well-being of the group. Shamans, medicine men astute in matters of human behavior and wise in the ways of nature, may have arisen through group recognition.

By about 3000 B.C. increasing numbers of Southwest foragers were following much the same lifeway, oriented to an unceasing search for food. While cultural change came slowly, they were understandably receptive to any additional foods that would afford more security. Thus, they were conditioned to accept the growing of corn, a plant evolved from a wild ancestor in central Mexico that had inched northward through the Sierra Madre Occidental to reach the Southwest. Likewise, squash and beans apparently followed shortly thereafter. The Mogollon highlands, with an environment similar to the Mexican interior, appear to have been important in the naturalization of these Mexican domesticates to the Southwest. From there they were dispersed north to the Colorado Plateau. The low deserts of Arizona may not have witnessed this earliest intrusion of domesticated plants because of the necessity for more heat-resistant varieties that presumably evolved later.

No immediate cultural change occurred among the foragers who failed to appreciate the possibilities of becoming full-time food producers. For many centuries the introduced plants were little more than minor dietary supplements. Nevertheless, their initial cultivation, together with improved hunting and gathering techniques and an apparent period of increased moisture, made possible larger groupings of people. More substantial habitations appeared in camps or semi-permanent settlements, accommodating perhaps thirty to fifty individuals and situated in the lee of cliffs or in the open. These were houses made of a light framework of poles, possibly covered with brush, grass, or even hides, placed over a shallow depression and equipped with hearth and storage pits.

The northward flow of cultural stimulation, begun with the diffusion of the fundamental idea of agriculture and its diagnostic plants — corn, squash, and beans — quickened about 500 B.C. A noticeable commitment to food producing was seen. This entailed more sedentary life in permanent villages with sturdier, below-ground homes and more storage chambers for food stockpiling. With this village life, kin groups, formerly made up of mobile social units, possibly were succeeded by organization geared to the new relations of family and community. Leadership likely became necessary to direct occasional group activities. Organized ritualism designed to assure the success of unpredictable dryland farming in the arid Southwest may have arisen.

Pottery making appeared in southern sectors of the Southwest by about 300 B.C. Even the simplest pottery had many advantages over traditional baskets, bags, and skin and gourd containers. Notwithstanding, in the ancient Southwest, pottery never entirely replaced basketry and other types of containers.

Repeated injections of objects and ideas from Mesoamerica continued sporadically for the next millennium. Some of these contributions to Southwest cultures are thought to have been carried unknowingly by peaceful traders, who were more active at some times than others. A few of these merchants had close tribal and economic ties to the central Mexican markets; others were more provincial middlemen with weaker connections to the primary sources of trade goods. The distance from donors, the number and complexity of intervening participants, and the state of cultural advancement of ultimate recipients accounted for uneven acceptance of the cultural adjuncts introduced into the Southwest. For example, pottery did not appear among the emerging northern, culturally disadvantaged farmers of the Colorado Plateau until about A.D. 400, centuries after it was a basic ingredient of more southerly households.

One notable exception to the diffusion-through-trade concept may have been an actual migration of people from the south into the Gila and Salt river valleys of southern Arizona about 300 B.C., bringing in a rich complex of Mesoamerican traits previously unknown in the Southwest. Some of these items greatly influenced people residing elsewhere within the province, while some remained localized but modified to the new cultural context that evolved. The elements introduced were certain pottery techniques and modes, figurines, trough metates, stone bowls, turquoise mosaics, shell ornaments, canal irrigation, and cremations.

The more than one thousand years that prehistoric Southwest culture existed fall naturally into several stages. Each is named for the predominant settlement pattern of the time but ultimately is based on its material inventory of both Southwest and foreign affiliation and its geographical distribution. Three core areas are recognized, coincident with the major environmental zones. The *desert zone* includes the lowland desert expanses about the middle stretches of the Gila and Salt rivers in southern Arizona. A second, the *mountain-valley zone*, encompasses the high mountains and more verdant deep valleys astride the southern New Mexico–Arizona boundary and the northwest Mexican cordillera. The third, the *plateau zone*, is situated along the San Juan, Little Colorado, and a part of the Colorado River drainages of the high pinyon- and juniper-clad Colorado Plateau region of the Four Corners, with an extension eastward into the upper Rio Grande valley. The boundaries of these focal areas expanded and contracted, bringing about different levels of exchange between peoples and, in some instances, complete dominance of one group over another. The basic, sedentary agricultural way of life and the informal regulated contacts between peoples were important factors in maintaining generally uniform culture throughout the region, although growth and regression did occur.

Hamlets (300/100 B.C. to A.D. 500/700)

When food production finally won over dependence upon wild resources, a new subsistence base was established from which issued the dramatic changes that were to distinguish the southwesterners from surrounding peoples. Anthropologists view this shift from nomadism to sedentism as the first great revolution in mankind's history. Though it took centuries, in the Southwest it certainly brought about a new lifeway.

In most parts of the province, the gradual acceptance of corn, squash, and beans, and the development of methods to efficiently grow and utilize them, prompted the slow gathering of previously wandering peoples into small hamlets. In one exception, the agricultural possibilities of the fertile desert river valleys may have attracted a migrant group of Mexicans who were already irrigation farmers and craft specialists. In general, the earliest appearance of these hamlets in the southern deserts, mountains, and valleys of the Southwest was due to their being closer to Mexico. It also took time for various groups to spread from south to north within the Southwest.

Groups lived in simple, family-sized dwellings with walls and roofs built over circular or rectangular pits. Posts were set in the floor or around the pit as a supporting framework for a domelike or sloping-sided superstructure with a flat roof. The roof was made of short sections of logs, poles, brush, and mud. Entrance usually was through a side opening or a short lateral passageway. Firepits or heating pits were located in the middle of hard-packed mud floors, with a smokehole in the roof for ventilation. Storage units either were cut into the floors or were built upon them. Rudimentary as these structures were, they provided shelter and sleeping places during bad weather. Their dimly lighted interiors were used at times for preparing meals, storing foodstuffs, and performing other everyday tasks. Some

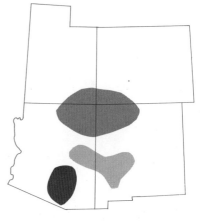

Hamlets

household duties likely took place on the flat roofs of the homes because much time was spent in the outdoors. In some of the eastern and plateau settlements an extra-large pithouse, or Great Kiva, seems to have served as a community meeting place for social and religious affairs.

Social and religious patterning probably was informal and likely did not extend beyond the family or small enclaves of several families. Most of it must have concerned maintaining family harmony and placating the erratic forces of nature. Only the desert hamlets, with their dependence on irrigation systems, might have required some secular leadership in a community.

Depending on several circumstances, the first communities were located in diverse settings. In the desert they were along rivers where nearby farm plots could be irrigated. In the mountains and valleys, selection of steep ridges suggests a concern for defense. On the plateau, large shallow caves or adjoining talus slopes were chosen for the first flimsy structures. Later, after houses became more substantial, open sites were utilized. Often the areas selected not only provided space suitable for gardening, but also were located near sources of game and native plants essential to existence.

The first pottery showed its Mesoamerican ancestry in being well-executed though simple in form and color. It seems to have been part of a ceramic tradition of undecorated brown- and red-slipped utility wares that arose in central Mexico and diffused north through the central Mexican highlands after 1000 B.C., finally to reach the southern border of the Southwest about 300 B.C. A sluggish diffusion, as well as the presence on the plateau of a tradition of fine basketry, forestalled its appearance in the north for nearly seven centuries.

By the end of the hamlet stage, each region had modified ceramic wares into distinctive local schools that continued to flourish. The desert people, the most advanced potters of the period, swung to a convention of buff ware with red designs; the mountain and valley folk continued the plain browns and reds but modified their surfaces with various types of tooling; and the plateau dwellers switched to a gray ware occasionally embellished with black designs. Not only did colors and habitual designs vary from center to center, but manufacturing techniques and firing methods also differed. Jar and bowl forms predominated.

The inhabitants of the Gila and Salt river drainages also excelled in other cultural aspects due to their rapid assimilation of additional traits from Mexico. Paramount to their existence in the arid deserts was irrigation farming. Contemporary southwesterners were less advanced, relying solely upon dry farming. Stone carving and polishing, and turquoise and shell working, were particularly well developed by the desert Indians. They also surpassed their peers in modeling small clay effigies, supposedly of ritualistic significance.

Stone, bone, and wooden artifacts were added to the basic tools. The growing importance of domesticated plant foods is reflected in the increase and improvement of milling implements used in the preparation of vegetal materials and in the presence of pits and cists for storing them. Better cutting, hammering, and piercing tools can also be related to the everyday tasks associated with sedentary life. The plateau people created many baskets, bags, and belts of fiber, but the seemingly greater abundance of such objects in the north may be due to better preservation. Cotton began to spread north from the desert valleys, where it was first cultivated. Clothing and sandals were fashioned from animal hides and various plant fibers. The atlatl and spear were replaced by the bow and arrow. Pipes and gaming pieces attest to lighter sides of life. Cremation was the burial custom in the lowlands; elsewhere inhumation was practiced. Offerings normally accompanied the deceased.

Villages (A.D. 500/700 to 1000/1100)

More people in larger communities, territorial expansion, and more elaborate ceremonialism typify this stage.

Houses built over or in pits continued to be in vogue in the southern deserts and eastern mountains and valleys, but the larger villages of the desert people were frequently placed farther from rivers, necessitating extension of the canal systems. Incorporated into some of their settlements were ballcourts and platform mounds, both Mexican traits associated with religious performances. Colonizing thrusts to the north, west, and east carried the desert variety of life to its maximum distribution. The mountaineers in the east moved their communities down into stream-watered valleys, enlarging them and continuing to include a Great Kiva in most villages.

On the plateau, surface houses gradually made their appearance. First constructed of posts and mud, the rectangular flat-roofed storage and living rooms were built side by side in a line. As stone masonry was introduced, compact pueblos of dozens of rooms placed in an angular plan about a courtyard or plaza became popular. Specialized features were added to the earlier pithouses, creating a kiva for the religious or social activities of small groups. One or more kivas were incorporated into every village. Larger Great Kivas for community functions also came into use. Growth of population and movement into previously unoccupied districts took plateau peoples throughout the Four Corners and southward, bringing them into contact with other Indians scattered through the deserts and mountains.

The dryland farmers became more efficient by setting up simple systems of terraces, rock alignments, and stone-bordered grids to distribute runoff waters and curtail erosion on slopes and in arroyos. However, nowhere did they approach the skills of the desert irrigation agriculturalists. As generations passed, more productive strains of corn evolved in the different ecological zones which, when combined with improved farming technology, resulted in greater yields. The domestication of the turkey in some localities may have provided a more dependable meat supply, as well as feathers for various purposes.

The makers of red-on-buff ceramics of the low country produced quantities of their traditional wares. Many featured designs of repeated naturalistic and geometric motifs. The plateau potters placed white slips on their gray vessels and decorated them with

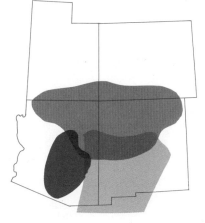

Villages

geometric and curvilinear black designs, a long-lived color preference. Here and there, black-on-red and red-on-orange pottery was locally significant. Gray containers with corrugated surfaces were retained for cooking and storage purposes. The mountain and valley inhabitants continued to produce plain reds and browns and manually textured pots, but painted red designs on some brown pieces. Northern influence inspired the use of white slips and poorly executed red or black patterns on forms that included large and small bowls and jars, pitchers, ladles, canteens, and an occasional effigy. Neighboring villages traded ceramics and certain raw materials of limited distribution. This trading was occasionally supplemented by more distant commerce between culture centers.

Evidence of even more far-flung, extra-territorial trading ventures is evident in the desert villages in an assortment of luxury commodities of stone, copper, and shell from Mexico. Throughout the Southwest the use of shell from the Pacific coast and Gulf of California for jewelry making also testifies to the importance of long-distance trade.

The partially sedentary marginal agriculturalists who lived south and east of the Colorado River in Arizona and in the desolation of southeastern California accepted a number of traits from their more settled neighbors. This imparted a superficial southwestern look to some of their material culture. Elsewhere, people from the core areas began to touch less advanced cultures with their pottery, house types, ornaments, and burial customs. Less tangible reciprocal influences in economic, social, and religious aspects of life also can be postulated. As a result, a distinct cultural shatter belt evolved about the San Francisco Mountains and in the Verde valley. On the northern and eastern fringes of the Southwest, intercourse with Great Basin and Plains groups produced comparable cultural fusion. Such relationships between donor and recipient groups continued well into the following cultural stage.

Southwestern villagers did not greatly alter earlier artifacts. Relatively minor changes included greater use of trough metates for pulverizing corn, and the adoption of the true loom, which increased the production of woven fabrics for a variety of objects. The unique process of etching was devised by the desert artisans for embellishing ornaments of shell. Burials generally followed the customs adhered to during the preceding period.

Marked changes in social and religious practices must have occurred throughout the Southwest coincident with the drawing together of large numbers of people into relatively permanent farming villages. Structures for more formalized religious rites, which undoubtedly called for full- or part-time religious leaders, became widespread. Perhaps these same individuals also provided direction for a growing number of social functions and communal projects.

Towns (A.D. 1000/1100 to 1450/1600)

The changes that came in the final stage of the prehistoric Southwest were many, consequential, and often devastating. The eastern mountain and valley cultures were peacefully overwhelmed by stronger northern neighbors. The desert farmers, already past their cultural prime, pulled back from the frontiers into their original homeland, where

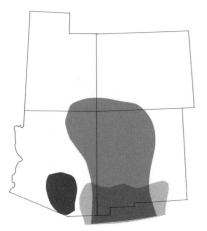

Early Towns

they experienced a cultural regression and dilution of their uniqueness, then final disappearance. The plateau people rose to new cultural heights, aggressively expanding into and dominating new lands. Plagued by misfortunes, they finally withdrew to reassemble in reduced numbers elsewhere. The period also saw the arrival of nomadic peoples, such as the Paiutes, Utes, Apaches, and Navajos, who subjected town dwellers to unaccustomed pressures. Lastly, the Spanish conquerors and settlers appeared, overcame the natives, and initiated rapid changes that eradicated or altered many aboriginal ways.

Architectural advances are the most obvious accomplishments of this period. Construction of great multistoried, many-roomed stone or adobe pueblos occurred on the plateau; erection of large, sometimes walled, communities of single- and several-storied mud buildings took place in the desert. The architecture probably evolved locally but may have received some inspiration from Mexican sources. A peppering of large towns grew up on the flatlands, mesas, and valley bottoms of northern New Mexico and northeastern Arizona. In a more restricted district encircling the Four Corners, similar structures were placed in the shallow caves eroded into canyon walls. Some of these communities had hundreds of storage rooms and living quarters, many kivas, and at least one Great Kiva. When placed in the open, they frequently grew to their final size and shape through an orderly addition of rooms. Rectangles of rooms usually were stepped back from plazas in terraces to heights of four or five stories. Those built in caves were constrained by the caves' outlines, making them appear less systematically arranged.

Where stone masonry was practiced in the north, decided regional variations in style and skill may be observed. The masons of Chaco Canyon excelled, and their pueblos were the grandest in the entire Southwest. At the other extreme, pueblos of the Rio Grande district used irregular blocks set in large amounts of mud mortar, or they depended completely on adobe because suitable building stone was rare. Spacious masonry pueblos (some with kivas and Great Kivas) and small cliff dwellings appeared in the mountains and valleys as the plateau people took over that territory.

In most cases, populous communities along the fertile lands near the southern desert watercourses were incongruous mixtures of the old pole-brush-and-mud-over-pithouses and clay-walled, one-story units of contiguous rooms, plus several Great Houses of adobe built on packed-earth platforms, all surrounded by an earthen wall. Ballcourts were sometimes included. Plateau and/or Mesoamerican influences probably were behind such deviations.

Canal irrigation remained a forte of the desert farmers, but improved systems for collecting and distributing runoff waters appeared among the plateau pueblo dwellers. Knots of population that crowded into some northern districts, such as at Mesa Verde and in Chaco Canyon, depended on being able to gather water from spring thaws and summer rains and direct it to farm plots or storage places by means of diversion dams, reservoirs, canals, and ditches.

In ceramics, the lowland red-on-buff tradition persisted, although plain red increased in popularity and an alien black-and-white-on-red polychrome appeared. On the plateau, black-on-whites were important, but other duochromes and black-and-white-on-red or

Late Towns

-orange polychromes were present in limited distribution. Gray utility wares continued. Plateau-style pottery replaced most of the established red and brown wares of the mountains and valleys when the northerners overran that area. Between about A.D. 1050 and 1200 the most extraordinary black-on-white pottery in the Southwest, featuring excellently executed geometric and naturalistic animal designs, was crafted in pueblos along the Mimbres River in southwestern New Mexico. Along the upper Rio Grande, duochromes and polychromes were painted with pigments that glazed upon firing. Bowls, jars, pitchers, ladles, and some effigies were common forms.

As for other artifacts, most southwesterners relied heavily upon the assemblage that had been in use for many generations. Certain specializations in materials and types are now useful for defining regional and temporal distributions.

In Chaco Canyon on the northern pleateau, a unique cultural brilliance shone for two centuries, beginning about A.D. 1000. There, an integrated political, social, and economic system characterized some sixteen towns and hundreds of smaller communities in and around the now desolate Chaco Wash in northwestern New Mexico. A network of roads and a series of outposts from where signals could be observed and relayed tied together many people from diverse zones. Possibly they functioned in a structured production and redistribution organization whose influences radiated in all directions, probably even as far as northern Mexico. From Mexico came several kinds of special goods in exchange for turquoise and other items valued by the southern traders. Certain Mesoamerican social and religious customs, the practice of making astronomical observations, the means of communication, and economic and architectural principles also seem to have been absorbed by the Chacoans. A high level of control and leadership, perhaps exercised through a stratified society, appears to have been necessary for the complex Chaco development to have prospered. Thus far, their outstanding achievements in so many endeavors appear unique. Architecture, communications, control and distribution of water, production and apportionment of resources, and probably social and ceremonial organization were areas in which the Chacoans excelled. It is likely that town dwellers elsewhere also evolved more complicated social and religious structures and patterns of leadership to cope with enlarged societies and the problems of sustaining them.

The intrusion of plateau people into the mountain and valley country along the southern Arizona–New Mexico border was one example of their urge for expansion during this town stage. Another group apparently moved down into the desert to take up a century-long residence among the southerners. During this time of cohabitation each faction clung to its established patterns of behavior. Two distinct architectural forms, pottery styles, burial modes, and perhaps agricultural techniques were thus brought together.

The long continuum of southwestern culture, which reached a climax among the desert craftsmen and farmers as early as A.D. 700 to 900 but did not attain a comparable elaboration among pueblo builders until several centuries later, began to experience a creeping decay as the town period progressed. Behind such decline was a tangle of physical, social, and moral reasons. Environmental and cultural exhaustion likely were

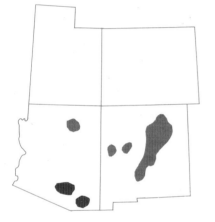

Contact

fundamental to any of them.

First to feel the adverse effects were groups along the northern plateau. The outstanding, but somewhat exotic, Chaco Phenomenon started to fall apart during the twelfth century, and by A.D. 1200, if not earlier, most Chaco Canyon residents had deserted their customary territory to drift southward. By 1300 the magnificent cliff dwellings and large pueblos of the Mesa Verde area were also abandoned by their residents who likewise moved south to settle among kinfolk. Elsewhere on the plateau, other pockets of farming Indians slowly retreated from former holdings to regroup into three principal locations by about 1450. One was in the vicinity of the Hopi mesas, a second was in the Zuni country, and a third was near the upper Rio Grande. It was in these regions that villages of Pueblo Indians, as they came to be designated by Spanish explorers and colonists, were found in the sixteenth century already on a downward cultural path. Many of them remain in these same regions. Ties between the ancient occupants of the plateau and historic Pueblo people have definitely been established, but no precise correlation between specific prehistoric and contemporary towns can be made. Nevertheless, many aboriginal patterns, especially some concerned with spiritual matters, remain viable ingredients of Pueblo life.

The fate of the desert dwellers is not as clearly discernible. As an archeological entity, their culture dwindled and disappeared by A.D. 1450 for many of the same reasons that underlay the demise of the northern version of Southwest culture. About 1700, when Spanish Jesuit priests first began to write accounts of the natives of southern Arizona, they identified the Tohono O'odham (Pima-Papago) as living along the Salt and Gila rivers and described them as practicing canal irrigation. Although this protohistoric cultural expression little resembles the past glory of the aboriginal occupants of the same area, it is likely that the Tohono O'odham are indeed the inheritors of that tradition.

Ancestors of the tribes along the lower Colorado River temporarily accepted a modicum of southwestern culture but reverted to their simple life once contacts with certain core areas ceased; they include the Mohave, Yavapai, Hualapai, Havasupai, and Maricopa. △

Present

ADDITIONAL READINGS

Cordell, Linda S.
  1979 Prehistory: Eastern Anasazi. *Handbook of North American Indians.* Vol. 9.
        Washington, D.C.: Smithsonian Institution. 131–151.
  1984 *Prehistory of the Southwest.* New York: Academic Press.
Eggan, Fred
  1979 Pueblos: Introduction. *Handbook of North American Indians.* Vol. 9.
        Washington, D.C.: Smithsonian Institution. 224–235.
Gumerman, George J., and Emil W. Haury
  1979 Prehistory: Hohokam. *Handbook of North American Indians.* Vol. 9.
        Washington, D.C.: Smithsonian Institution. 75–90.
Irwin-Williams, Cynthia
  1979 Post-Pleistocene Archeology, 7000–2000 B.C. *Handbook of North American*

Indians. Vol. 9. Washington, D.C.: Smithsonian Institution. 31–42.

Jennings, Jesse D.
    1989 *Prehistory of North America.* Third Edition. Mountain View, California:
            Mayfield Publishing Company.

Jones, Dewitt, and Linda S. Cordell
    1985 *Anasazi World.* Portland, Oregon: Graphic Arts Center Publishing Company.

Kelley, J. Charles
    1966 Mesoamerica and the Southwestern United States. *Handbook of North*
            American Indians. Vol. 4. Archaeological Frontiers and External Connections.
            Austin: University of Texas Press. 95–110.

Kidder, Alfred V.
    1962 *An Introduction to the Study of Southwestern Archaeology.* Reprint of 1924.
            New Haven, Connecticut: Yale University Press.

Lipe, William D.
    1983 The Southwest. *Ancient North Americans.* New York: W. H. Freeman. 421–494.

Martin, Paul S.
    1979 Prehistory: Mogollon. *Handbook of North American Indians.* Vol. 9.
            Washington, D.C.: Smithsonian Institution. 61–74.

Noble, David Grant, Editor
    1991 *The Hohokam, Ancient People of the Desert.* Santa Fe, New Mexico: School of
            American Research.

Plog, Fred
    1979 Prehistory: Western Anasazi. *Handbook of North American Indians.* Vol. 9.
            Washington, D.C.: Smithsonian Institution. 108–130.

Schroeder, Albert H.
    1979 History of Archeological Research. *Handbook of North American Indians.* Vol.
            9. Washington, D.C.: Smithsonian Institution. 5–13.
    1979 Prehistory: Hakataya. *Handbook of North American Indians.* Vol. 9.
            Washington, D.C.: Smithsonian Institution. 100–107.

Woodbury, Richard B.
    1979 Prehistory: Introduction. *Handbook of North American Indians.* Vol. 9.
            Washington, D.C.: Smithsonian Institution. 22–30.

Woodbury, Richard B., and Ezra B. W. Zubrow
    1979 Agricultural Beginnings, 2000 B.C.–A.D. 500. *Handbook of North American*
            Indians. Vol. 9. Washington, D.C.: Smithsonian Institution. 43–60.

All-Southwest Overview

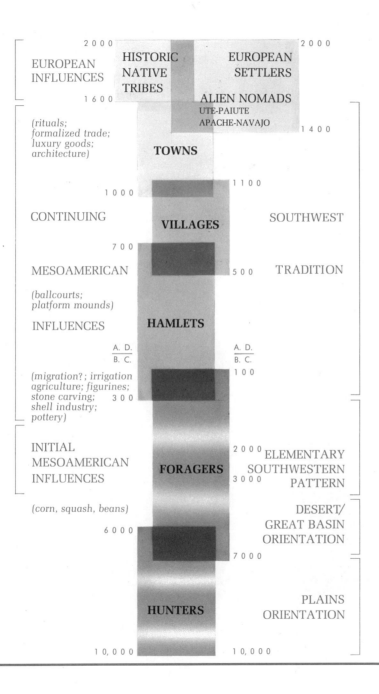

EUROPEAN
INFLUENCES

2000

HISTORIC
NATIVE
TRIBES

EUROPEAN
SETTLERS

2000

1600

ALIEN NOMADS
UTE-PAIUTE
APACHE-NAVAJO

1400

*(rituals;
formalized trade;
luxury goods;
architecture)*

TOWNS

CONTINUING

1000

1100

VILLAGES

SOUTHWEST

MESOAMERICAN

700

500

TRADITION

*(ballcourts;
platform mounds)*

INFLUENCES

HAMLETS

A. D.
B. C.

A. D.
B. C.

*(migration?; irrigation
agriculture; figurines;
stone carving;
shell industry;
pottery)*

300

100

INITIAL
MESOAMERICAN
INFLUENCES

FORAGERS

2000

3000

ELEMENTARY
SOUTHWESTERN
PATTERN

(corn, squash, beans)

6000

DESERT/
GREAT BASIN
ORIENTATION

7000

HUNTERS

PLAINS
ORIENTATION

10,000

10,000

Cultural associations represented in the national parks and monuments.

Traditional Archeological Classification	ALL-SOUTHWEST INTERPRETATION		
	HAMLETS	*VILLAGES*	*TOWNS*
HOHOKAM	Montezuma Castle (Well) Organ Pipe Cactus Saguaro	Organ Pipe Cactus	Casa Grande Organ Pipe Cactus
MOGOLLON	Carlsbad El Malpais Gila Cliff Dwellings Guadalupe Mountains Petrified Forest	El Malpais Gila Cliff Dwellings Petrified Forest	Petrified Forest
ANASAZI	Arches Bandelier Canyon de Chelly Canyonlands Chaco El Malpais Glen Canyon Grand Canyon Mesa Verde Natural Bridges Navajo Pecos Petrified Forest Zion	Arches Bandelier Canyon de Chelly Canyonlands Chaco El Malpais Glen Canyon Grand Canyon Mesa Verde Natural Bridges Navajo Pecos Petrified Forest	Aztec Bandelier Canyon de Chelly Chaco El Malpais El Morro Hovenweep Mesa Verde Yucca House Navajo Pecos Petrified Forest Petroglyph Salinas Pueblo Missions
IN-BETWEENS AND OUTLIERS	Bryce (Fremont) Capitol Reef (Fremont) Colorado (Fremont) Dinosaur (Fremont) Glen Canyon (Fremont) Zion (Fremont)	Capitol Reef (Fremont) Glen Canyon (Fremont) Grand Canyon (Hakataya) Montezuma Castle (Hakataya) Petrified Forest (Hakataya) Sunset Crater (Hakataya) Walnut Canyon (Hakataya) Wupatki (Hakataya)	Montezuma Castle (Hakataya) Tonto (Salado) Tuzigoot (Hakataya) Wupatki (Hakataya)

Petroglyphs, Salt Creek, Arches National Park. DAVID MUENCH.

Horse Canyon, Canyonlands National Park. DAVID MUENCH.

White House Ruin, Canyon de Chelly National Monument. DAVID MUENCH.

Tyuonyi Ruin, Bandelier National Monument. DAVID MUENCH.

Pueblo Bonito, Chaco Culture National Historical Park. DAVID MUENCH.

Atsinna Ruin, El Morro National Monument. DAVID MUENCH.

Square Tower House, Mesa Verde National Park. DAVID MUENCH.

Spruce Tree House, Mesa Verde National Park. DAVID MUENCH.

Stronghold Ruin, Hovenweep National Monument. DAVID MUENCH.

Inscription House, Navajo National Monument. DAVID MUENCH.

Montezuma Castle National Monument. DAVID MUENCH.

Kiva and mission, Pecos National Historical Park. DAVID MUENCH.

Mission and pueblo ruins, Gran Quivira, Salinas Pueblo Missions National Monument. DAVID MUENCH.

Wupatki Ruin, Wupatki National Monument. DAVID MUENCH.

Fremont pictographs, Courthouse Wash, Arches National Park. DAVID MUENCH.

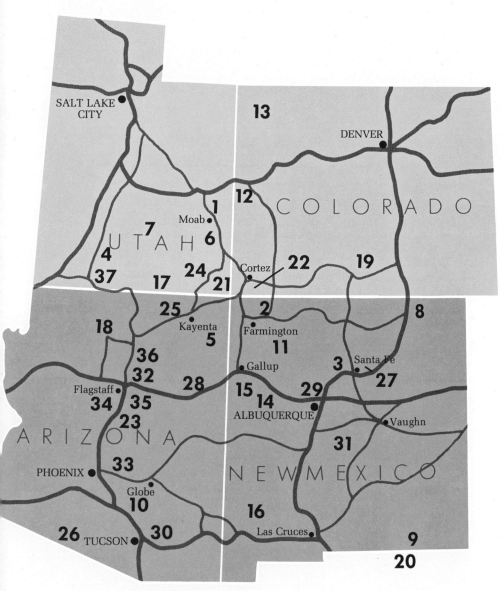

(1) Arches National Park
(2) Aztec Ruins National Monument
(3) Bandelier National Monument
(4) Bryce Canyon National Park
(5) Canyon de Chelly National Monument
(6) Canyonlands National Park
(7) Capitol Reef National Park
(8) Capulin Volcano National Monument
(9) Carlsbad Caverns National Park
(10) Casa Grande Ruins National Monument
(11) Chaco Culture National Historical Park
(12) Colorado National Monument
(13) Dinosaur National Monument
(14) El Malpais National Monument
(15) El Morro National Monument
(16) Gila Cliff Dwellings National Monument
(17) Glen Canyon National Recreation Area
(18) Grand Canyon National Park
(19) Great Sand Dunes National Monument

(20) Guadalupe Mountains National Park
(21) Hovenweep National Monument
(22) Mesa Verde National Park
(23) Montezuma Castle National Monument
(24) Natural Bridges National Monument
(25) Navajo National Monument
(26) Organ Pipe Cactus National Monument
(27) Pecos National Historical Park
(28) Petrified Forest National Park
(29) Petroglyph National Monument
(30) Saguaro National Monument
(31) Salinas Pueblo Missions National Monument
(32) Sunset Crater Volcano National Monument
(33) Tonto National Monument
(34) Tuzigoot National Monument
(35) Walnut Canyon National Monument
(36) Wupatki National Monument
(37) Zion National Park

SOUTHWESTERN ARCHEOLOGY IN THE NATIONAL PARKS AND MONUMENTS

A large measure of the allure that the opening of the West held for most nineteenth-century Americans was that it was not merely the highest mountains, deepest canyons, wildest rivers, and serest deserts that were being proclaimed as common property, but also an intriguing lost world of a vanquished race. Or so it seemed. Within a period of about fifty years such antiquities had been encountered from the Rockies to the Gulf of California, the portion of the nation to become known as the Southwest. Their discovery aroused a healthy curiosity about the human parade that had passed that way before the arrival of Europeans, but it also produced a less admirable treasure hunting fever that threatened to wipe out in a few decades what had lain undisturbed for centuries.

It was the public's good fortune that many of the significant finds were first made known by people with scientific interests who appreciated the inherent intellectual value of their discoveries and embarked on serious research. As a result, the discipline of southwestern archeology was born in the minds of those stalwart few. It was of more enduring consequence that the federal government adopted a policy of protecting this irreplaceable heritage from the casual offender to preserve it for all. Although such action came too late in some areas, the creation of national preserves of Southwest antiquities provided archeologists a chance to study what otherwise might have been lost forever. It also provided citizens an opportunity to learn in pleasant surroundings, which also were often spectacularly scenic. Education never has been made so easy because in no other nation in the world has such an archeological alliance between government, science, and the general public been formed.

Because each National Park Service installation in the Southwest is an independent unit, a visitor may come away with the misconception that each spotlighted site or group of sites was a simple aboriginal world unto itself. In actuality, all the federally maintained southwestern sites once were meshed cogs in a greater Indian universe. The accounts to follow assign each to its proper niche (or niches) as defined in the general reconstruction of the regional prehistory of sedentary peoples; they consider the modern discovery of each and the archeological and preservation activities that have taken place within it, and offer suggested readings for greater detail. ▲

Anasazi granary, Lake Powell side canyon, Glen Canyon National Recreation Area. GEORGE H. H. HUEY.

ARCHES, CANYONLANDS, AND CAPITOL REEF NATIONAL PARKS/NATURAL BRIDGES NATIONAL MONUMENT/GLEN CANYON NATIONAL RECREATION AREA, UTAH

Cultural Significance and Archeological Classification

The region in which these National Park Service areas are located was important in the pioneering days of southwestern archeology, especially in defining the early stages of Anasazi culture. Subsequent research has extended the record of human occupation back to the period of the earliest Archaic hunters and gatherers. Fiber and charcoal samples have dated these Archaic remains from ca. 7000 B.C. to A.D. 400. Both Basket Makers and Fremont peoples making the transition to a subsistence pattern sustained by horticulture evolved out of this cultural base. Anasazi affiliated with the Kayenta tradition moved northwest of the Colorado River gorge in Pueblo II and early Pueblo III times, while others following Mesa Verdean modes settled in the canyons and mesas north of the San Juan and east of the Colorado rivers.

Outstanding examples of rock art may be examined in many places, particularly in Canyonlands and Capitol Reef. Prior to the creation of Lake Powell, Glen Canyon and its tributaries were subjected to a comprehensive survey and excavation program to recover specimens and data from ruins now covered by waters of the lake.

Explorations and Investigations

These five areas in southwestern Utah are noted primarily for a breathtaking landscape eroded from the extensive, red sandstone formations of the Colorado Plateau by millions of years of the action of water, wind, frost, and sun. But it was an agonized terrain that did not attract early penetration or settlement by Spaniards or Mexicans, who considered it a formidable barrier better skirted than crossed. The broken country along the Colorado River above Lees Ferry remained terra incognita to Spaniards. Not until 1776, while seeking a passage connecting the Spanish provinces of New Mexico and California, did Franciscan priests Francisco Atansio Domínguez and Silvestre Vélez de Escalante ride through parts of this wilderness to cross the Green and Colorado rivers. The so-called Crossing of the Fathers in Glen Canyon soon became an important ford for traders and trappers, who by 1840 had become acquainted with much of the forbidding land sliced by the upper Colorado and its tributaries.

After the United States assumed control of the region in 1848, the Colorado River was considered a possible water route from the Rocky Mountains to the west coast, where growth had been accelerated by the discovery of gold. In the 1850s several government explorations looking into the navigability of the Colorado were led by Captain Lorenzo Sitgreaves, Lieutenant Joseph Ives, and Captain J. N. Macomb. The first accurate description of the canyons of the Green and Colorado rivers and much of the adjacent

Archaic: *Desert Culture*
Anasazi: *Basket Maker II, III; Pueblo I, II, III*
In-betweens and Outliers: *Fremont culture (San Rafael)*
All-Southwest: *Hamlets and Villages, plateau zone*

Sherd of corrugated pottery showing finger prints on the construction coils. FRED MANG, JR., NATIONAL PARK SERVICE

territory, along the more than one thousand winding miles from Green River, Wyoming, to the lower end of the Grand Canyon in Arizona, was provided by John Wesley Powell as a result of his two exploratory trips in 1869 and 1871–72. His writings mentioned prehistoric remains encountered along the route, which bisected Canyonlands National Park and traversed the length of Glen Canyon National Recreation Area. The Colorado River from Arches National Park to its confluence with the Green River in Canyonlands National Park was first described after it was explored by a railroad survey party in 1889.

Accumulation of accurate archeological knowledge of the region commenced with the work of several Hayden Survey parties of the U.S. Geological and Geographical Survey of the Territories in 1873–76. William H. Holmes, artist, geologist, and later chief of the Bureau of American Ethnology, and William H. Jackson, famous for his photographs of the West, participated in some of the reconnaissances and described and depicted Indian remains.

Public awareness of the archeological wealth of the Four Corners area developed in the late 1880s after the discovery and popularization by the Wetherill brothers of Indian structures tucked in the cliffs of the Mesa Verde. Their haul of "relics" from the sites was displayed at museums and fairs and was sold to antiquarians. As a result, during the late nineteenth and early twentieth centuries the Colorado Plateau emerged as a favored spot for a growing number of archeologists. They crisscrossed the mesas and gorges hoping to locate important aboriginal remains and obtain materials from them for institutions in the East. Rivaling their exploits and fortitude were numerous local collectors bent upon lucrative sales to the highest bidder of items removed from the ruins. In some instances wealthy patrons and resident enthusiasts joined forces in scouring what commonly was regarded as the public domain. To their credit, sometimes they were spurred on by the altruistic goal of giving their finds to a reputable museum. One such arrangement led to work in Butler Wash, Cottonwood Wash, and Grand Gulch, all side canyons of the San Juan River that proved to be of great significance in the developing discipline of southwestern archeology.

In 1893 Richard Wetherill and his brothers had completed their explorations and excavations in the cliff houses of Mesa Verde and were eager to examine new territory. Richard had heard stories and seen pictures of abandoned sites in Grand Gulch which reminded him of those at Mesa Verde. He had also seen a large assortment of fine Cliff Dweller artifacts from the sites. He determined to see Grand Gulch and sought financial backing from two young, wealthy brothers from New York, Frederick and Talbot Hyde. He had first met them when they came to the Wetherill ranch in Mancos, Colorado, on their way to visit Mesa Verde. A partnership was formed in which Richard would lead a party, the Hyde Exploring Expedition, into Grand Gulch, and the Hydes would finance the effort. Whatever was recovered would be given to the American Museum of Natural History in New York. Richard realized that he was undertaking something for which he lacked training or education. Because of his former experiences with scientists at Mesa Verde, he knew that the value of any possible Grand Gulch collection would depend entirely upon documentation of his excavations and all specimens recovered. He prepared forms so he could note the location, depth, and catalog number of every object. A permanent catalog number was to be placed on each article. Plans were to be drawn of every ruin investigated, each room in a site was to be numbered, and important features would be photographed before and after excavation.

With his brothers Al and John and several others, Richard left the Wetherill Alamo Ranch in November on horseback. Supplies were lashed into two-hundred-pound packs on mules. Fortunately, the winter of 1893–94 was mild, allowing the party to work steadily for four months in the sand and rubble of more than one hundred caves in Grand Gulch, Cottonwood Wash, Butler Wash, and a few localities south of the San Juan River. At the end of this time, a collection weighing well over a ton and numbering 1,216 specimens had been amassed. It was packed out to Bluff City, Utah, transferred to wagons, and taken back to the ranch. There, Richard worked over the collection, studying and cataloging specimens before crating them for shipment to the New York museum.

Not only were the Hyde brothers and the American Museum of Natural History pleased with the Wetherill collection, but during the course of the expedition an incident took place that had a long-lasting effect upon southwestern archeology. Richard was aware that Charles McLoyd and C. C. Graham of Durango, Colorado, after making the first exploration of Grand Gulch in 1890–91 and bringing out a number of ancient artifacts, had noted that some of the mummies and specimens seemed different from those of the Cliff Dwellers. They speculated that they may have belonged to another, more primitive "race." Richard's party was digging in caves in Cottonwood Wash when he, too, began to find evidence that a people with a distinct culture had used the caves before the Cliff Dwellers. These remains, which he routinely found in deposits below those left by the Cliff Dwellers, were unlike anything he had seen before. The earlier people had long, narrow, undeformed skulls and buried their dead in pits or abandoned storage cists dug into cave floors. They made excellent baskets, had no pottery, used spears propelled by an atlatl, and wore unique sandals. The later Cliff Dwellers had skulls that had been flattened in childhood through use of a hard cradle board. In addition, they had pottery, used the bow and arrow, and wore a style of sandal different from that of their predecessors. Upon these few tatters from the hazy past was based the reconstruction of a long, pulsating pageant of human endeavor.

Richard Wetherill was convinced that he had made a significant discovery. From his field camp in Cottonwood Wash he wrote to the Hydes with news of this and other finds. In reply to Talbot Hyde's request for more specific information, Richard referred to the "Basket People" to distinguish the older folk from the Cliff Dwellers. Later, Hyde wrote that it might be better to call them "Basket Makers," although notes accompanying Al Wetherill's autobiography imply that the Wetherill brothers may have used that term from their first recognition of the pre–Cliff Dweller culture.

Thus, the early stage of what archeologists later were to call the Anasazi culture was recognized and labeled Basket Maker. However, many archeologists were prejudiced against Richard Wetherill's claims and interpretations because to them he was only an untrained cowboy with a reputation for collecting and selling antiquities. It was not until

Pictographs at Peekaboo Springs, Canyonlands National Park.
GEORGE H. H. HUEY.

Anasazi corrugated jar. TOM
MASAMORI, COURTESY OF COLORADO
HISTORICAL SOCIETY.

several years later, after similar finds had been made and reported upon by professionals, that Wetherill's keen deductions were verified and his term Basket Maker, for the first sedentary farmers of the Colorado Plateau, was generally adopted by the academic community. Successive and more advanced stages of what came to be recognized as an Anasazi cultural progression subsequently were designated Pueblo to replace the original, more limited term, Cliff Dweller.

Other Wetherill brothers played leading roles in ruin hunting in southeastern Utah. At Richard's urging, Clayton Wetherill explored Moqui Canyon, a tributary of Glen Canyon, seeking Basket Maker remains. Sometimes accompanied by Al, he also spent many summers guiding T. Mitchell Prudden, an eastern physician turned archeologist, who enjoyed traveling and examining Indian ruins of the San Juan basin. From 1906 until his death in 1944 John Wetherill served as guide, packer, and advisor for nearly every scientific party that entered the Kayenta area.

Beginning about the turn of the century, Byron Cummings and his students began a long exploration program into the basins of the upper Colorado and lower San Juan rivers. Known as the "Dean" because he served for a time as a dean at the University of Utah, his reports upon the country's archeological and geological resources were instrumental in the establishment of several national monuments. One was Natural Bridges National Monument, set aside in 1908 to protect the weathered arches in White Canyon and the prehistoric ruins in the vicinity. Another was Rainbow Bridge National Monument, established in 1910, after he had played an important part in discovering that natural wonder. After he left the University of Utah for the University of Arizona, where he nurtured an active archeology department, he continued his researches in the Navajo country and was one of the first to publicize its grandeur and archeological richness. He also left records of his work in Canyonlands, Natural Bridges, and Glen Canyon.

Cummings's contemporaries likewise were attracted to southeastern Utah and neighboring states to delve into the region's mysteries. Their remarkable work filled gaps in the accumulating information about the ancient people who had dwelt there. One relationship between a prominent New York cottonbroker with an avid passion for exploration and a group of archeologists and veteran southwestern guides eventuated in a series of organized treks much like the earlier Hyde expedition. In fact, the work was similarly undertaken on behalf of the American Museum of Natural History, which received all notes and artifacts.

For more than a decade, beginning in 1920, New Yorker Charles L. Bernheimer made fourteen pack trips through the remote canyons, plateaus, and deserts of the Four Corners. To his advantage, at various times he secured the archeological services of Earl Morris, an eager young researcher, and was guided by John Wetherill and Ezekiel "Zeke" Johnson. A resident of Blanding, Utah, Johnson rivaled Wetherill in his familiarity with the lower San Juan country. In later years he was appointed the first custodian of Natural Bridges National Monument. Bernheimer's wanderings covered much of the area's most inhospitable and little-known corners, including portions of Natural Bridges and Glen Canyon. And even though he successfully charted a southern approach to Rainbow Bridge, scientifically the results of his work were minimal. Several popular magazine articles and a book were published.

By the late 1920s archeologists realized that some areas north of the Colorado River in Utah, the northern periphery of the Southwest, possessed prehistoric remains that differed somewhat from the better-known cultural manifestations of the San Juan drainage. At the suggestion of Alfred V. Kidder, considered by many to have been the foremost early figure in southwestern archeology, the Peabody Museum of Harvard University placed four expeditions in that country between 1927 and 1930 to learn more of its antiquities. Their widespread surveys and excavations took them into districts of Canyonlands National Park, Capitol Reef National Park, and Glen Canyon National Recreation Area. Called the Claflin-Emerson Expedition after its Boston sponsors, its field staff included Donald Scott, Noel Morss, and Henry Roberts. Although the complete results of the expedition's fieldwork were not made available, Morss promptly reported his efforts in the Fremont and Dirty Devil drainages in which he defined the Fremont Culture. This he considered an aberrant form of the more common southwestern mode. His key sites now lie within the boundaries of Capitol Reef National Park. Years later, in 1969, James H. Gunnerson prepared a lengthy monograph synthesizing all available data on the Fremont Culture and the northern frontier, including a belated report of the accomplishments of the Claflin-Emerson Expedition. Shortly after, in her paper on the rock art of Utah, Polly Schaafsma included information gathered during those field trips by Donald Scott.

The possibility of further exciting archeological finds in a setting of such harsh magnificence continued to lure both scholars and adventurers throughout the 1930s. The Rainbow Bridge–Monument Valley Expedition spent six summers conducting extensive scientific investigations, some of which were published.

The next important archeological undertaking was a statewide survey initiated in 1949 by the University of Utah. Various participants in this continuing program have inventoried ancient remains in parts of southeastern Utah, among them sections of Canyonlands, Capitol Reef, and Arches. Investigations in Beef Basin revealed an area of high site density with scientific promise.

Congressional authorization in 1956 for construction of Glen Canyon Dam and several other dams in the upper Colorado River basin set in motion one of the most comprehensive emergency archeology programs ever attempted up to that time in this country. Through research contracts administered by the National Park Service, work on the Glen Canyon Project of the Upper Colorado River Basin Archeological Salvage Program was shared by the University of Utah and the Museum of Northern Arizona. It was anticipated that the flooding of some 153,000 acres in Glen and San Juan canyons would seriously threaten archeological resources. Therefore, farsighted research projects were launched in order to salvage materials and data pertinent not only to prehistory but also to ethnohistory, geology, history, climatology, paleontology, and biology. The ultimate goal was to prepare a natural history of the Glen Canyon region showing how human behavior is tied to and modifies other resources of a land.

With the closing of the gates of Glen Canyon Dam in 1963, the program's fieldwork ended. Behind the dam, Lake Powell extends 183 miles with 1,800 miles of shoreline confined between majestic sandstone cliffs and buttes. The canyon bottoms, where teams of researchers toiled in heat, sand, rain, and hardship, are completely obscured. The Glen Canyon Project amassed a solid body of new data from a vast area, making Glen Canyon one of the best-known archeological areas of comparable size in the West.

Survey teams working from boats, on foot, with saddle horses and pack animals, and in four-wheel-drive vehicles, along with excavation crews isolated for weeks at a time in remote places, charted the precise location and attributes of more than two thousand sites and exposed several dozen representative ruins. The majority of the archeological resources identified in Glen Canyon and its tributaries are now submerged beneath Lake Powell. Some prehistoric trails and steps, rock art panels, and remnants of storage and habitation structures were not flooded and are still visible to boaters and hikers.

As soon as the waters of Lake Powell began rising behind the dam, the lake and environs became an increasingly popular recreation spot. The dam is operated by the Bureau of Reclamation, but in 1971 administration of the recreation facilities was assigned to the National Park Service. Since then National Park Service archeologists and interpreters have labored to protect and preserve accessible examples of rock art and ruins and to develop an interpretive program, including floating wayside exhibits.

The most intensive work was carried out between 1984 and 1987 by researchers from Northern Arizona University under the direction of Phil R. Geib. This latest archeological effort covered almost 19,000 acres to record 489 sites, of which 20 were tested. Without the time constraints associated with the preinundation surveys and with the advancement during the intervening twenty years of techniques and dating methods, it was learned that the Glen Canyon region had supported an Archaic population for an estimated eight thousand years. About A.D. 200 a Fremont culture slowly emerged from this background. Seven hundred years later, Anasazi expansion out of northern Arizona and southwestern Colorado dominated the area.

After its establishment in 1964, one of the first steps in the development of Canyonlands National Park was to appraise the park's archeological holdings. University of Utah archeologists inventoried a portion of the park, concentrating on the Needles District. That area, which is east and southeast of the Colorado River, and Island-in-the-Sky, between the Colorado and Green rivers, were surveyed again in 1989 to record 477 sites. Late Archaic, Pueblo II, and Pueblo III occupation are most commonly represented but, because of the rugged dry terrain, appear to have been seasonal and small-scale.

Spectacular rock art features colossal human figures with elongated or trapezoidal bodies, various animals, and geometric designs. Fine examples occur in the Maze and Needles components of Canyonlands, but more outstanding are those on massive, vertical sandstone cliffs deep in Horseshoe Canyon, a detached unit west of the park.

Capitol Reef became a national monument in 1937. Its boundaries were later adjusted, and in 1971 it was designated a national park. In geologic terms, a reef is a ridge of rock that forms a barrier. The reef for which the park is named has a prominent dome, Capitol Dome, resembling the United States Capitol—hence, Capitol Reef. The first aboriginal

Anasazi structure at Kachina Bridge, Natural Bridges National Monument. GEORGE H. H. HUEY.

works in Capitol Reef to attract scrutiny were the distinctive pictographs and petroglyphs of the Fremont River gorge and vicinity. The most striking characteristic of the typical rock art is a large anthropomorphic figure with headdress, facial decoration, necklaces, and ear ornaments. A figure carrying a shield also is depicted frequently. The rock art, together with other diagnostic elements found at sites in that region, led Noel Morss in 1931 to define the Fremont Culture.

The first archeological program directed specifically at Capitol Reef National Park was a thorough inventory of areas assumed suitable for past human occupancy along or near water sources. Through the work of University of Utah archeologists in the 1960s, fifty-eight sites were identified. More recently, emergency surveys along the right-of-way of the road paralleling the Waterpocket Fold and following the line of a proposed irrigation system found additional localities. All the surveys have revealed nearly ninety sites in the park. It is probable that all the major sites along primary drainages are known, but undoubtedly smaller, more remote sites remain to be found.

Arches is another National Park Service installation that progressed from monument to park status. Although its geologic and scenic wonders earned it national monument status in 1929, its commonplace aboriginal remains did not entice early professionals and amateurs. The park contains no evidence of long habitation; there is no evidence that the essential combination of arable land and reliable water supply existed. Most spots of aboriginal use are camps either in the open or beneath rock shelters, quarries that furnished raw materials for stone tools, and rock art panels. The Barrier Canyon style of the latter, often including front-facing, long, tapering torsos without appendages, is considered to be of Archaic age. While Arches was still a monument, National Park Service personnel recorded some sites in the backcountry. After Arches National Park was created in 1971, the National Park Service contracted with the Office of the Utah State Archeologist for a systematic examination of the northeastern portion of the reserve. These two endeavors have resulted in a list of eighty-eight sites.

From the earliest white settlement in southeastern Utah in the 1880s, the region's numerous antiquities attracted the curious and the acquisitive. It was in the great chasms sharply knifed through evergreen Cedar Mesa where wonderfully preserved masonry houses of the Cliff Dwellers were found to override burial cists of an earlier folk whom the diggers named the Basket Makers. Consequently in 1908, when the government sought to protect three nearby majestic spans of sandstone (now known as Sipapu, Kachina, and Owachomo bridges) through the establishment of Natural Bridges National Monument, concern was expressed for comparable protection of whatever prehistoric remains might be present in that particular part of Cedar Mesa. William B. Douglass, U.S. Examiner of Surveys, was instructed to document evidence of prehistoric occupation within the monument boundaries. Prior explorations anticipated his success in certifying ancient life in the vicinity of the stone arches.

Fifteen years passed before Ezekiel Johnson was named the first custodian of Natural Bridges National Monument. During Johnson's tenure from 1923 to 1941, he thoroughly explored this wild, remote, northern corner of the Colorado Plateau. One old house he found in White Canyon was named Horsecollar Ruin because of an associated pair of intact surface granaries whose open mouths suggested that gear. In 1937 Charlie Steen, National Park Service archeologist who carried out some excavations there, was more interested in a well-preserved rectangular kiva complete with entrance ladder.

For the past thirty years a series of intensive reconnaissances of the canyons and mesa tops within the monument have confirmed the presence of such aboriginal features as hearths, middens, rock foundations and walls, rock art panels, and modest houses and granaries. After a substantial Basket Maker II and Basket Maker III use of the area, an unexplained hiatus occurred until about A.D. 900. At that time Anasazi farmers returned and stayed until the middle of the thirteenth century. Their numbers never were great, probably because of limited arable land.

Artifact collections from the numerous archeological programs in and about these five federal holdings are housed mainly in the institutions that performed the fieldwork. Major assemblages of specimens are to be found in the Peabody Museum of Harvard, the American Museum of Natural History, the University of Utah, the National Park Service Midwestern Archeological Center, and the Museum of Northern Arizona. Minor collections are displayed or stored in the visitor centers of the respective areas.

A large number of comprehensive reports covering various aspects of the research of the University of Utah's Glen Canyon Project have been issued. For brevity, only several of general nature are included in the following suggested readings. ▲

ADDITIONAL READINGS, Arches, Canyonlands, and Capitol Reef National Parks/Natural
    Bridges National Monument/Glen Canyon National Recreation Area
Crampton, C. Gregory
    1959 *Outline History of the Glen Canyon Region, 1776–1922*. Anthropological Papers
        No. 42. Salt Lake City: University of Utah.
    1973 *Standing Up Country: The Canyon Lands of Utah and Arizona*. New York:
        Alfred A. Knopf.
Gunnerson, James H.
    1969 *The Fremont Culture: A Study in Cultural Dynamics of the Anasazi Frontier*.
        Papers, Peabody Museum of American Archaeology and Ethnology, Vol. 59,
        No. 2. Cambridge, Massachusetts: Harvard University.
Jennings, Jesse D.
    1966 *Glen Canyon: A Summary*. Anthropological Papers, No. 81. Salt Lake City:
        University of Utah.
McNitt, Frank
    1966 *Richard Wetherill: Anasazi*. Reprint of 1957. Albuquerque: University of New
        Mexico Press.
Petersen, David
    1990 *Of Wind, Water, and Sand: The Natural Bridges Story*. Moab, Utah: Canyonlands
        Natural History Association.

Schaafsma, Polly
1971 *The Rock Art of Utah; from the Donald Scott Collection.* Papers, Peabody Museum of American Archaeology and Ethnology, Vol. 65. Cambridge, Massachusetts: Harvard University.
Sharrock, Floyd W.
1966 *An Archaeological Survey of Canyonlands National Park.* Anthropological Papers, No. 83. Salt Lake City: University of Utah. 49–84.

Pictographs at Horseshoe Canyon, The Great Gallery, Canyonlands National Park.
GEORGE H. H. HUEY.

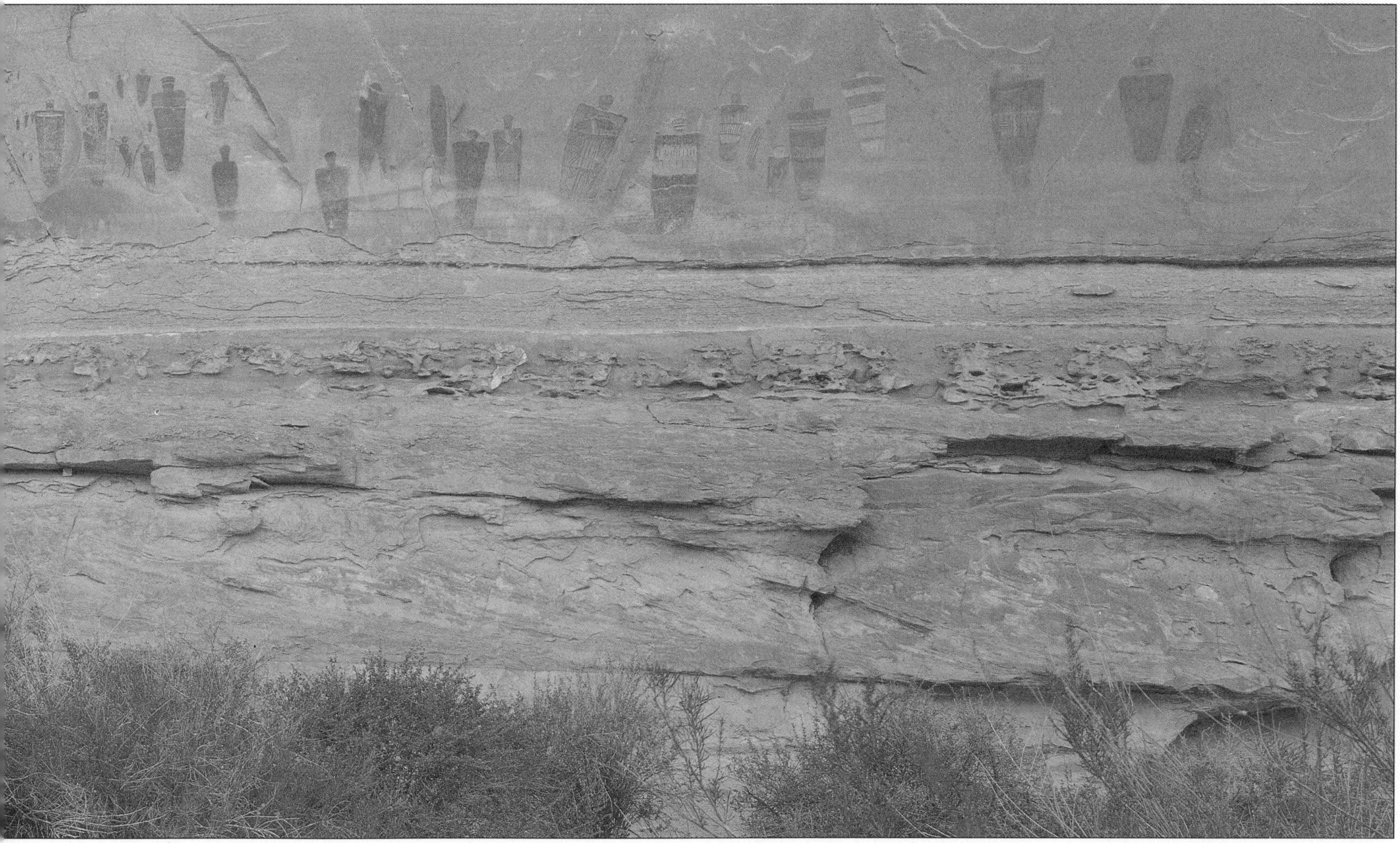

West Ruin at Aztec Ruins National Monument, with reconstructed kiva. The roof is now dismantled. GEORGE A. GRANT, NATIONAL PARK SERVICE, 1946.

AZTEC RUINS NATIONAL MONUMENT, NEW MEXICO

Cultural Significance and Archeological Classification

The excavated Aztec West Ruin and its adjacent unexcavated East Ruin are prime examples of the town building of classic Anasazi times. Additonally, they represent a pair of outliers created in the twelfth century to support the Chaco Phenomenon, probably with foodstuffs grown in a fertile valley coursed by perennial waters. A roadway separating the settlements and connecting them to indigenous, smaller cobblestone villages on the adjacent river terrace is suspected. After being abandoned, both sandstone-masonry house blocks were remodeled and reoccupied by Mesa Verdeans, thereby affording an unusual exhibit of extensive interaction between Anasazi in neighboring areas. The restored Great Kiva, the only one of its kind in existence, shows how these massive chambers for communal social, religious, and perhaps economic activities may have been finished inside and out, how they were roofed, and how skilled and industrious their builders were.

Anasazi: *Pueblo III*
All-Southwest: *Towns, plateau zone*

Explorations and Investigations

In the first half of the nineteenth century the Spanish defeat of the Aztec Indians of central Mexico had received exhaustive popular treatment (*The Conquest of Mexico* by William H. Prescott) which kindled widespread fascination with American Indian remains. As Americans became familiar with their new western lands, a number of the antiquities encountered there were attributed to the Aztecs. This opinion was fortified by the knowledge that the Aztecs themselves considered their origin to have been in "the north." Such was the case when, in the 1870s, white settlers moved into the Animas valley in what is now northwestern New Mexico. The largest group of stone ruins found heaped on terraces of the Animas River became known as Aztec Ruins. However, the Aztec Indians' roots were no farther north than the north-central Mexican plateau. In fact, as a recognizable entity, they postdated the Animas ruins by several centuries. The builders of the Aztec Ruins were the same predecessors of the modern Pueblo Indians responsible for hundreds of other contemporary settlements scattered over the Colorado Plateau.

The earliest known reference to ruins in the region appears on a map of the route of the Escalante and Domínguez expedition from Santa Fe, New Mexico, into Colorado and Utah, 1776–77. On that simply drawn document is written a notation near the Animas and Florida rivers that their waters were sufficient to have supplied the many ancient towns in the vicinity. The Escalante-Domínguez party probably never actually visited the Aztec Ruins. Considering discrepancies in the map and interpretation of the written account, it appears that they traveled well to the north of Aztec.

After the United States acquired the New Mexico Territory in the mid-nineteenth century, a trickle of scientists visited the Aztec Ruins during the next fifty years and left descriptions of them. John S. Newberry, a geologist, came in 1859 as part of the exploratory expedition from Santa Fe to the junction of the Colorado and Green rivers. He was

Anasazi, Pueblo III, black-on-white-pottery fragments. FRED MANG, JR., NATIONAL PARK SERVICE.

followed sixteen years later by another geologist, Frederic M. Endlich, a member of the Hayden Survey. Lewis H. Morgan, a prominent anthropologist, toured the mounds in 1878 while on an extensive southwestern trip. Warren K. Moorehead, a teacher at Phillips Academy in Andover, Massachusetts, on a mission of collecting data for an exhibit at the 1892 Chicago World's Fair, camped for two weeks at the largest cluster of ruins. Each of these men added a few details to the growing body of knowledge of the Animas antiquities.

Meanwhile, white settlers moving down out of the Rockies encountered numerous remains of former occupation along the entire Animas valley. Schoolboys on an outing broke into the largest of these, now called West Ruin, and found undisturbed rooms containing burials with clothing, baskets, pottery, ornaments, tools, and weapons. They and older members of the community indiscriminately looted many intact chambers, fortunately breaching only those that required little digging. However, shaped building stones and roof timbers were hauled away for construction purposes. After the property on which the largest mounds stood was acquired in 1890 by John A. Koontz and later was sold to Henry D. Abrams, this practice was stopped.

In 1915 Nels C. Nelson of the American Museum of Natural History traveled to Aztec to inspect the ancient remains. Recognizing their potential for further investigation, he soon convinced his institution that the largest unit of the Aztec group, the West Ruin, should be the scene of a major excavation program. Owner Abrams gave the American Museum of Natural History excavation rights, with the provision that he be allowed to retain some of the recovered specimens. Philanthropist Archer M. Huntington, owner of the Southern Pacific Railroad, agreed to fund what was anticipated to be a long-term undertaking. A budding young archeologist, Earl H. Morris, who had grown up in the Animas valley, been educated at the University of Colorado, and who was well versed in the antiquities of the region, was chosen to head the project. From 1916 through 1922 Morris devoted his energies to excavating the major portion of the West Ruin.

At the outset the museum intended to completely clear the prehistoric settlement and to strengthen or stabilize all walls or other features in need of repair. However, interrupted by World War I and shortage of funds, excavation of only about two-thirds of the rectangular, multistoried town was completed. As revealed by the excavations and surface evidence, the building originally had at least 220 ground-floor rooms, 119 second-story rooms, and probably more than 12 third-story rooms. There were twenty-nine kivas and one Great Kiva. Foundations for a second Great Kiva underlying the cleared example suggest an earlier aborted effort.

In addition to the principal mound of the site, Morris tested some of the associated ruins. Since his time, the National Park Service has opened a few additional units in the West Ruin and sections of other sites in conjunction with preservation and stabilization measures. In 1934, under National Park Service sponsorship, Morris directed the complicated project of refurbishing the Great Kiva which he had dug years earlier.

The Hubbard Site, a small but significant ruin at the northwest corner of the monument, was cleared by National Park Service archeologists in 1953 to learn more about a particular type of archeological feature peculiar to the region along the upper San Juan River. Its primary element is a triple-walled complex encircling a kiva, which is believed to have been employed in religious activities.

The American Museum of Natural History purchased the small tract of land on which the West Ruin is situated in 1920 and subsequently donated it to the government. On January 23, 1923, Aztec Ruins National Monument was established by proclamation of President Warren G. Harding. Morris was its first custodian. Later additions to the monument brought it to a total of twenty-seven acres within which are six major archeological complexes and seven or eight smaller mounds, some of which may merely be refuse dumps from the settlements.

In 1966 the Aztec Ruins National Monument was placed on the National Register of Historic Places. Additional recognition came in 1987 when the United Nations Educational, Scientific, and Cultural Organization included Aztec Ruins with the Chaco Culture National Historical Park as a World Heritage Center. Finally, in 1988 the size of the monument was increased to 319 acres to incorporate adjacent farmlands in order to halt damage from irrigation waters to the fragile cultural resources and uncultivated terraces to the west and north where many Anasazi ruins have been threatened by vandalism. Included in long-term plans is the conversion of a portion of the present visitor center, originally a house Morris built with materials from West Ruin, into a museum devoted to pioneer southwestern archeologists and additional exhibit space.

Most of the artifacts obtained by the American Museum of National History excavations still are deposited in that institution in New York. National Park Service collections include specimens from all sites in the monument, particularly the West Ruin and the Hubbard Site, and in addition contain items from surrounding locations donated by local residents. The Abrams family collections remain in private hands. ◭

ADDITIONAL READINGS, Aztec Ruins National Monument
Corbett, John M.
    1963   *Aztec Ruins National Monument, New Mexico.* Historical Handbook Series, No.
            36. Washington, D.C.: National Park Service.
Lister, Florence C., and Robert H. Lister
    1977   *Earl Morris and Southwestern Archaeology.* Reprint of 1968. Albuquerque:
            University of New Mexico Press.
    1993   *Earl Morris and Southwestern Archaeology.* Reprint of 1977. Tucson, Arizona:
            Southwest Parks and Monuments Association.
Lister, Robert H., and Florence C. Lister
    1987   *Aztec Ruins on the Animas: Excavated, Preserved, and Interpreted.*
            Albuquerque: University of New Mexico Press.
    1990   *Aztec Ruins National Monument: Administrative History of an Archeological
            Preserve.* Professional Papers, No. 24. Santa Fe, New Mexico: Southwest
            Cultural Resource Center, National Park Service.

Morris, Earl H.
    1919 *The Aztec Ruin.* Anthropological Papers, Vol. 26, Pt. 1. New York: American Museum of Natural History.
    1921 *The House of the Great Kiva at the Aztec Ruin.* Anthropological Papers, Vol. 26, Pt. 2. New York: American Museum of Natural History.
Vivian, R. Gordon
    1959 *The Hubbard Site and Other Tri-walled Structures in New Mexico and Colorado.* Archeological Research Series, No. 5. Washington, D.C.: National Park Service.

Custodian Faris and workmen Tatman and Howe at Aztec during 1933–34 repairs. Funded by Civil Works Administration.
NATIONAL PARK SERVICE.

Interior of reconstructed Great Kiva, Aztec Ruins National Monument. GEORGE A. GRANT, NATIONAL PARK SERVICE, 1940.

Partially reconstructed talus village, Bandelier National Monument. GEORGE A. GRANT, NATIONAL PARK SERVICE, 1934.

BANDELIER NATIONAL MONUMENT, NEW MEXICO

Cultural Significance and Archeological Classification

After a limited Archaic presence followed by a long hiatus, a major Anasazi occupation of the verdant Pajarito Plateau began in the eleventh century and reached peak expansion in the thirteenth and fourteenth centuries. Remains consisted of tiny fieldhouses, pueblos with more than a hundred rooms, rooms in alcoves, rock shelters, and lesser features such as cists, hearths, rock art, trails, and check dams.

The large and small talus communities for which Bandelier National Monument is best known demonstrate the adaptation of pueblo architecture to the Pajarito Plateau, where the soft volcanic deposits provided poor building material for stonemasons but whose cliffs were such that cavities could easily be quarried into them. Communities with walls of irregularly shaped building blocks set in large amounts of mud mortar were built against the bases of cliffs, into which additional connecting rooms were carved. Some large pueblos, such as Tyuonyi and Tsankawi, dating from about A.D. 1400–1550, were placed away from the cliffs in canyon-bottom or mesa-top locations.

The coalescence of Pueblo population along the Rio Grande in late prehistoric times is exemplified by these and many other ruins in the vicinity. Reading Adolph Bandelier's *The Delight Makers*, an ethnohistoric novel set in Frijoles Canyon, gives an insight into fifteenth-century Pueblo life and the peoples' struggle against nomadic newcomers.

Archaic: *Oshara*
Anasazi: *Pueblo III, IV*
All-Southwest: *Hamlets, Villages, Towns, plateau zone*

Explorations and Investigations

Adolph F. Bandelier was born in 1840 in Berne, Switzerland. When he was eight, the Bandeliers moved to Highland, a small Illinois town. His father became a partner in a local bank and was prominent in civic affairs. Young Adolph apparently received his primary education in Highland, but from childhood was stimulated by his family's social connections, wide-ranging scientific inquiry, and mastery of foreign languages. Nevertheless, to prepare him for a career similar to his father's, he was sent back to Berne to study law at the university. As a young married man, he assisted at the bank, became active in community matters, and was headed toward a successful business career.

However, Bandelier's latent fascination with natural history and ancient societies, and the influence of newly acquired scientific associates, prompted him at age forty to embark vigorously in the disciplines of southwestern anthropology and history.

Bandelier arrived in Santa Fe in the summer of 1880 and started immediately upon his first fieldwork, which took him to the ruins of Pecos pueblo, the modern pueblos of Santo Domingo and Cochiti, and finally to the canyon of El Rito de los Frijoles. His journal entry for October 23, 1880, describes this initial foot and horseback trip with a group of Cochiti Indians across a series of deep, lava-strewn canyons and sharp mesas to the Rio Grande and then into Frijoles Canyon. Bandelier's enthusiasm for the area was immediate; El Rito de los Frijoles that cut into the Pajarito Plateau and wound through thick pines, oaks, and cottonwoods was always one of his favorite places. The region and its antiquities were described in seven of his scientific reports. It was the setting for his only novel, written first in German as *Die Koshare* but published in 1890 in English as *The Delight Makers.*

The name El Rito de los Frijoles, or Bean Creek, was applied to the stream and its canyon long before Bandelier knew it. Today, it is commonly called simply Frijoles Canyon. By 1800 the canyon had been designated El Rito de los Frijoles, and plots of it were under cultivation periodically, especially in beans, hay, and grain. Archives of a few years later state that cattle thieves banded together to occupy caves in the canyon like those used by the "barbarians." Apparently this was the earliest reference to the aboriginal lodges of the area.

Edgar L. Hewett, first director of the School of American Research and the Museum of New Mexico, both in Santa Fe, followed Bandelier's circuitous trails on the Pajarito Plateau. Beginning in 1896 and continuing for several years, he and his Indian guides tramped over the country exploring, mapping, and making preliminary archeological inquiries. In 1907 Hewett began digging at some of the region's larger, more promising sites, first Puyé, on the Santa Clara Indian Reservation, and then in Frijoles Canyon. There he and his colleagues and students worked for many seasons.

At Frijoles Canyon Hewett's summer field camps served as training grounds for aspiring students of archeology and as a study and conference center for scholars, writers, artists, and others. Tyuonyi, one of the four canyon-bottom community houses, was excavated, and others were tested. Tyuonyi proved to be a large, oval-shaped pueblo, built about a central plaza, completely enclosed except for a narrow entryway. It had more than 250 ground-floor, cell-like rooms made of blocks of the volcanic tuff that forms the crust of the Pajarito Plateau, and may have stood three stories high in places. Three kivas were sunk into its plaza.

Several talus villages in Frijoles Canyon also were cleared. These are ruins of small terraced masonry pueblos set against the base of a vertical cliff where the talus slope meets the wall of the canyon. The floor and ceiling beams of the rear rooms rested in holes cut into the tuff. Sometimes additional interior rooms were created by cutting doorways in the rear rock walls and then expanding the excavation into room-shaped cavities. The volcanic tuff was easily removed with stone or even wooden tools. These ruins are not cliff dwellings in the usual sense, but are more correctly pueblos built into the cliff.

Hewett's crews also dug in Ceremonial Cave situated high on the canyon escarpment, which contains a well-preserved kiva and a few associated rooms. Outside Frijoles Canyon they made limited tests in some of the larger pueblo ruins, such as Otowi, Tsankawi, and Tshirege.

Bandelier's research called attention to the need to protect the fragile ruins of the Pajarito Plateau. In 1902 legislation was introduced in the U.S. Congress to create a Cliff Dwellers National Park, but objections from loggers and ranchers prevented passage of the bill. It was not until Hewett's archeological program further demonstrated the cultural significance of the region, and he had committed himself to a dogged campaign to have the area set aside as a preserve, that the national holding was proclaimed in 1916. President Wilson fittingly named it Bandelier National Monument.

Under National Park Service administration, some minor excavations, such as in Rainbow House, have been completed. Beginning in the 1930s, emphasis was placed on cleaning up the ruins and preserving those in disrepair.

A series of archeological surveys and salvage excavations in the Rio Grande canyon along the monument's southeastern border was initiated in the mid-1960s in conjunction with the construction of the Cochiti Dam by the U.S. Army Corps of Engineers. The reservoir waters have impacted many archeological sites in and south of the monument. These investigations, handled by the University of New Mexico, the Museum of New Mexico, and the National Park Service, have enhanced the understanding of the monument's prehistory.

In 1977 a disastrous wildfire broke out in Bandelier that raged out of control ten days despite the efforts of more than fifteen hundred firefighters. Before it was finally extinguished, fifteen thousand acres of dense forest in and around part of the monument had been consumed. A unique role was played by archeologists during the firefighting, as they accompanied bulldozers clearing fire lanes through trees and scrub growth. The archeologists ranged on foot ahead of the bulldozers, identifying unexcavated ruins and relaying their locations so they would not be obliterated. Once the fire was out, the archeologists returned to the ash-covered, charred landscape to record the many small ruins that previously had been hidden by the thick forest cover. They also tested their contents to determine what effects the fire had had upon the ruins and artifacts. The most obvious damage was to the volcanic tuff used both as unshaped and shaped blocks by Anasazi masons as their basic wall-construction material. Heat caused the soft tuff to spall and disintegrate.

A positive result of the La Mesa conflagration was that it made administrators aware of their lack of knowledge of the volume or exact kind of cultural resources existent within the monument. Therefore, ten years later government funding was obtained to conduct the area's first systematic archeological reconnaissance. Nearly two thousand sites were tabulated, many of them previously unknown.

Most of the collections resulting from the early excavations in the monument by the School of American Research and the Museum of New Mexico are in those institutions in Santa Fe. The National Park Service's Southwest Cultural Resoures Center, also in Santa Fe, the University of New Mexico, and the Museum of New Mexico have materials from survey and salvage projects. A small assortment of artifacts remains in the monument's visitor center. ▲

ADDITIONAL READINGS, Bandelier National Monument
Bandelier, Adolph F.
1976 *The Delight Makers*. Reprint of 1890. New York: Harcourt Brace Jovanovich.
Barey, Patricia
1990 *Bandelier National Monument*. Tucson, Arizona: Southwest Parks and

Ceremonial Cave, Bandelier National Monument. GEORGE H. H. HUEY.

Monuments Association.

Bousman, C. Britt, Paul Larson, and Frances Levine
1974 *Archaeological Assessment of Bandelier National Monument.* Archaeology Research Program. Dallas, Texas: Southern Methodist University.

Hendron, J. W.
1940 *Prehistory of El Rito de los Frijoles, Bandelier National Monument.* Technical Series, No. 1. Coolidge, Arizona: Southwestern Monuments Association.

Hewett, Edgar L.
1938 *Pajarito Plateau and its Ancient People.* Albuquerque: University of New Mexico Press.

Hubbell, Lyndi, and Diane Traylor, Editors
1982 *Bandelier: Excavations in the Flood Pool of Cochiti Lake, New Mexico.* Denver, Colorado: Interagency Archeological Services Division, National Park Service.

Lange, Charles H., and Carroll L. Riley
1966 *The Southwestern Journals of Adolph F. Bandelier, 1880–1882.* Albuquerque: University of New Mexico Press.

Noble, David G., Editor
1980 *Bandelier National Monument, Geology, History, Prehistory.* Santa Fe, New Mexico: Exploration, Annual Bulletin of the School of American Research.

Wing, Kittridge A.
1955 *Bandelier National Monument, New Mexico.* Historical Handbook Series, No. 23. Washington, D.C.: National Park Service.

Tyuonyi, large canyon-bottom community, Bandelier National Monument. GEORGE A. GRANT, NATIONAL PARK SERVICE, 1934.

White House Ruin, Canyon de Chelly National Monument. GEORGE A. GRANT, NATIONAL PARK SERVICE, 1940.

CANYON DE CHELLY NATIONAL MONUMENT, ARIZONA

Cultural Significance and Archeological Classification

Although overshadowed by an awe-inspiring natural setting, its extraordinarily long record of human occupation and abundance of perishable artifacts make Canyon de Chelly National Monument a unique archeological experience. Plentiful Basket Maker remains, numerous late Pueblo II and Pueblo III structures, protohistoric Hopi and Navajo shelters and goods, and a rich array of rock art of all ages confirm the importance of these canyons to the Anasazi and later Native American peoples. The many unexcavated sites available for future study enhance the value of the monument.

Anasazi: *Basket Maker II, III; Pueblo I, II, III, IV (?)* All-Southwest: *Hamlets, Villages, Towns, plateau zone*

Explorations and Investigations

Located on the high plateau of northeastern Arizona near the center of the Navajo Reservation, Canyon de Chelly National Monument encompasses three of the Southwest's most spectacular red-walled canyons—Canyon de Chelly, Canyon del Muerto, and Monument Canyon. The area that became a national monument in 1931 is named for its main declivity, Canyon de Chelly, thought to be a corruption of the Navajo word "tsegi," meaning rocky canyon. It is administered by the National Park Service as a joint-use area with the Navajo Nation.

Scattered on the evergreen canyon rims, in bottom lands, in shallow alcoves, and on high ledges along the canyon walls are remains of some fifteen hundred years of human occupation. These range from early pithouses to silent cliff dwellings marooned high on slick rock, to the hogans of the Navajos who farm the canyon bottom in summer. Exactly when this remnant of civilization became known to the Europeans occupying the Rio Grande valley is uncertain, but a 1776 Spanish map clearly indicates the location of Canyon de Chelly. Certainly within a quarter-century Spanish troops had entered the region, but any observation of antiquities was secondary to their task of bringing the Navajos to justice.

The Navajo Indians are thought to have filtered into the de Chelly area in the mid-1700s from north-central New Mexico, where contact with Hispanic settlers had introduced them to horses, sheep, and goats and gradually changed their way of life. Formerly the Navajos existed by hunting small game, gathering wild plants, and raising a few patches of corn or beans. The acquisition of livestock converted them into full-time pastoral herdsmen who found it easier to raid neighboring farmers than to grow their own crops. Anglo towns along the Rio Grande and the Pueblo Indian villages especially tempted them, with the result that the century between the 1770s and the 1860s saw almost continual friction.

The Spanish method of trying to cope with the Navajos was to offer them bribes and, if that failed, to send punitive expeditions against them. One such foray occurred in 1805, when a military column entered the Canyon de Chelly country bent upon engaging fleeing

Navajos in combat, hoping to take some captives. Led by Lieutenant Antonio Narbona, later governor of the province of New Mexico, the troopers fought a day-long battle with Navajo men, women, and children fortified on a deep shelf near the top of a wall of Canyon del Muerto. His official report listed the killing of ninety warriors and twenty-five women and children, and the capture of eight adults and twenty-two children. This carnage gave the rock shelter its name of Massacre Cave.

When this part of the Southwest came under American control in 1848, it became the United States forces' turn to handle the Navajos. To most contemporaries, military or civilian, that meant unconditional surrender or extermination. A concerted thirty-seven-year army campaign against the Navajos had had little lasting success.

With the outbreak of the Civil War and withdrawal of troops for duty elsewhere, conflicts between Anglos and Navajos intensified. To meet this growing crisis, a plan proposed by Brigadier General James H. Carleton, Commander of the Department of New Mexico and a veteran Indian fighter, was adopted. His earlier experiences with Indians had convinced him that the only way to get the rebels to settle down was to confine and educate them. In 1863 a forty-square-mile reservation, three hundred miles away at Fort Sumner on the Pecos River in central New Mexico, was made ready. Military directives for rounding up and moving the Navajos to the fort were set in motion.

General Carleton ordered Colonel Christopher "Kit" Carson's forces, which consisted of eight hundred men of the New Mexico Volunteers and two hundred Ute guides and scouts, to begin the operation against the Navajos in June 1863. They were instructed to destroy the Navajos' flocks, fields, orchards, and homes to force their surrender. If they resisted, they were to be captured. Constant military pressure and battles throughout the winter left many of the Navajos destitute. Small groups began to surrender. A particularly demoralizing blow that winter was an army detachment's penetration of Canyon de Chelly, which the Navajos had considered their most secure refuge. Although only about one hundred prisoners were taken, it convinced the Navajos that Carson could flush them out anywhere. Broken in spirit, many turned themselves in at Fort Defiance.

By early March 1864, approximately twenty-five hundred Navajos had straggled into the fort. This group, with wagons and livestock, was the first to be escorted on the "Long Walk" to the Bosque Redondo reservation at Fort Sumner. There were enough wagons and horses only for the aged, infirm, and very young; all others covered the three hundred miles on foot. Within six weeks two additional large groups, more than four thousand people, followed.

The governor of New Mexico proclaimed the end of the Navajo war on April 9, 1864, but some renegades managed to avoid Carson's men to continue their harassment and retaliation. However, most were placed in exile at Fort Sumner. They suffered extreme hardships from disease, food shortages, homesickness, and attempts to force foreign ways of life upon them. By 1868 Carleton's experiment had been judged a failure. As a substitute measure, the government then set aside a new reservation of three-and-one-half million acres in the former Navajo homeland in northeastern Arizona and northwestern New Mexico. Those interned at Bosque Redondo were allowed to return home.

A new treaty, signed by twenty-nine Navajo chiefs and council members, stated that the tribe and the United States were at peace and that the Navajos would stop their raiding. For ten years the government would provide the tribe with schools, emergency food rations, sheep and goats, and agricultural tools and supplies. It was hoped this would encourage the Navajos to accept fixed abodes and farming pursuits.

Because of the shared experiences of the four years of captivity and the impact of the Anglo world upon them, the Navajos began to see themselves as a single united group rather than as numerous bands. But recovery from the Bosque Redondo ordeal was long and painful. Government promises were slow in being fulfilled, and the old pattern of life changed little. Goat and sheep herding continued to be important, supplemented by income from weaving and silversmithing. In time, Navajo blankets, silver and turquoise jewelry, and wool and mohair were taken to market in nearby towns. Additionally, trading posts were opened on the reservation to furnish supplies to the Navajos and provide outlets for their products.

The first license to operate a trading post to serve the Canyon de Chelly Navajos was granted to Lorenzo Hubbell and C. N. Cotton early in 1886. They opened for business at Chinle, at the west mouth of the canyon, in an abandoned stone hogan. A succession of traders followed Hubbell and Cotton, adding more posts as the market warranted.

The twentieth century has witnessed a remarkable turn of events for the Navajos, brought about mainly by their ability to integrate traits and ideas from other groups into their traditional culture, by assistance from federal programs, and by the exploitation of extensive deposits of coal, gas, oil, and uranium on their reservation. Though the Bureau of Indian Affairs still maintains some financial and political authority over tribal matters, the Navajo Nation steadily is increasing its responsibility for its own people and their destinies. A tribal government, headquartered at Window Rock, Arizona, is headed by a set of elected officials, consisting of a chairman and tribal council; local government functions through chapter houses located throughout the reservation. As United States citizens, Navajos also may vote in state and federal elections.

A few Navajo families still reside in Canyon de Chelly. Their homes, fields, and orchards stand out as oases in the desolate, sandy-bottomed, massively walled canyons. Some are employed by the National Park Service and the Thunderbird Lodge to interpret the remarkable archeological remains of the old pueblos and their own culture and history.

Understandably, the living inhabitants of Canyon de Chelly have always been of most immediate interest to the area's visitors. Even so, fairly accurate descriptions of some of the ruins that predated the Navajo occupation by many centuries were made soon after American military exploration parties and punitive forays against the Navajos swept across the territory. Occasionally those expeditions included men with scientific training assigned to gather information about the regions penetrated. Such was the case in 1849 when Lieutenant James H. Simpson, of the Corps of Topographical Engineers, kept a record of a reconnaissance of part of Canyon de Chelly. Simpson described several of the archeological sites in the canyon, including one which he called Casa Blanca because of a conspicuous white-plastered room in its upper portion. This name translates to White

The unstable corner of the Mummy Cave tower was repaired for the National Park Service by Earl Morris soon after Canyon de Chelly National Monument was established. The perilous condition of the three-story structure may be noted in the early photograph on the opposite page.

Morris is shown in three photographs on this page in campaign hat, riding pants, and puttees. He and his skilled crew carefully replaced missing ceiling beams, rebuilt the fallen corner, and tied the walls to the cliff with metal rods.

A Navajo bucket brigade carried mortar up to the cave for masonry repairs.

Buttresses were built beneath rocks supporting sections of the tower, and the style of ancient masons was meticulously copied in joining the side and front together as a unit.

The wounds of reconstruction healed so successfully, as shown in the lower photograph, that few realize the modern efforts which were expended upon the old house.

PHOTOGRAPHS BY EARL MORRIS, NATIONAL PARK SERVICE, 1932.

House, by which the site presently is known. He also noted similarities between the construction methods used in this region and those in the ruined pueblos of Chaco Canyon, which he had previously visited. During the next two decades other military parties, including those of Colonel Kit Carson's 1863–64 Navajo campaign, wandered the canyons collecting more archeological information.

Since that time, the prehistoric remains of Canyon de Chelly have been subjected to a parade of investigations, from mere collecting treks for the benefit of museums or private individuals to broad scientific projects. The first such effort occurred in 1873 because of a reconnaissance by the U.S. Corps of Engineers Wheeler Survey, at that time engaged in compiling topographical information and mapping large sections of the West. The survey also gathered data on climate, vegetation, mineral resources, Indian groups, and antiquities. The Wheeler Survey reports contained a photograph of White House with an account of the ruin. About a decade later parties from the Bureau of American Ethnology, led by Colonel James Stevenson and brothers Cosmos and Victor Mindeleff, explored the canyons. Their combined labors located 140 ruins, many of which were mapped, sketched, and photographed. The specimens they exhumed from jumbled structures in several caves were deposited at the Smithsonian Institution. In one site the party stumbled upon two human burials weathered from the ancient trash that spilled down from the mouth of the overhang. They named the alcove and the ruin in it Mummy Cave. The canyon which cut below it became Canyon del Muerto, or Canyon of Death. Cosmos Mindeleff was particularly intrigued with the defensive location of many of the old communities and their distance from lands suitable for farming.

Around 1900, when looting ruins was a rampant practice, Canyon de Chelly became a magnet for collectors. Portions of collections gathered by Chinle traders Charles Day and his son Sam were sold to the Brooklyn Museum of National History where occasionally they have been exhibited.

When anthropologists examined the Day collection in the museum, they found that it contained some Hopi materials. This provided the first clue that in late prehistoric or early historic times (Pueblo IV?) the Hopi had been in the canyons. Subsequent studies of Hopi legends, combined with archeological evidence, suggest several possible interpretations. Some of the modern Hopi once may have lived in Canyon de Chelly and migrated from there to the Hopi mesas, where they now reside. Certain Hopi clans may have traveled from the Hopi villages to Canyon de Chelly and lived there intermittently. During times of drought on the Hopi mesas, some Hopi families may have moved to Canyon de Chelly to raise crops on the bottomlands. Or, perhaps the Hopi artifacts recovered in Canyon de Chelly indicate that the Hopi traded with either the late pre-Hispanic Pueblos or the area's more recent Navajo residents.

From 1923 to 1929 Earl H. Morris conducted the most extensive excavation program in de Chelly and del Muerto, sponsored principally by the American Museum of National History in New York with some assistance from the Carnegie Institution of Washington, the Bureau of American Ethnology, and the University of Colorado. The initial season's survey and test excavations showed that earlier pothunting had not completely eliminated

Turkey feathers from Antelope House, Canyon de Chelly National Monument. NATIONAL PARK SERVICE.

further archeological research in many of the ruins. In fact, the prospects were so promising that Morris returned several seasons to dig intensively, particularly in sites producing specimens of and information about the Basket Makers.

Morris excavated and dug exploratory trenches in Big Cave, Mummy Cave, Pictograph Cave, Sliding Rock Ruin, White House, Antelope House, Battle Cave, Ledge Ruin, and many lesser sites; surveyed unexplored lengths of the canyons; collected some tree-ring specimens for dating the ruins: and examined an assortment of Navajo remains. When he found the tower of Mummy Cave in a precarious state, he designed a way to preserve it. This delicate work commenced in 1924 and continued sporadically. In 1932 Morris returned to Canyon del Muerto on a special assignment for the National Park Service to finally complete the job. Stabilization measures also were taken at White House while excavations in the lower section of that ruin were being conducted.

Although Morris successfully located and dug numerous examples of well-preserved Basket Maker remains, including some special burial furnishings, he was disappointed that most of the deposits had been disturbed by later prehistoric occupants of the same caves. Churned archeological debris did not provide clear-cut answers about the Basket Makers and their ties, if any, with the Pueblo peoples who succeeded them. Consequently, few technical reports on the long endeavors at Canyon de Chelly were written, even though both Earl and his wife, Ann, authored popular accounts. Nevertheless, the research provided Morris with useful firsthand knowledge that helped define the Basket Maker stage and its relevance to the cultural sequence. Train cars loaded with the extensive Morris collection from de Chelly were dispatched to the American Museum of Natural History; a few other specimens were deposited in the University of Colorado Museum in Boulder.

During the 1930s many of the major ruins in Canyon de Chelly National Monument were dated from tree-ring specimens obtained by several programs fielded by Gila Pueblo, a private archeological research foundation in Globe, Arizona. These dates substantiated the cultural evolution theorized by Morris and others.

Surveys carried out mainly after World War II have systematically inventoried the archeological resources of a large portion of the monument. Techniques have varied from the "blanket" approach, which involves carefully covering on foot every bit of a designated area, to sampling only selected transects in a region and statistically expanding the data for the entire area. David L. de Harport, of the Peabody Museum, Harvard University, intensively covered about twenty-seven miles of Canyon de Chelly. Reports from his survey not only located and described nearly four hundred sites but also correlated patterns of settlement with environmental factors over the long period of use. In the 1970s Don P. Morris of the National Park Service conducted a photographic reconnaissance of certain canyon walls and a transect sampling survey in Canyon del Muerto to obtain data about site types and locations and the natural resources available to the aborigines. With the approximately three hundred sites he recorded, the total number of known sites in Canyon del Muerto and its tributaries then totaled about six hundred. A few other surveys designed to locate ruins threatened with destruction by road building in the monument have resulted in opening several small sites in the road alignments.

Since the 1950s, National Park Service stabilization specialists have been strengthening and preserving architectural elements of such important structures as Mummy Cave, White House, Antelope House, and Sliding Rock Ruin, and taking steps to prevent further damage by erosion and other natural forces or trampling by Navajo livestock. In 1949 and 1950 Tse-ta'a, a canyon-bottom village beneath a protective rock overhang in Canyon de Chelly, was excavated by Charlie R. Steen of the National Park Service because it had been severely damaged and was threatened with total eradication by periodic floods from Canyon de Chelly wash. Steen found the deeply stratified deposits to be a complex set of superimposed habitations spanning a long time, from Basket Maker pithouses and storage cists, through a group of Pueblo rooms and kivas, to Hopi and Navajo remains.

The second ruin excavated under the auspices of the National Park Service was Antelope House. The Antelope House Project, directed by Don P. Morris, was in the field during the summers between 1970 and 1973. Even though some prior digging had been done at the site, the National Park Service excavators uncovered a series of structures dating from Basket Maker through Pueblo times. Pueblo remains, including large quantities of well-preserved plant material, predominated. A fairly complete record of the growth of the village from the eighth through the thirteenth centuries, environmental conditions prevailing during occupation, and the mode of life of its inhabitants, particularly their dietary habits, was recovered. Analysis of its structure and artifacts makes Antelope House the most thoroughly investigated site in Canyon de Chelly. Definitive reports upon the people, cultural stages, and their relationships to the archeology of Canyon de Chelly and other parts of the Southwest have been prepared by the staff of the Western Archeological and Conservation Center. Antelope House was stabilized after excavation to provide one of the leading prehistoric exhibits in the monument.

In order to instigate future, comprehensive resource management by the National Park Service, the most intensive, multi-faceted reconnaissance of the monument thus far attempted began in 1991 in Canyon del Muerto. Survey of canyon bottomlands, cliff faces, ledges, and alcoves is adding dozens of previously unknown sites and rock art panels to the cultural inventory. Of special interest is an abundance of what appear to be Basket Maker II remains, which include many cists gouged out of indurated alluvium deposits in alcove floors, some of which are still roofed with matting and smeared with a greenish shale plaster. Great Kiva depressions, farmsteads, and wall stubs of large masonry pueblos nearly obliterated by centuries of floodwaters have been identified. Detailed assessments of site conditions, contour maps with elevations, suggestions for conservation procedures, and measurements and stylistic analyses of rock art are being compiled. For the first time, Hopi and Navajo utilization of the canyon is being seriously studied.

The extensive collections and records from Antelope House and other National Park Service excavations and surveys are deposited in the Western Archeological and Conservation Center. Additional materials from Canyon de Chelly include those in the

Antelope House in Canyon del Muerto, Canyon de Chelly National Monument. GEORGE A. GRANT, NATIONAL PARK SERVICE, 1934.

American Museum of Natural History, New York; the U.S. National Museum and the Smithsonian Institution, both in Washington, D.C.; the Southwest Museum, Los Angeles; the Brooklyn Museum; Peabody Museum, Harvard University; Museum of Northern Arizona; and the University of Colorado Museum, Boulder. ▲

ADDITIONAL READINGS, Canyon de Chelly National Monument
Bradley, Zorro A.
    1973 *Canyon de Chelly: The Story of its Ruins and People*. Washington, D.C.: Office of Publications, National Park Service.
Grant, Campbell
    1978 *Canyon de Chelly: Its People and Rock Art*. Tucson: University of Arizona Press.
Lister, Florence C., and Robert H. Lister
    1977 *Earl Morris and Southwestern Archaeology*. Reprint of 1968. Albuquerque: University of New Mexico Press.
    1993 *Earl Morris and Southwestern Archaeology*. Reprint of 1977. Tucson, Arizona: Southwest Parks and Monuments Association.
McDonald, James A.
    1976 *An Archeological Assessment of Canyon de Chelly National Monument*. Publications in Anthropology, No. 5. Tucson, Arizona: Western Archeological Center, National Park Service.
Morris, Ann A.
    1978 *Digging in the Southwest*. Reprint of 1933. Santa Barbara, California, and Salt Lake City, Utah: Peregrine Smith.
Morris, Don P.
    1986 *Archaeological Investigations at Antelope House*. Washington, D.C.: National Park Service.
Morris, Earl H.
    1925 Exploring in the Canyon of Death. *National Geographic Magazine*, Vol. 48, No. 3. 263–300.
Steen, Charlie R.
    1966 *Excavations at Tse-Ta'a, Canyon de Chelly National Monument, Arizona*. Archeological Research Series, No. 9. Washington, D.C.: National Park Service.
Supplee, Charles, Douglas Anderson, and Barbara Anderson
    1971 *Canyon de Chelly: The Story Behind the Scenery*. Las Vegas, Nevada: KC Publications.

CAPULIN VOLCANO NATIONAL MONUMENT, NEW MEXICO

Cultural Significance and Archeological Classification   Paleo-Indian: *Folsom*

About ten thousand years ago a band of Paleo-Indian hunters may have watched in terror as the earth convulsed to produce a thousand-foot-high symmetrical cinder cone on the steppes of northeastern New Mexico, now called Capulin Volcano. Their presence at that time and place was revealed only through another cataclysmic event, a roaring flood that tore away many feet of soil deposited in millennia of erosion to expose their stone spear points and bones of their prey. That find in 1926–27 was the first authenticated association in North America of man-made tools with extinct *Bison antiquus* and represented a major archeological breakthrough. The site and the distinctive spear points recovered there became known as Folsom, after a tiny ranching town nearby which in the late 1800s was the most important cattle shipping center west of Texas.

Explorations and Investigations

Capulin Volcano, now green with a stunted pinyon-juniper woodland, looms above a sweep of flat prairie and distant mesas that in good summers is a crazy quilt of wild flowers and short grasslands. The landscape is so scenic that it was set aside as a natural preserve as early as 1891. In 1916 it became part of the young National Park Service system. The beauty of nature notwithstanding, for archeologists the Capulin vicinity is especially important because that is where not so long ago the history of mankind in the Western Hemisphere took a dramatic turn.

Scientific advancement often contains an element of chance. Such was the case in 1908 when a black cowboy, George McJunkin, riding down a dry arroyo bed on the New Mexico cattle ranch where he worked, spotted extraordinarily large animal bones weathering out of an embankment which a recent flood had cut some ten feet below the surface of the surrounding tableland. Because the size of these bones was unusual, he took a few back to his bunkhouse. For years they collected dust on a fireplace mantle, added to occasionally by other oversized specimens picked up at the same place—the Bone Pit, as McJunkin called it. McJunkin died in 1922 but not before telling several acquaintances how to locate the boneyard. In due time these men found the arroyo and dug out some specimens for themselves. Four years passed before one of them took a sample to Denver to show to J. D. Figgins, curator at the Colorado Museum of Natural History.

Figgins immediately recognized the bones as belonging to an extinct species of bison. Since he was one of a handful of scientists who then entertained the possibility of modern humans having been in the Americas more than just several thousand years, perhaps even at a time when these mammals roamed the plains, he promptly launched an exploratory expedition to the site. His efforts were rewarded in 1926 when several stone spear points were taken from loose fill surrounding more bison bones. More conclusive proof of the contemporaneity of weapons and bones came the next season with the uncovering of a

Where Folsom hunters once roamed, Capulin Volcano National Monument. GEORGE H. H. HUEY.

point securely lodged between two bison vertebrae. Scientists summoned to verify the find in situ were convinced that *Homo sapiens* indeed had been in the New World by Late Pleistocene times.

Ultimately, remains of twenty-three fossil bison were identified, together with nineteen fluted spear points used to dispatch them as they were trapped in a natural blind. George McJunkin never had the pleasure of knowing the significance of his accidental recovery of old bleached bones some nineteen years previous.

The Folsom points are of a distinctive, easily recognized type. They are delicate, skillfully flaked to razor-sharp edges, and grooved longitudinally on each face. They now have been found in a number of localities, primarily along the western reaches of the great interior plains of North America, where bison were killed or processed. The flood of research following the Folsom discovery, however, has shown that the makers and users of these particular weapons were preceded by thousands of years by earlier peoples who depended upon other, now-extinct mammals. No evidence of these most ancient hunters was found at Folsom, but what was recovered will remain historically significant in opening up a new chapter in the prehistory of the Southwest. ▲

ADDITIONAL READINGS, Capulin Volcano National Monument
Cordell, Linda S.
    1984 *Prehistory of the Southwest.* New York: Academic Press.
Folsom, Franklin
    1973 *The Life and Legend of George McJunkin: Black Cowboy.* Nashville, Tennessee:
        Thomas Nelson.
Jennings, Jesse D., ed.
    1978 *Ancient Native Americans.* San Francisco, California: W. H. Freeman.

Natural cavern entrance, Carlsbad Caverns National Park. GEORGE H. H. HUEY.

CARLSBAD CAVERNS NATIONAL PARK/GUADALUPE MOUNTAINS NATIONAL PARK, NEW MEXICO, TEXAS

Cultural Significance and Archeological Classification

The topographically diverse backcountry of these two parks experienced prehistoric human utilization for perhaps as long as ten thousand years, but throughout that long period it remained a cultural backwater. While camping in the protection of caves or rock shelters in the craggy uplands, successive peoples from Paleo-Indian to Jornada Mogollon (A.D. 840–1450) hunted megafauna or lesser game on the surrounding flatlands, or took advantage of the more than six hundred wild plant species native to this part of the Chihuahuan Desert. Although the most recent groups acquired use of the bow and arrow and traded for pottery made elsewhere, none advanced technologically beyond a generic Archaic level. Only rudimentary storage and living chambers were erected. The environment may not have been conducive to higher achievements or, more likely, it may have been that the region was situated too far on the outer eastern fringes of the Southwest Tradition, further cut off from effective contact with the Rio Grande valley and its more aggressive inhabitants by the rugged Guadalupe and Sacramento mountains.

Explorations and Investigations

Other than surface artifact collecting by amateurs, little attention was paid to regional prehistoric remains until the 1930s. Carlsbad Caverns, established as a national monument in 1923 and upgraded to a national park in 1930, then was receiving international publicity. Aside from its geologic wonders and its enormous bat colony, the curiosity of those concerned with the human past was piqued by the discoveries near the main cave entrance of several Indian burials, mescal roasting pits, and a few pictographs. The original information about these finds was lost, but surely the bowels of the dark, dank caverns would have been avoided by the aborigines as evil places. Nevertheless, at the same time widespread interest in regional archeology had been generated by the concurrent recognition at Folsom, New Mexico, that human beings had been in the Southwest thousands of years longer than previously believed. To a handful of researchers, the numerous caves and alcoves along the eastern flanks of the Guadalupe Mountains south of the underground honeycomb of Carlsbad seemed promising places to look for more clues in the unfolding mystery of ancient humanity. A half-dozen expeditions were led by William Burnet, Archaeological and Historical Society of Carlsbad; Edgar B. Howard and Mary Y. Ayer, University of Pennsylvania Museum and the Philadelphia Academy of Natural Sciences; and H. P. Mera, Laboratory of Anthropology, and Edwin N. Ferdon, Museum of New Mexico, both in Santa Fe. Their intensive work in several dozen sites outlined the basic archeological chronology for the region.

After the interruption of World War II, National Park Service personnel initiated the

Paleo-Indian: *Folsom*
Archaic: *Cochise*
Mogollon: *Jornada*
All-Southwest: *Hamlets, intermediate between mountain-valley zone and plains*

Prehistoric projectile points, Carlsbad Caverns National Park.
GEORGE H. H. HUEY.

second phase of research by expanding investigations to the park tablelands. During the 1960s John Greer, University of Texas, made a thorough study of midden circles in the Carlsbad area. Barney T. Burns, a student at the University of Arizona, wrote a synthesis of Carlsbad archeology in 1967. Southern Methodist University completed another survey in 1973.

Meanwhile, as the government was acquiring title to what was to become the Guadalupe Mountains National Park in 1972, park service archeologists carried out further investigations there. They were followed in 1970 by Susan M. Riches, a student at the University of Wisconsin, who used a six-week survey and small excavation in the park as background data for a thesis. In operating a field school in 1974, Paul and Susanna Katz, Texas Tech University, walked over miles of the high country looking for additional sites. Harry J. Shafer and his team from the University of Texas added 139 previously unknown sites to the growing list. Ultimately, by 1987 a total of almost three hundred places of archeological importance had been recorded within the park confines. Most of these were prehistoric, but others had been left by nineteenth- and early twentieth-century enterprises such as mining, ranching, and stagecoach operations.

Collections and notes resulting from regional archeological work are at the Museum of New Mexico, Santa Fe; University of Pennsylvania Museum, Philadelphia; and the Western Archeological and Conservation Center, Tucson. ▲

ADDITIONAL READINGS, Carlsbad Caverns National Park and Guadalupe Mountains National Park
Bousman, C. Britt
    1974 *An Archeological Assessment of Carlsbad Caverns National Park*. Dallas, Texas: Southern Methodist University.
National Park Service, Southwest Regional Office
    1976 *Final Environmental Statement/Proposed Master Plan, Guadalupe Mountains National Park*. Santa Fe, New Mexico: Southwest Regional Office, National Park Service.
Sierra Club
    1984 *Sierra Club Guides to the National Parks of the Desert Southwest*. New York: Stewart, Tabori, and Chang.

Mescalero Apache pictographs in backcountry cave, Carlsbad Caverns National Park. GEORGE H. H. HUEY.

Casa Grande, Casa Grande Ruins National Monument. GEORGE A. GRANT, NATIONAL PARK SERVICE, 1934.

CASA GRANDE RUINS NATIONAL MONUMENT, ARIZONA

Cultural Significance and Archeological Classification

Archeological features of Casa Grande Ruins National Monument played an important role in defining one of the three major components of the ancient sedentary culture of the Southwest. In addition, the monument preserves the only remaining example of a Great House, a feature common in the once numerous Classic Hohokam towns along the river oases of southern Arizona. Casa Grande tells the story of adaptation to an arid environment which permitted a large population of irrigation farmers to prosper for many centuries.

Hohokam: *Pioneer, Colonial, Sedentary (Snaketown), Classic (Casa Grande)*
All-Southwest: *Hamlets, Villages (Snaketown), Towns (Casa Grande), desert zone*

Explorations and Investigations

Seventeenth-century Jesuit missionary Fray Eusebio Kino was the first European to visit the site and refer to it as the Casa Grande, or Great House. While visiting Indian villages on the northern border of his sweeping territory, called the Pimería or land of the Pima Indians, Kino heard tales of a "casa grande" on the banks of the Gila River. Aided by Indian guides, he reached the ruin in 1694, said mass within its towering crumbling walls, and wrote an account in his journal. He saw it as a four-story building as large as a castle or any church then in Sonora. He also noted thirteen smaller ruined houses in the immediate vicinity.

Kino returned to the Casa Grande several other times. In 1697 he was accompanied by Captain Cristóbal Martín Bernal and a detachment of soldiers. Bernal's narrative provides a few more details about the Casa Grande and notes the existence there of an ancient canal estimated to be ten yards wide and four yards deep.

During the eighteenth and first half of the nineteenth centuries, the Casa Grande became a landmark for other Spanish and American travelers following the Gila River across the desolate stretches of southern Arizona. Some of them wrote accounts that recorded in word and sketch what they saw and how they felt about the unusual structure.

At the time of the war between the United States and Mexico, General Stephen Kearny commanded the Army of the West, which explored and established a string of fortifications across the Southwest to California. The army moved down the Gila and camped at a group of Tohono O'odham (Pima) villages near the Casa Grande in November 1846. Two of Kearny's officers, Lieutenant William H. Emory, a topographical engineer, and Captain A. R. Johnston, examined the ruin, drew ground plans and elevation sketches, and entered notes in their journals. Johnston observed that the massive earthen structure contained plastered walls four feet thick at their bases that curved inward as the upper levels were reached. The first of the four stories was filled with rubbish. He saw wooden joists for the other levels still in place, although at some time floors and roof had been burned. Their charred ends lacked any evidence of having been cut with metal tools.

By the 1880s references to the Casa Grande began to indicate that vandalism, such as removal of wood and wall material and the scratching of graffiti on the plastered walls, was increasing. It was stimulated in part by the completion of the Southern Pacific Railroad through the area, which placed the ruin only twenty miles by a well-traveled road from Casa Grande station. Fortunately, a growing national consciousness of archeology and serious efforts to protect aboriginal sites prevented further destruction of the site and brought professional archeologists to the scene. Staff members of two research institutions founded in 1879, the Archaeological Institute of America and the Bureau of Ethnology, became involved with the Casa Grande.

During an extensive survey in June 1883, Adolph F. Bandelier, under auspices of the Archaeological Institute of America, spent several hot days measuring and mapping the Casa Grande and contiguous structures, examining artifacts from the ruins in the vicinity, and interviewing local Indians about their way of life and their ideas about the ruin. His journal and later reports suggested that the Casa Grande proper could have functioned either as a domestic edifice or as a fortress.

The next scholar to concern himself with the Casa Grande was Frank H. Cushing, leader of the Hemenway Southwestern Archaeological Expedition. This group conducted systematic excavations in the Gila-Salt basin during 1887 and 1888. The expedition, privately sponsored by Mrs. Mary Hemenway, accomplished the first organized archeological work in the Southwest, not only in southern Arizona but later in ruins near Zuni, New Mexico. After examining the Casa Grande and no doubt having been influenced by his earlier study of Zuni, Cushing decided that it had been the assembly place of the priesthood of a highly organized, stratified society.

Agitation for the protection of the Casa Grande began in 1887, along with a proposal to establish an archeological society in Arizona. Congress was petitioned to preserve antiquities on federal lands, but the legislation met with numerous setbacks and delays in Washington. Finally, in 1889 congressional approval for the preservation of the Casa Grande was obtained, together with funds for a stabilization project. Jesse W. Fewkes, who succeeded Cushing as head of the Hemenway party, went to the Casa Grande in 1891 to document the extent of destruction. He observed the damage caused by curious travelers but understood that erosion undercutting construction joints was the principal cause of past destruction and, if allowed to continue, might lead to collapse of the structure.

Cosmos Mindeleff was dispatched in late 1891 by the Bureau of Ethnology to study the Casa Grande before the stabilization was initiated. He made the first accurate topographical maps of the site, drew a scaled ground plan of the building, and wrote one of the most perceptive descriptions of its architecture. Preservation followed. These efforts included clearing debris from within the ruin and underpinning a number of badly weathered wall sections with cement and bricks. Two-by-fours were placed over the doorways, and the south wall was braced with metal tie rods and a wooden beam. The next year 480 acres encompassing the Casa Grande and several other archeological units were made the first federal reservation for a prehistoric site in the United States. When Congress appropriated additional funds for the Casa Grande, Fewkes returned from 1906 to 1908 to prepare it for exhibition to the American public. He excavated the remaining ruins in Compound A, the enclosed complex that included the Casa Grande, as well as several other mounds in the environs.

An important name in the history of the Casa Grande as a public educational attraction is that of Frank H. Pinkley. As a youth in 1901, he was named caretaker of the Casa Grande Ruins shortly after it was placed under the authority of the General Land Office. He served as its manager, protector, and interpreter the rest of his life, during which time the status of the area changed to a national park and finally in 1918 to a national monument. With meager funds he strove to maintain the ruins and improve their accessibility to visitors. Also in 1918 he initiated the first trenching of a depression near the Casa Grande that later was identified as a ballcourt, and he tested several other structures in nearby sites.

Frank Pinkley was not only in charge of the Casa Grande, but he assumed responsibility for other monuments as they began to be set aside. Ultimately in 1924 the National Park Service named him superintendent of all southwestern national monuments. Under his leadership, custodians, rangers, and scientists set about to protect, preserve, and interpret the ruins and missions and to develop visitor and staff facilities. Among the new improvements was a modern roof, erected in 1930–31, to protect the Casa Grande from rain. "The Boss," as Pinkley was warmly known to his men, maintained his headquarters at the Casa Grande.

Continuing studies of the role of the Casa Grande in regional prehistory have involved surveys of the monument, and test excavations in Compound A and several other villages by the Southwest Museum, the Los Angeles County Museum, and the National Park Service. Of narrower focus were observations made in 1969 by John Molloy, a University of Arizona graduate student, in an attempt to demonstrate that some of the openings in the high walls of the principal structure had been used to observe certain celestial events, such as solstices and equinoxes. That information would have been essential to setting up a calendrical system for regulating ceremonial cycles and agricultural routines. It is known that the Pueblo Indian priesthoods, as well as some among Mexican Indians, make such observations.

Even in dry environments, buildings made of sun-dried mud are vulnerable to the elements, making continual care of the Casa Grande imperative. Ways to arrest further erosion and also to reinforce its walls so that they could survive a severe earthquake have been investigated by soil scientists, chemists, and civil engineers. One proposal involves placing a steel grid framework bonded with epoxy in the walls so the building could withstand earth tremors.

In light of this or other potential protective procedures and their resulting disturbance of archeological deposits, the National Park Service called for a definitive architectural study of the Casa Grande. The research was done in 1975 and 1976 by David R. Wilcox and Lynette O. Shenk of the Arizona State Museum of the University of Arizona. Their reports address many questions about the Casa Grande and contain the most detailed analysis ever made of the multistoried house. In an effort to resolve conflicting ideas about such aspects of the site as its time of occupation, method of construction, original height, and purpose, Wilcox and Shenk reached certain conclusions and presented recommendations. Lacking

The original protective roof over Casa Grande. GEORGE A. GRANT, NATIONAL PARK SERVICE, 1925.

tree-ring dates, but using chronological data from archeological materials at the site and making comparisons with better-dated antiquities in the vicinity, they believe it likely that the Casa Grande was built and occupied between A.D. 1300 and 1450. The entire edifice was built at one time using local soil with beams of juniper, ponderosa pine, fir, and mesquite, some of which were obtained at great distance.

Walls were made of lenses of stiff mud piled up in courses lacking internal reinforcing members. The present height of the house closely approximates the original height of four stories. The first story was purposefully filled in during construction; the second and third stories each had five rooms; a single room or tower comprised the fourth story; and a low parapet may have surrounded the uppermost roof levels. The function of the Casa Grande remains unclear, although it may have been a communal dwelling similar to other structures in Compound A. The "observation holes" in some rooms suggest a more special, but undetermined, use.

Within twenty-five miles northwest of the Casa Grande is a large archeological zone called Snaketown. From a scientific point of view, it completely overshadows its neighbor. Because it does not have a dominant, easily recognizable feature such as a Great House, it was of little interest during early explorations and settlement. Once comprehensive archeological investigations got under way in southern Arizona, however, its potential for fruitful research became obvious. As a result, two periods of excavation there have contributed as much to understanding the ancient sedentary peoples of the low desert as the cumulative efforts of all other research in the Southwest.

When Harold S. Gladwin opened his research facility at Gila Pueblo in 1928, he already was on the track of the people responsible for the prehistoric remains of the Gila-Salt basin. The sprawling, unvandalized ruins at Snaketown, covering more than half of a square mile, became known to him years before while he was working through trash mounds at the Casa Grande. Because he was dealing with a new and little-known culture, he postponed digging there until he had better defined its characteristics. Not until he had dug several small ruins and visited and collected from more than twelve thousand prehistoric sites throughout the greater Southwest did he tackle Snaketown.

Aided chiefly by Emil W. Haury and E. B. Sayles of his Gila Pueblo staff, Gladwin excavated portions of Snaketown during 1934 and 1936. Rounded trash mounds, some ten feet high, were conspicuous in the flat desert. Stratigraphic trenches, carefully dug into three of the approximately sixty mounds dotting the site, yielded enormous quantities of potsherds and other artifacts. These were chronologically arranged to help refine and expand upon the generally accepted stages of cultural evolution. Forty single-roomed habitations, obscured by trash and soil, were located and excavated. All had been built in shallow circular to rectangular pits having inclined or vertical walls. They had flat roofs supported and framed with timbers, covered with smaller timbers and earth. Variations of this basic plan distinguished the house types of different periods. Another major find at Snaketown was two ballcourts, a feature commonly found at sites in Mexico and Central America where a game with religious connotations was played. Also present were sections of a canal that had delivered water from the Gila River to garden plots. Development of an irrigation system obviously had been fundamental to the survival of these desert farmers. Ashy remains from cremation of the dead, together with funerary offerings, were found in areas that appeared to have been used only for burial.

Analyses of new findings provided insight into the regional prehistory but left some basic problems unanswered. One nagging question was the time of occupation. Tree-ring dates were not available because they could not be determined from the charred timbers. Hence a chronology was devised based upon trade pottery from cultures which had been dated by tree-rings. A lifetime of some fourteen hundred years was postulated for the village, beginning about 300 B.C. If that date were correct, the initial stage of the Hohokam predated that of other known southwestern cultures.

Gladwin theorized that the regional culture, as exemplified by Snaketown, evolved from an indigenous hunting and gathering group. Over a period of several centuries, epecially from about A.D. 500 to 900, the adaptation of local traditions and the absorption of traits from outside sources stimulated cultural advances. Notable among these were agricultural techniques, arts and crafts, and religious practices. According to the Gladwin reconstruction, after about A.D. 1300, in a stage not represented at Snaketown, people with a somewhat divergent lifestyle moved from the Tonto basin down into the Gila basin and merged with the original inhabitants. The two peoples occupied the same villages. The newcomers built multistoried communal houses such as at the Casa Grande, made a different kind of pottery, and buried rather than cremated their dead. After about a century of coexistence, the immigrants seem to have moved on, leaving the territory to its first occupants, who probably evolved into the modern Tohono O'odham. Other members of the Gila Pueblo staff identified Mexico as the main source of alien traits that enriched the native culture of southern Arizona.

After the initial research at Snaketown, Gladwin re-evaluated his original interpretations and, in 1942 and 1948, he revised the chronology upward in time, pictured the early stage at Snaketown as not ancestral to the more complex culture of southern Arizona, and set the beginning of the Hohokam presence at about A.D. 700. He believed this date better coincided with the infusion of new elements from Mexico. Other concepts had the local peoples being invaded by the Hohokam from Mexico sometime between A.D. 500 and 900. Emil Haury, who had left Gila Pueblo after the Snaketown excavations to become chairman of the Department of Anthropology at the University of Arizona, held to the chronology and general scheme of interpretation as it had been outlined in 1937. Thus, there were sharp differences of opinion among the experts as to the identity of the first farmers of the desert Southwest, and a variation of about one thousand years in estimates for the age of the early stages of Hohokam culture.

In an attempt to resolve the problems, Haury decided to reinvestigate Snaketown and returned in 1964 and 1965 to explore the points of contention. Haury and his crew employed some excavation and dating procedures developed after Gila Pueblo's original work at the site. These included use of mechanical earth-moving equipment and radioactive carbon and archeomagnetic methods for dating certain kinds of remains. Haury also was able to draw on a large body of archeological data of the greater Southwest which had accrued since 1937. Particular attention was paid to a review of the Snaketown chronology, the questions of Hohokam origins and Mexican influences, and the history of irrigation agriculture. Extensive probing in previously undisturbed areas was undertaken in more than one hundred sixty houses, several large trash mounds and rubbish-filled pits, portions of canals, cremation areas, wells, and caches. After more than a decade of laboratory analysis and report preparation, in 1976 the results of Haury's reexamination of Snaketown and the Hohokam appeared.

Haury concluded that the original chronology for Snaketown, a stretch of time from about 300 B.C. to A.D. 1100, could be substantiated. He determined that irrigation agriculture had been practiced at Snaketown from the time it was founded. In a dramatic turn of mind, he decided that the Hohokam themselves had been a migrant group from Mexico. According to this theory, while searching for a new home, the Hohokam had arrived in the Gila basin bearing a diluted version of central Mexican culture dependent upon irrigation agriculture. Once settled in the new surroundings, in effect they were an aberrant Mexican society acting as a donor culture to other southwesterners.

Together Snaketown and the Casa Grande present a rich record of Hohokam cultural evolution. A slow cultural ripening from beginning to climax is scattered over and beneath the sands of Snaketown. Its later stages, when foreigners or influences from elsewhere in the Southwest engulfed the Hohokam, are present at the Casa Grande.

A number of Hohokam artifacts are exhibited at Casa Grande Ruins National Monument. Others have been deposited in the Western Archeological and Conservation Center in Tucson. The Arizona State Museum, University of Arizona, has the large collections from Snaketown. ▲

ADDITIONAL READINGS, Casa Grande Ruins National Monument
Gladwin, Harold S., Emil W. Haury, Edwin B. Sayles, and Nora Gladwin
    1965 *Excavations at Snaketown: Material Culture*. Reprint of 1937. Tucson:
            University of Arizona Press.
Haury, Emil W.
    1976 *The Hohokam: Desert Farmers and Craftsmen. Excavations at Snaketown,
            1964–1965*. Tucson: University of Arizona Press.
Noble, David Grant
    1991 *The Hohokam, Ancient People of the Desert*. Santa Fe, New Mexico: School of
            American Research.
Wilcox, David R., and Lynette O. Shenk
    1977 *The Architecture of the Casa Grande and its Interpretations*. Archaeological
            Series, No. 115. Tucson: Arizona State Museum.

Emil W. Haury at Snaketown during excavation. HELGA TEIWES, ARIZONA STATE MUSEUM, UNIVERSITY OF ARIZONA.

North wall of Pueblo Bonito, Chaco Culture National Historical Park after repairs of damages from the 1880s. GEORGE A. GRANT, NATIONAL PARK SERVICE, 1929.

CHACO CULTURE NATIONAL HISTORICAL PARK, NEW MEXICO

Cultural Significance and Archeological Classification

Chaco Canyon includes the largest and some of the most significant and thoroughly studied prehistoric communities in the Southwest. In their desolate surroundings, these remains record a cultural evolution that parallels that of other plateau people until about A.D. 1000. At that time an amazing fecundity resulted in complex economic development and advancement of certain skills unique in the ancient Southwest. One interpretation is that the Chaco Phenomenon that evolved was an integrated system of perhaps as many as seventy-five cooperating communities which produced and assembled goods for local consumption and for widespread distribution over an area of thirty thousand square miles. Another is that there was a politico-religious basis for the obvious regional linkage of eastern Anasazi under the domination of those at Chaco Canyon. Particularly noteworthy in Chaco are the outstanding architectural and construction accomplishments of the builders of the great towns, the networks of roads and visual signaling stations that linked the Chaco world, and the means for harnessing and distributing runoff waters. A hierarchical social system undetected in other contemporary Anasazi societies is implied in these communal endeavors. Physical, social, economic, and moral factors combined to bring the decline and fall of this unusual divergence from the normal Anasazi pattern.

Explorations and Investigations

A presidential proclamation of March 11, 1907, included Chaco Canyon National Monument among a group of eighteen areas reserved during Theodore Roosevelt's tenure. By that time the great ruins of Chaco Canyon had been popularized in fact and fantasy, probed for years by an organized archeological expedition, and subjected to heated debate between those who wished to continue unrestrained digging and those who opposed it.

On December 19, 1980, the U.S. Congress enlarged the monument by 12,500 acres and changed its name to Chaco Culture National Historical Park. An additional system to preserve and protect thirty-three outlying Chacoan sites was proposed. The canyon and its satellite territories are a diamond in the rough compared to other well-manicured national properties, mainly because they are accessible only over rutted dirt roads that at times are impassable. At this writing, improvements are being made.

The ruins of Chaco Canyon likely were known in the seventeenth century to Spanish occupants of northern New Mexico. Military forays already had sallied forth against the Navajos who, long after the first dwellers had deserted their arid canyon lands, had settled in and near the Chaco. Few archival records exist for the years before 1680, when most such documents fell victim to an Indian uprising. In the middle of the next century knowledge of Chaco is confirmed by requests of several men for land near there and by

Archaic: *Oshara*
Anasazi: *Basket Maker III; Pueblo I, II, III*
All-Southwest: *Hamlets, Villages, Towns, plateau zone*

Anasazi, Pueblo III, black-on-white effigy vessel. ROBERT H. LISTER, EARL MORRIS MEMORIAL COLLECTION, UNIVERSITY OF COLORADO MUSEUM.

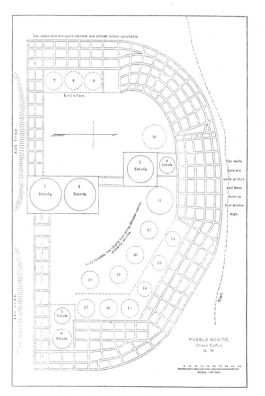

William H. Jackson's map of Pueblo Bonito prepared during his visit to Chaco Canyon in 1877. FROM THE TENTH ANNUAL REPORT OF THE UNITED STATES GEOLOGICAL AND GEOGRAPHICAL SURVEY OF THE TERRITORIES.

the name "Chaca" inscribed on a 1774 Spanish map of the canyon's vicinity.

Military action against the Navajos was responsible for additional knowledge about Chaco Canyon in the early nineteenth century. Soldiers departing from Santa Fe and its vicinity for the Navajo domain usually traveled most of the length of Chaco Canyon.

The first substantive report on the ruins in Chaco came in 1849 shortly after the opening of the American era. Lieutenant James H. Simpson, a member of a U.S. Army outfit pursuing marauding Navajos, spent several days in the canyon. He carefully described seven of the larger ruins, gave them names used by his Indian and Mexican guides, had drawings and measurements made of them, and noted their bleak surroundings. The massiveness of the sites, the excellent engineering skills evident in their construction, and the immense effort involved in erecting and occupying such sizable communities in the demanding environment greatly impressed him.

Slightly more than a quarter-century later the U.S. Geological and Geographical Survey of the Territories sent a field party into northwestern New Mexico. In May 1877, led by photographer William H. Jackson, the group entered Chaco Canyon. Jackson devoted about five days to reconnoitering, mapping, sketching, photographing, and taking notes. Unfortunately, none of the more than four hundred exposures he tediously made with a cumbersome eight-by-ten camera turned out. Jackson re-examined the ruins that Simpson had identified and found and named several others. He was the first to recognize the existence of stairways, which the Chacoans had cut into the cliffs so they could move in and out of the canyon. And he was also the first to comment on the appreciable amount of sedimentation and erosion that had taken place on the canyon floor after the towns were vacated.

The next chapter in the voluminous saga of investigations into Chaco Canyon's prehistory was dominated by a preeminent figure in the opening of this part of the Southwest, Richard Wetherill. Following the pioneering archeological work he and his brothers accomplished at Mesa Verde and Grand Gulch, he brought the Hyde Exploring Expedition to Chaco Canyon in 1896, where it conducted excavations for four years.

Nominally, the Hyde party was directed by Professor F. W. Putnam of the American Museum of Natural History and Harvard University; he actually visited the canyon only twice during the undertaking. The field supervisor was George H. Pepper, one of Putnam's students. With Wetherill as foreman, work commenced at the prominent ruin of Pueblo Bonito. At the end of the fourth and final season, 190 rooms, kivas, and other features had been cleared, and 10,000 pieces of pottery, 5,000 stone implements, 1,000 bone and wooden objects, a few fabrics, a small number of copper bells, and a great mass of turquoise beads, pendants, and mosaic sets had been recovered and shipped to the American Museum of Natural History.

The cost to Talbot and Frederick Hyde had been in the neighborhood of twenty-five thousand dollars, but the materials collected probably exceeded any previous similar effort in this country. On the side, the Hydes set up a string of trading posts across the Navajo Reservation, and marketed Indian rugs and jewelry in the East.

While working at Pueblo Bonito, Wetherill filed a homestead claim on land in Chaco

Canyon. When the expedition concluded, he and his family remained there as ranchers and trading post operators. In June 1910, Wetherill was shot to death by a Navajo after an argument over a horse. He was buried in a small windswept cemetery within sight of Pueblo Bonito.

After the years of activity resulting from the Hydes' scientific and business operations and the excitement engendered by Wetherill's murder, Chaco Canyon fell into its characteristic solitude despite its designation as a national monument. Archeological investigations resumed in 1921, when the National Geographic Society chose Chaco Canyon for an intensive program. Neil M. Judd of the U.S. National Museum was named director of the expedition. For seven summers he and his staff again considered Chaco's prehistory. They cleared the remaining half of Pueblo Bonito, excavated about fifty rooms and kivas of Pueblo del Arroyo, and tested numerous small ruins and isolated remains in the vicinity. Biological and geological studies were correlated with archeological findings to reconstruct the past environment and man's relationship with it. In seeking reasons behind the rise and fall of Chaco culture, special attention was paid to the vegetation patterns and arroyo cutting associated with the time of the aboriginal presence.

In 1929 Frank H. H. Roberts, Jr., formerly a member of Judd's staff, returned to Chaco Canyon on behalf of the Smithsonian Institution to examine what appeared to be a concentration of pithouses on the south rim of the canyon nine miles east of Pueblo Bonito. He uncovered evidence of numerous small habitations that had consisted of a shallow pit over which had been built walls and a roof of poles, brush, and mud. Called Shabik'eshchee Village (Navajo for a large petroglyph near the site), it was a fine example of a community of late Basket Makers, predecessors of the later Pueblos who had erected the villages and towns in Chaco.

Several New Mexico institutions became interested in Chaco Canyon archeology during the 1930s through the efforts of Edgar L. Hewett. He brought students from the University of New Mexico, the Museum of New Mexico, and the School of American Research in Santa Fe to excavate Chetro Ketl. This was an imposing derelict town of jagged wall stubs, filled kivas, and mounded refuse just east of Pueblo Bonito. The situation at Chetro Ketl proved complex. Much of the present ground-level structure was found to have been superimposed over earlier, sometimes deeply buried, phases of the community. In eight seasons of digging, Hewett and his crews covered less than half of Chetro Ketl, or 130 rooms in all, eleven kivas, and two Great Kivas. Trenches were dug in the large trash heap so that its potsherds and bits of charcoal could be used to tell more about the habitation of Chaco.

In addition, various lesser ruins were excavated or tested, sections of the park were surveyed, and smaller archeology or ecology projects were accomplished. Certain architectural features were suggested to have parallels in ancient sites in Mexico and Central America. The excavation and repair of Casa Rinconada, the largest Great Kiva in Chaco directly across the canyon from Pueblo Bonito, was handled by Gordon Vivian under Hewett's direction.

In the late 1930s and 1940s the University of New Mexico's anthropology department conducted well-attended summer research and student training programs, whose staff and trainees cleared a group of small ruins just east of Casa Rinconada. Some of these small rural sites are included in the general chronology used by the National Park Service in interpreting the evolution of Chaco culture. They are pivotal in demonstrating their contemporaneity and interaction with the urbanized Pueblo Bonito and Chetro Ketl.

The appearance and condition of most of the park's exposed ruins and those unexcavated sites with standing walls are due to an intensive stabilization program begun by the National Park Service in 1933. Concurrent with his excavations, Judd had completed some preservation and reconstruction at Pueblo Bonito. Hewett had done likewise in Chetro Ketl. Though the methods they employed were common at the time, they did not prove satisfactory and in some instances actually were detrimental. To remedy this situation, the National Park Service sought other preservation procedures which would not alter the appearance of the edifices but would secure them for the future. Gordon Vivian and a trained crew of Navajos undertook the task of stabilizing and strengthening the masonry walls and wooden elements of the old buildings. They tried to erase all signs of previous preservation endeavors and to realign the natural drainages around the ruins so that moisture damage would be minimal. After many years of work, initial stabilization was realized. Still, maintenance and perfection of methods continue.

Natural forces proved more than a match for the stabilizers on one occasion. National Park Service engineers fruitlessly attempted to arrest the movement of Threatening Rock, a huge, thirty-thousand-ton wedge of sandstone that had towered precariously behind Pueblo Bonito from the time it was built. After centuries of almost undetectable shifting, the enormous monolith finally fell on January 22, 1941, crushing the finest part of the north wall of the town and all or parts of sixty-five rooms. The Pueblo Bonito trail is built over and around the great jumble of boulders and rubble left after that catastrophe.

Nature was met more evenly with the halt of the rapid erosion of the banks of Chaco Wash. Some one hundred thousand trees were planted along the watercourse, eliminating one threat to archeological evidence.

The close scrutiny of Chaco Canyon antiquities by these many representatives of highly respected institutions had resulted in a reasonably full accounting of the area's prehistory. Information concerning probable cultural evolution and the physical environment had been painstakingly gathered. But many questions, some dating from the earliest fieldwork, remained to be answered. Meanwhile, research in surrounding sectors was pushing ahead. As American archeology matured, new theoretical and technical methods had come into use which had not been applied to Chaco. In 1971 the National Park Service, in cooperation with the University of New Mexico, launched a campaign to take a modern, in-depth look at human achievements in Chaco. Robert H. Lister directed the resulting research facility, the Chaco Center, for six years. He was succeeded by W. James Judge.

The first order of the Chaco Center's business was a thorough, three-season reconnaissance of the park to determine the exact number of sites present, their location, characteristics, and cultural affiliation. The surveyors walked the forty-three square miles within and immediately adjoining National Park Service lands. More than two thousand sites were recorded, ranging from camps of the earliest nomadic foragers, through the pithouse to pueblo sequence of the sedentary farmers, to historic Navajo remains. Numerous other traces of past human activity included rock-cut stairways, small circular basins cut into bedrock, water-control devices, and examples of rock art.

The survey results indicated shifting settlement patterns that could be related to climatic fluctuations and changing cultural attributes. A network of line-of-sight signaling stations linking the entire population was defined. Data were also obtained on conditions of sites, their presumed age, their geographic setting, and their promise for further investigation. This information was essential in selecting representative sites for future testing or excavation.

Although the park proper represents the nuclear area of Chaco culture, later surveys encountered a number of comparable Chacoan house blocks a considerable distance away. Three notable such structures on government lands in Colorado are as many as 150 miles from Chaco Canyon. These are Chimney Rock near Pagosa Springs, the Escalante-Domínguez ruins near Dolores, and the Lowry Ruin west of Pleasant View.

The Chaco Center used remote sensing, a specialized analysis of various types of aerial photography, which proved of utmost importance in charting an elaborate, far-flung pattern of prehistoric roads that connected the principal Chaco centers and tied them to nearby small settlements or areas with resources unavailable in the canyon. It also aided in locating canals, reservoirs, and garden plots that had been part of an ingenious form of irrigation agriculture. Site plans and profiles and area maps prepared from aerial photos proved to be accurate, faster to produce, and cheaper than by conventional survey. Archeomagnetic dating, a technique based upon alignment of iron particles in relation to the magnetic north pole, helped date hearths or old conflagrations and thus, by extension, periods of occupation. A concerted effort to collect cores from all original wood construction elements will provide tree-ring dates to help establish building episodes within each structure. Various electronic machines were used for subsurface exploration to determine the presence and extent of buried features.

The Center's major effort was excavation of a series of sites representing each ancient cultural stage at Chaco Canyon. Efforts focused on horizons for which there had been little or no previous information. Most ruins were dug for data only and were backfilled after clearing. A few, such as the large north-rim structure of Pueblo Alto and a group of small houses in Marcia's Rincon, were opened with the intention that they be used as interpretive exhibits. More than twenty-five individual ruins or ruin complexes, including one Navajo homesite, ultimately were excavated. Additionally, minor investigations of some isolated elements and nonhabitation items were carried out. Consideration of these data and preparation of reports continue.

Astronomers and archeologists have become increasingly interested in a widely held theory that ancient southwesterners, possibly those who called Chaco Canyon home, made observations of the sun and other celestial bodies to formulate calendars and regulate ritual and farming cycles. In Chaco such efforts have been devoted to locating what may have been solstice observation stations and to identifying rock art depictions of heavenly bodies and means of reckoning time. One pictograph in a protected overhang at the west end of the canyon is believed to record the supernova of July 4, 1054.

The American Museum of Natural History in New York retains most of the huge Hyde Exploring Expedition collection. In Washington, D.C. the U.S. National Museum has most of the specimens recovered by Neil Judd, although the National Geographic Society kept some of the finer objects. The Museum of New Mexico, Santa Fe, and the Maxwell Museum of Anthropology, University of New Mexico, Albuquerque, have collections resulting from their Chaco investigations. Most artifacts and records assembled by various National Park Service endeavors are housed in the Chaco Center, also in Albuquerque. ▲

ADDITIONAL READINGS, Chaco Culture National Historical Park

Frazier, Kendrick
    1986 *People of Chaco, a Canyon and Its Culture.* New York: W. W. Norton.
Hayes, Alden C., David M. Brugge, and W. James Judge
    1981 *Archeological Surveys of Chaco Canyon, New Mexico.* Publications in
        Archeology, No. 18A. Washington, D.C.: National Park Service.
Judd, Neil M.
    1954 *The Material Culture of Pueblo Bonito.* Smithsonian Miscellaneous Collections,
        Vol. 124. Washington, D.C.
    1964 *The Architecture of Pueblo Bonito.* Smithsonian Miscellaneous Collections,
        Vol. 147. No. 1. Washington, D.C.
Lekson, Stephen H.
    1984 *Great Pueblo Architecture of Chaco Canyon, New Mexico.* Publications in
        Archeology, No. 18B. Albuquerque, New Mexico: National Park Service.
Lister, Robert H., and Florence C. Lister
    1981 *Chaco Canyon, Archaeology and Archaeologists.* Albuquerque: University of
        New Mexico Press.
McNitt, Frank
    1966 *Richard Wetherill: Anasazi.* Reprint of 1957. Albuquerque: University of New
        Mexico Press.
Mathien, Frances Joan
    1985 *Environment and Subsistence of Chaco Canyon, New Mexico.* Publications in
        Archeology, No. 18E. Albuquerque, New Mexico: National Park Service.
Noble, David G., Editor
    1984 *New Light on Chaco Canyon.* Santa Fe, New Mexico: Exploration, Annual
        Bulletin of the School of American Research.
Powers, Robert P., William B. Gillespie, and Stephen H. Lekson
    1983 *The Outlier Survey: A Regional View of Settlement in the San Juan Basin.*
        Reports of the Chaco Center, No. 3. Albuquerque, New Mexico: National Park
        Service.

Vivian, Gordon, and Paul Reiter
    1960 *The Great Kivas of Chaco Canyon and Their Relationships.* Monograph, No. 22.
        Santa Fe, New Mexico: School of American Research.
Vivian, R. Gwinn
    1990 *The Chacoan Prehistory of the San Juan Basin.* New York: Academic.
Windes, Thomas C.
    1987 *Investigations at the Pueblo Alto Complex, Chaco Canyon, New Mexico; Vol. I,
        Summary of Tests and Excavations.* Publications in Archeology, No. 18F. Santa
        Fe, New Mexico: National Park Service.

Cluster of kivas in eastern portion of Pueblo Bonito, Chaco Culture National Historical Park. GEORGE A. GRANT, NATIONAL PARK SERVICE, 1929.

Archaic: *Desert Culture*
In-betweens and Outliers:
Fremont (San Rafael)
All-Southwest: *Hamlets,
plateau zone*

COLORADO NATIONAL MONUMENT, COLORADO

Cultural Significance and Archeological Classification

Enigmatic, undated Archaic/Fremont remains comprise the limited prehistoric resources of Colorado National Monument. They represent the easternmost distribution of the latter culture.

Explorations and Investigations

The broad valley at the northern base of the ruddy spired cliffs of Colorado National Monument through which the Colorado River flows attracted white settlers as soon as the Utes were removed to a more distant reservation in the early 1800s. They created farms and canals, and set about building the town of Grand Junction. The rugged canyon country and whatever human secrets it held were of little concern to most of them.

An exception was John Otto, a 1906 arrival who was enthralled with the area, built trails into it, and ceaselessly lobbied to have it federally protected. Success was his in 1911 when more than twenty thousand acres became a national monument. For the ensuing sixteen years he served as official custodian. However, there is no record of Otto having been more than casually interested in trace evidence of previous Indian presence. This situation prevailed until 1963 when the National Park Service contracted with the University of Colorado for the first archeological survey.

Meanwhile, as interest in southwestern archeology grew in the 1930s, local avocational archeologists identified a number of sites in Glade Park, a ranching area along the Colorado-Utah state line, southwest of the monument. Several test trenches in the fill of two promising caves were dug in 1940 by C. T. Hurst, a professor at Western State College in Gunnison. In the belief that information about the prehistory of the surrounding region might be forthcoming, this initial work was followed up in 1951 by University of Colorado staff members Robert H. Lister, who further excavated Luster and Roth caves, and Herbert W. Dick, who examined three nearby sites exposed by arroyo cutting. The cultural deposits turned out to be relatively thin, with a restricted artifact yield from which it was determined that the occupation probably had been Fremont. The presence of cobs and kernels of corn indicated some farming economy, but no habitations were found. Gray pottery was present, as was a variety of stone, bone, leather, and fiber materials. A large petroglyph panel in Sieber Canyon conforms to others identified as Fremont. Based upon tool typology and stratigraphy, suggested dating of the sites ranges from about sixteen hundred to seven hundred years ago.

The archeological survey of Colorado National Monument, carried out in 1963 by graduate students from the University of Colorado, produced much the same kind of materials as those from Glade Park. Seventy-five aboriginal sites were noted within the monument, none large or with extant dwelling structures. These were twenty-four rock shelters in the canyons or along escarpments and on the mesa top, forty-one open camp sites near intermittent stream beds or large rocks that would have provided shelter, two caves, eight chipping areas lacking habitations or hearths, isolated storage cists, and three petroglyph panels. Limited testing was done at two localities. Surface collections included projectile points, blades, scrapers, manos, metates, cordage, potsherds, basketry, and corncobs. The surveys suggested an Archaic into Fremont occupation with a hunting-gathering lifestyle dominating throughout.

Artifacts and notes are housed at the University of Colorado and with the National Park Service. ◆

ADDITIONAL READINGS, Colorado National Monument
Madsen, David E.
    1989 *Exploring the Fremont.* Salt Lake City: Utah Museum of Natural History.
Lister, Robert H., and Herbert W. Dick
    1952 Archaeology of the Glade Park Area, a Progress Report. *Southwestern Lore*, Vol.
        17, No. 4. Boulder: Colorado Archaeological Society. 69–92.
Wormington, H. M., and Robert H. Lister
    1956 *Archaeological Investigations on the Uncompahgre Plateau.* Proceedings,
        No. 2. Denver, Colorado: Denver Museum of Natural History.

Fremont petroglyph, Colorado National Monument. NATIONAL PARK SERVICE.

Petroglyphs at McKee Springs, Dinosaur National Monument. NATIONAL PARK SERVICE.

DINOSAUR NATIONAL MONUMENT, COLORADO-UTAH

Cultural Significance and Archeological Classification

Caves, terraces, and parks along the Green and Yampa rivers in the corners of northeastern Utah and northwestern Colorado were utilized for approximately six or seven thousand years. Archaic remains are of a generalized Desert Culture, which was being replaced as early as A.D. 100 by a Uinta Basin variant of the Fremont. While adhering to a basic hunting-foraging subsistence pattern, the latter practiced some horticulture, built rudimentary storage chambers and pithouses, and made simple, gray, utilitarian pottery. Their rock art was particularly notable. By about A.D. 1150 these Fremont may have been absorbed into the ancestral Shoshonean (Paiute, Ute, Shoshone) stock later to dominate the Great Basin and northern Colorado Plateau. Today the Northern Ute Indian Reservation shares the Uinta Basin.

Archaic: *Desert Culture*
In-betweens and Outliers: *Fremont (Uinta Basin)*
All-Southwest: *Hamlets, plateau zone*

Explorations and Investigations

Dinosaur National Monument was established in 1915 by proclamation of President Woodrow Wilson to protect a remarkable dinosaur boneyard discovered six years earlier by paleontologist Earl Douglass of the Carnegie Museum in Pittsburgh. The spectacular dinosaur quarry and the unspoiled wild beauty of the monument overshadow the area's prehistory. However, for many centuries its varied topography and wealth of plant and animal resources provided a favorable environment for small bands of people. The limited traces they left behind went unnoticed by the early explorers.

The Spanish Escalante-Domínguez expedition dispatched in 1776 from Santa Fe to find a westward route to San Francisco forded the Green River near the modern quarry site without noting any evidence of ancient people. In 1825 mountain man William H. Ashley and six trappers floated the Green River and through the dangerous Lodore Canyon, as did John Wesley Powell and his party in 1869 and again in 1871. That sheer-walled gorge always had been too difficult for human occupation. At the end of the nineteenth century a handful of white settlers took up holdings in the tiny meadows locked within the canyon fastness. They may have seen Indian remains but were not as interested as Charley Mantle.

Mantle was a pioneer rancher who arrived in Castle Park on the Yampa River in 1919 and soon became aware of artifacts weathering out of the blanket of earth in various caves or along the ridges. He later shared this information with scientists, who in the 1920s and 1930s took note of the antiquities of Dinosaur National Monument. J. A. Jeancon, Colorado State Historical Society; F. Martin Brown, Colorado Biological Survey; Hugo Rodeck and Charles R. Scoggin, University of Colorado Museum; Earl H. Morris, Carnegie Institution of Washington; and a party of National Park Service administrators were among those who visited the canyons during this period in order to appraise the possibilities of future archeological research there. Finally, in 1940 Scoggin and Edison P. Lohr conducted the first excavations in Castle Park, but their studies were halted by World War II.

Following the war, teams from the University of Colorado, headed by Robert F. Burgh, Robert H. Lister, and Herbert W. Dick, returned to Castle Park to complete work on the deposits of Mantle, Marigold, and a half-dozen unnamed caves, and to trench a deeply stratified refuse dump called Hells Midden, where lower levels were pre-agricultural and pre-ceramic. From 1963 through 1965 David A. Breternitz and students from the same institution undertook an intensive archeological survey of the monument and dug in twenty-two sites of various kinds in the Cub Creek area. Twenty years later a National Park Service archeologist was stationed at the monument. His work both substantiated and refined earlier findings and added new information. An especially significant excavation at Juniper Ledge Shelter in the archeologically rich Jones Hole/Ely Creek district yielded evidence of nearly a millennium of human presence.

Archeological specimens from Dinosaur National Monument are housed at the University of Colorado Museum, Boulder, and with the National Park Service. ▲

ADDITIONAL READINGS, Dinosaur National Monument
Breternitz, David A.
   1970 *Archaeological Excavations in Dinosaur National Monument, Colorado-Utah, 1964–1965*. University of Colorado Studies, Series in Anthropology No. 17. Boulder: University of Colorado.
Burgh, Robert F., and Charles R. Scoggin
   1948 *The Archaeology of Castle Park, Dinosaur National Monument*. University of Colorado Studies, Series in Anthropology No. 2. Boulder: University of Colorado.
Lister, Robert H.
   1951 *Excavations at Hells Midden, Dinosaur National Monument*. University of Colorado Studies, Series in Anthropology No. 3. Boulder: University of Colorado.
   1955 The Ancients of the Canyons. *This is Dinosaur*, edited by Wallace Stegner. New York: Alfred A. Knopf. 48–57.
Madsen, David B.
   1989 *Exploring the Fremont*. Salt Lake City: Utah Museum of Natural History.
Truesdale, James A.
   1990 Archaeological Investigations of the "Uinta Basin" Fremont in Dinosaur National Monument (1988–1990). Paper presented at Plains Anthropological Society Conference, Norman, Oklahoma, November 1–2, 1990.

EL MALPAIS NATIONAL MONUMENT, NEW MEXICO

Cultural Significance and Archeological Classification

Prehistoric occupation within El Malpais National Monument extends from the Archaic through Pueblo III periods. Pueblo II sites are the most numerous. Candelaria, formerly Las Ventanas Ruin, at the Sandstone Bluff Overlook on the east side of the monument is the most southeasterly Chaco outlier thus far identified. Although the structures at this location are unexcavated, eventually they will be made accessible to the public and the Chaco Phenomenon will be an interpretive theme.

Explorations and Investigations

Five craggy lava flows that engulfed the San Jose valley of central New Mexico, and now form the heart of El Malpais National Monument, made travel between two important prehistoric centers of population difficult but not impossible. The Anasazi in the Acoma area to the east of the badlands, and those in the Zuni area to the west, beat an east-west trail across a tongue of all five flows. When a deep break in the layers interrupted their preferred route, resourceful men threw chunks of the rock into the opening to create a bridge. Further, because it was easy to get lost amidst the sea of black lava, they stacked up cairns of rock as markers.

The earliest recorded reference to the lava fields, *malpais* as the Spaniards called them, was made in 1582 by a scribe with the Rodríguez-Chamuscado expedition. Since he did not mention the ancient trail, it is assumed he never saw it. However, the parade of Hispanics who later traveled west from the Rio Grande and paused to note their passage on the cliff at El Morro probably made use of the Indian shortcut. Neither they nor the American soldiers and surveyors who explored along the thirty-fifth parallel during most of the second half of the nineteenth century commented on any regional antiquities.

It remained for Adolph Bandelier, while traversing the Acoma-Zuni trail in 1882, to first document the large Candelaria ruin and mention remains of twenty to thirty small houses in the environs. Together they form a substantial concentration of Anasazi habitations but were given little professional attention until the next century.

During the 1970s the possibility of a federal preserve and nearby highway improvements stimulated the first serious archeological surveys by the School of American Research, the Bureau of Indian Affairs, and the Museum of New Mexico. No substantial excavations resulted. Meanwhile, because the scattering of antiquities had become common knowledge among residents of districts peripheral to the badlands, pothunting took place. Candelaria suffered the most severe damage. With the establishment in 1987 of El Malpais National Monument, administered by the National Park Service, and the surrounding National Conservation Area, under control of the Bureau of Land Management, this destructive activity has ceased.

Archeological surveys confirmed a sequence of Archaic-Pueblo development similar

Archaic: *Oshara*
Anasazi: *Basket Maker III; Pueblo I, II, III*
Mogollon: *1, 2, 3*
All-Southwest: *Hamlets, Villages, Towns, intermediate between plateau and mountain-valley zones*

to that found elsewhere on the eastern Colorado Plateau. Researchers noted a pattern of increased concern with agriculture, shifting residence through time to take advantage of favorable ecological situations, and progression from single-unit pithouses, to small surface dwellings, to multiroomed masonry structures. Whenever excavations are undertaken, it is anticipated that the architectural details and material culture will resemble contemporary occupation on Cebolleta Mesa and east of the monument conservation lands. There, at some periods (especially early Pueblo II) an important interaction with Mogollon peoples to the south has been detected. Judging from surface indications, the malpais was abandoned by the Anasazi during Pueblo III times. They may have migrated eastward to Cebolleta Mesa and other highlands, where they congregated into large, defensible communities such as Acoma pueblo. A significant Pueblo IV presence in this area was in place when the Spaniards arrived.

The most outstanding of the malpais habitations is Candelaria. It sits on a sandstone bluff overlooking the forbidding McCarty flow to the west. Its placement on a prominence within an indigenous settlement is typical of Chaco outliers. Other Chacoan diagnostic features include two house blocks built with core and veneer masonry walls. Although the structure remains in mounded condition, its two units are estimated to contain about eighty-nine rooms. One unit was two stories in height and incorporated a tower kiva. Nearby is the depression of a Great Kiva with four surface alcoves. At the time of Bandelier's visit, six circular sandstone disks that had been used as seating for the kiva roof supports were present. They have since disappeared. A segment of a prehistoric road with some stone curbing runs along the east base of the McCarty flow before coming to an end at the Candelaria mound.

Geological opinion is that the McCarty flow occurred from seven hundred to one thousand years ago. If the former age is correct, the Anasazi had left the region. However, archeological evidence suggests they occupied the Candelaria bluff after that episode of vulcanism. The lava spread in such a way as to block drainages flowing west off Cebolleta Mesa, thereby creating catchments that subsequently filled with alluvium. Some researchers believe these formations became desirable garden plots which made the Candelaria community possible. Some of the stone used in the lower levels of the Chacoan structure is vesicular basalt. Since the customary sandstone was readily available, the choice of basalt must mean that it also was near at hand. Moreover, the road obviously was laid out along the foot of the lava escarpment. Many of the southern Chaco outliers date to the second half of the eleventh century, preceding construction of the road network.

Specimens recovered in the various surveys are housed at the sponsoring institutions.

ADDITIONAL READINGS, El Malpais National Monument
Ireland, Arthur K.
　　1988　Cultural Prehistory of the El Malpais National Monument and National Conservation Area. Draft Manuscript. Santa Fe, New Mexico: Southwest Regional Office, National Park Service.

Mangum, Neil C.
   1990 *A History of Occupation in El Malpais Country.* Southwest Cultural Resources
         Center, Professional Papers No. 32. Santa Fe, New Mexico: Cultural Resources
         Center, National Park Service.
Marshall, Michael P., John R. Stein, Richard W. Loose, and Judith E. Novotny
   1979 *Anasazi Communities of the San Juan Basin.* Joint Publication of the Public
         Service Company of New Mexico and the Historic Preservation Bureau,
         Planning Division. Santa Fe: State of New Mexico.
Ruppe, R. J. Jr., and A. E. Dittert
   1952 The Archaeology of Cebolleta Mesa and Acoma Pueblo; a Preliminary Report
         Based on Further Investigation. *El Palacio*, Vol. 59, No. 7. Santa Fe: Museum of
         New Mexico. 191–217.

Inscription Rock, El Morro National Monument. GEORGE A. GRANT, NATIONAL PARK SERVICE, 1940.

EL MORRO NATIONAL MONUMENT, NEW MEXICO

Cultural Significance and Archeological Classification

    Although only partially excavated, the large ruin on top of Inscription Rock in El Morro National Monument shows the characteristics of many others in the vicinity. These towns were densely populated while most parts of the northern Southwest were being abandoned beginning in the twelfth century. Hawikuh is one of these towns.

Anasazi: *Basket Maker III; Pueblo I, II, III, IV*
All-Southwest: *Hamlets, Villages, Towns, plateau zone*

Explorations and Investigations

    This message is scratched at the base of the jutting promontory of yellowish tan sandstone that is the heart of El Morro National Monument. The Spanish name means headland or knob. The cliff is known as Inscription Rock because from at least 1605 it provided a convenient register for many who paused there to enjoy a natural reservoir of cool water. The Simpson-Kern entry represents the first recording of the 250-year-old roster.

    Legible Spanish inscriptions date from that of Juan de Oñate, the first governor of New Mexico, cut on the soft massif in April 1605 or 1606, followed by many other records of visits by soldiers, priests, and administrators.

    Inscriber Simpson found no English words on the rock, but after his time, travel past El Morro seems to have become popular. Names of many American emigrants, ranchers, soldiers, engineers, and prospectors were left on the smooth cliffs. Simpson also observed the presence of aboriginal petroglyphs on the rock surfaces and the existence of two ruined pueblo structures on top of the prominence.

Once publicized, this unusual historical catalogue attracted the curious, even though they found getting there difficult. Writer Charles Lummis returned many times after his first visit in 1885. Calling it the "stone autograph album," he made copies of many of the inscriptions and tried to verify their authenticity. Shortly after his first visit, he wrote a preliminary report, never published, in which he discussed the Oñate recording. He felt that its date should be interpreted as April 16, 1605. An earlier inscription that Lummis observed, possibly from the year 1580, is no longer discernible.

The area was made a national monument in December 1906. In 1912 representatives of the Bureau of American Ethnology, headed by Frederick W. Hodge, made photographs and paper molds of all inscriptions of historical interest. Plaster casts secured from the molds were placed in the U.S. National Museum.

In prehistoric times, the region around El Morro was occupied by Zuni ancestors. The ruins atop Inscription Rock are just two of a great number of villages and towns used by a dense, shifting population scattered along the Continental Divide in western New Mexico. At first contact with the Europeans in 1539, the Zunis were living in six major communities on the Zuni River. Following the Pueblo Revolt of 1680, fearful of Spanish reprisals, the Zuni took refuge on defensible mesa tops, especially Dowa Yalanne, or Corn Mountain. Once the Vargas reconquest of New Mexico had taken place in 1692, the Zunis consolidated into a single town, the modern Zuni pueblo about forty miles west of El Morro. Abundant ruins in the area, existence of detailed historical accounts of European contacts with the Zuni, and the fact that the Zuni people have maintained their ceremonialism and world view have stimulated a century of archeological and ethnographical studies among them.

In the 1880s Victor Mindeleff prepared a plan of Zuni pueblo and mapped other sites in the area. The Hemenway Southwestern Archaeological Expedition of 1888–89 did some digging in Halona, the prehistoric and historic town that is now Zuni, and also at the pre-Hispanic town of Heshotauthla. Systematic archeological research began with Alfred Kroeber's 1916 study of the potsherds at ruins near Zuni. Expanding on these findings, Leslie Spier demonstrated that all styles of pottery decoration had begun in small frequency, increased to maximum frequency, and gone out of use. He believed that Zuni's geographical isolation gave a specific "Zunian character" to the locally made pottery.

The most ambitious archeological program attempted in the area was that of the Hendricks-Hodge Expedition under auspices of the Museum of the American Indian, Heye Foundation. From 1917 to 1923 work was carried on at the historic site of Hawikuh, which had been a thriving Zuni pueblo in 1539. In that year Fray Marcos de Niza led a reconnaissance north from Mexico to verify rumors of the existence of "Seven Cities of Cíbola," a group of walled cities reputed to be extremely wealthy. When a few members of Fray Marcos's advance party entered Hawikuh, apparently ostentatiously, a Negro companion of Niza, Estéban, was killed by the inhabitants. The frightened Spaniards decided to view the town from a safe distance before retracing their steps to Mexico. Marcos de Niza exaggerated about seeing "seven fair-looking settlements in the distance," which were said to contain gold and jewels. He also allegedly stated that the city of Cíbola

(Hawikuh) was twice the size of Seville and contained fine four-story houses.

Because of Niza's overblown stories, an expedition was organized on behalf of the Spanish crown to thoroughly explore the borderlands believed to offer such brilliant prospects. Aristocratic young Francisco Vásquez de Coronado, governor of Nueva Galicia, was selected to head the expedition. Setting out from Culiacán, Sinaloa, in February 1540 with a small army of three hundred soldiers and eight hundred friendly Indians and Indian servants, the straggling assembly made its way slowly north, surely one of the most exotic contingents ever to penetrate the United States.

In July Coronado, with an advance force, finally reached Hawikuh. Although tired and hungry, they defeated the natives in a fierce battle. Coronado and his followers then assigned names to many native groups, gave them their first knowledge of certain domestic animals and material goods, and acquainted some of them with Christianity and European mores.

Coronado's disappointment was great when he learned that the Zuni pueblos were not golden cities. Instead, he had conquered humble farming communities. Undaunted, he sent out several exploratory parties, which found the Hopi villages, the Grand Canyon, Acoma, and the Rio Grande pueblos where the expedition spent the winter of 1540–41. In the spring a force was dispatched east to the impressive pueblo of Pecos and to the plains beyond on an ill-fated search for Quivira, another place of supposed riches. Nowhere did Coronado find the gold and treasure the Spaniards so avidly sought. Nevertheless, the Zuni pueblos and the region around them became known as Cíbola. Beset with increasing hardships and disappointments and faced with insurrection among his command, Coronado retreated to Mexico in the spring of 1542.

Nearly forty years later authorities in Mexico City sent another force into New Mexico. The 1581 route through Chihuahua and up the Rio Grande blazed by the Rodríguez-Chamuscado Expedition became the *camino real*, or royal road, for later soldiers, priests, colonists, and supply and commercial caravans.

After the 1600s, Zuni was not on the main caravan route between Mexico and the northern frontier of Spanish civilization. Nevertheless, travelers from Santa Fe to the Hopi villages and farther west usually passed by Acoma, El Morro, and Zuni. Many records of those trips are carved into Inscription Rock. The populous Zuni villages attracted the Spaniards for two reasons: productive farmland at Cíbola and natives available for religious conversion. Missionary labors began in June 1629, when a house in Hawikuh was purchased for use as a mission. Construction of the permanent church, La Purísima Concepción, was started the same year. Another church was built at Halona. Missionary activities and administrative dealings with the Zunis followed the same pattern as elsewhere in New Mexico.

The residents of Hawikuh, like those in the other Zuni pueblos, went through a half-century of sparring with Spanish civil authorities and resident priests. On at least one occasion the populace revolted, killed the attendant priests, burned the church, and left their homes for the mesa-top stronghold of Dowa Yalanne as they had done in Coronado's time. They were persuaded to return to their valley town by promises of better treatment from their oppressors, and the church was refurbished. The final destruction of the Hawikuh church was caused either by an Apache raid in 1672 or by the local inhabitants at the time of the Pueblo Revolt of 1680. Hawikuh never was reoccupied. Thereafter, the Zunis came together at Zuni pueblo.

It was Hawikuh to which Frederick Hodge turned his attention in 1917 in one of the main archeological activities of the first quarter of this century. Even though Pueblos had lived there for centuries before the arrival of the Spanish, Hodge restricted his research to the town as it existed from the time of its discovery by the Iberians until it was vacated. Evidence of occupancy beneath the historic remains was not investigated. When the project terminated six years later, 370 rooms had been cleared, the large mission church and its friary almost completely excavated, at least 1600 whole or restored pottery vessels recovered, about 1000 burials exhumed, and large quantities of potsherds and artifacts of native and Spanish derivation collected.

This inscription was supposedly done by Governor Eulate. It translates:

"I am the Captain General of the Province of New Mexico for the King our Lord, passed by here on the return from the pueblo of Zuni on the 29th of July the year of 1620, and put them at peace at their humble petition, they asking favor as vassals of his Majesty and promising anew their obedience, all of which he did, with clemency, zeal, and prudence as a most Christianlike (gentleman) extraordinary and gallant soldier of enduring and praised memory."

Although Hodge never wrote a general report on the archeology of Hawikuh, he did author several articles and produced an important volume on its history based primarily upon archival research. After Hodge's death, Watson Smith and Richard and Nathalie Woodbury utilized his notes and the materials recovered to put together a thoughtful report on Hawikuh exclusive of certain objects of Spanish or Mexican origin.

For the past decade Zuni pueblo has been sponsoring its own archeological and ethnohistorical programs in the vicinity of the town, as well as farther afield. A crew of professional scientists and Zuni workmen is studying the total range of local culture. In time, the history of ancient life in this sector of the Colorado Plateau, culminating in the modern community, will be known in greater detail than that of any of the contemporary pueblos.

Details of the prehistory of the wider Zuni region, including El Morro, began to emerge with a series of excavations between 1931 and 1940 by Frank H. H. Roberts, Jr. of the Smithsonian Institution. He noted an uninterrupted cultural growth from small, eighth-century pithouse villages to large, many-storied complexes of the contact period. He postulated a link between the Zuni and Chaco Canyon cultures. Roberts dug the Village of the Great Kivas, twenty-two miles northwest of El Morro, a large settlement of three masonry room blocks, seven ordinary kivas, and two Great Kivas. This profusion of ceremonial chambers suggests than an unusually large number of ritual performances may have taken place there.

Archeological investigations in El Morro National Monument took place in 1954 and 1955 when Richard Woodbury cleaned out part of one of the ruins on top of Inscription Rock. Known as Atsinna, Zuni for "writing on the rock," it is typical of many thirteenth- and fourteenth-century Zuni villages in that it is situated on a crest with commanding views in all directions. Atsinna was a large rectangular building of masonry with nearly one thousand rooms, arranged in ascending tiers from the central plaza to three stories around the exterior walls. Its occupants probably got their water from the same pool at the base of Inscription Rock that attracted so many travelers in colonial times. Rooms and kivas in one wing of the site have been stabilized by the National Park Service and may be examined by park visitors. Several other ruins near El Morro, some partially excavated, exhibit similarities to Atsinna and probably are the same age.

Some artifacts from Atsinna are displayed in the monument visitor center, but most are housed in the Western Archeological and Conservation Center in Tucson. Specimens obtained from the Village of the Great Kivas are at the Smithsonian Institution. Those from Hawikuh are at the Museum of the American Indian, New York. Zuni pueblo retains materials from its excavations. ▲

ADDITIONAL READINGS, El Morro National Monument
Noble, David G.
1983 *Zuni and El Morro, Past and Present*. Santa Fe, New Mexico: Exploration, Annual Bulletin of the School of American Research.
Roberts, Frank H. H., Jr.
1932 *The Village of the Great Kivas on the Zuni Reservation, New Mexico*. Bulletin, No. 111. Washington, D.C.: Bureau of American Ethnology.
Smith, Watson, Richard B. Woodbury, and Nathalie F. S. Woodbury
1966 *The Excavation of Hawikuh by Frederick Webb Hodge: Report of the Hendricks-Hodge Expedition, 1917–1923*. Contributions, No. 20. New York: Heye Foundation, Museum of the American Indian.
Woodbury, Richard B.
1979 *Zuni Prehistory and History to 1850*. In *Handbook of North American Indians*. Vol. 9. Washington, D.C.: Smithsonian Institution. 467–473.

Cliff dwellings, Gila Cliff Dwellings National Monument. NATIONAL PARK SERVICE.

GILA CLIFF DWELLINGS NATIONAL MONUMENT, NEW MEXICO

Cultural Significance and Archeological Classification

Gila Cliff Dwellings National Monument has the only Mogollon ruins on exhibit in the National Park Service system. However, the small cliff dwellings, wedged into caves high on the wall of a verdant narrow canyon, were built after the Anasazi had expanded into Mogollon territory along the mountains and valleys of the Arizona–New Mexico border region and implanted many of their traditions. One of these introduced traits was the erection of structures in shallow caves. In addition to other examples of this Anasazi-dominated period, the monument contains some unexcavated ruins of earlier, unadulterated Mogollon pithouse villages.

Mogollon: *1, 2, 3 (pithouses), 4 (cliff dwellings)*
All-Southwest: *Hamlets, Villages, mountain-valley zone*

Explorations and Investigations

In late 1883 Adolph Bandelier made a twelve-day round trip by foot, horseback, and wagon from the mining camp at Mimbres in southern New Mexico to the headwaters of the Gila River to view some cliff dwellings. To reach his destination, he endured sub-freezing weather, a sore foot that made walking painful, and rough mountainous trails. But his goal was reached, and his visit produced an early description of the Gila cliff dwellings.

These were small, roofless cells almost hidden in four irregular overhangs on a cliff high above a confined canyon. Wooden lintels were still in place over doorways. Domestic trash, such as bits of pottery, corncobs, and a discarded sandal, lay scattered about. The style of architecture impressed Bandelier because it was the same he had seen in ruins around Mimbres, but the Gila settlement housed fewer people because of the lack of arable land in the mountain valley.

The upper Gila region was Apache territory during Spanish colonial and early American times, and local white settlers claimed that the Indians had damaged the cliff dwellings. It is unlikely that they were the sole culprits because white cattlemen, soldiers, and drifters are known to have climbed to the ruins also. One casual visitor claimed to have removed stone axes, turquoise beads, red and gray pottery jars, and the desiccated corpse of a child from one house. In 1885 Lieutenant G. H. Sands, from Fort Bayard near Silver City, found a few specimens by grubbing with his hunting knife. Undoubtedly more startling was the mountain lion that jumped over him as he crouched, intent upon his finds.

Nomadic Apaches moved into the Gila headwaters region several centuries after the prehistoric village dwellers had withdrawn. The river's name likely is a Spanish corruption of the Apache word for mountain; one early Spanish document referred to the local inhabitants as "Apache de Xila."

Apache bands, striking out from their camps in the rough mountains along the Continental Divide, grew increasingly warlike under pressure of white colonization. They took to terrorizing and raiding as a means of survival. When pursued, they vanished into the knot of hidden canyons and high plateaus that later became the Gila Wilderness Area.

With American occupation of the Territory of New Mexico in 1846, the United States government soon learned that it had inherited a serious problem in dealing with these natives. For forty years military forces and civil agents fought against, made treaties with, set up reservations for, and encouraged agriculture among the Apache. The federal forces also were guilty of mismanagement, which worsened relationships.

Geronimo, for a decade the feared leader of a small band of the most rebellious Apaches, had been raised on the upper Gila. He frequently crossed the international boundary to avoid capture by Mexican or American forces. These troops had to have official permission to cross the border in either direction. Geronimo, of course, sought no such permission. At last, time ran out for the Apaches. In 1886 a truce and terms of surrender for Geronimo and his renegades were agreed upon, but at the last moment the band fled again to the Sierra Madres in Mexico. It took another six months before General Miles succeeded in rounding them up and forcing them to capitulate, thus putting an end to several centuries of bloodshed. Geronimo and his entire band of about 340 were deported as prisoners of war first to Florida, then to Alabama, and finally to Fort Sill, Oklahoma, where Geronimo died in 1909.

The cliff dwellings of the Gila River were made a national monument in 1907. Because of their location deep in the broken country of the Gila National Forest, they remained relatively unknown. Progress at last brought in a paved road in 1966. Inevitably, increased visitation to both the antiquities and the surrounding Gila Wilderness Area made it necessary to name a full-time superintendent. Gila Cliff Dwellings National Monument was transferred from the National Park Service to the Forest Service in 1975.

One thousand years of widespread cultural development that archeologists now call Mogollon is represented at Gila Cliff Dwellings. Earliest in the sequence are several pithouse villages. One such village, whose material objects were diagnostic of the Mogollon from about A.D. 400 to 600, was excavated because a proposed road would have cut through the site. Another threatened ruin proved to be a complex of fourteen pithouses dated about A.D. 900 to 1000. Both these semi-subterranean villages had been covered by later surface houses erected from A.D. 1000 to 1100, when influence from the Pueblo world to the north had drifted into the region. As masonry architecture then became common, larger towns of many rooms and several stories were erected either within shallow caves or on bottomland terraces. The cliff dwellings for which the monument is named yielded roof beams dated in the A.D. 1280s. The houses continued to be occupied into the middle of the next century. An unexcavated contemporaneous site, the T. J. Ruin, spreads over several acres a short distance behind the visitor center. It is estimated to contain about two hundred rooms in five house blocks, in part erected over earlier pithouses. The cultural stratification represents some nine hundred years of occupation.

Since 1942 the National Park Service has repaired damage to the cliff dwellings engendered by nature and humans. In the course of these efforts some potsherds, and artifacts of stone, bone, wood, fiber, and shell have been reclaimed.

Artifacts from Gila Cliff Dwellings are kept at the Western Archeological and Conservation Center of the National Park Service in Tucson. ▲

ADDITIONAL READINGS, Gila Cliff Dwellings National Monument
McFarland, Elizabeth
     1967 *Forever Frontier: The Gila Cliff Dwellings.* Albuquerque: University of New
           Mexico Press.
McKenna, Peter J., and James E. Bradford
     1989 *The TJ Ruin, Gila Cliff Dwellings National Monument.* Southwest Cultural
           Resource Center, Professional Papers, No. 21. Santa Fe: New Mexico: Southwest
           Cultural Resources Center, National Park Service.
Martin, Paul S.
     1979 Prehistory: Mogollon. In *Handbook of North American Indians*, Vol. 9.
           Washington, D.C.: Smithsonian Institution. 61–74.

Animals were needed to pack materials into the caves when the Gila cliff dwellings were repaired.
NATIONAL PARK SERVICE.

The ruins at Nankoweap, Grand Canyon National Park. JOHN RICHARDSON.

GRAND CANYON NATIONAL PARK, ARIZONA

Cultural Significance and Archeological Classification

Grand Canyon National Park was a meeting ground of several southwestern cultures, some of which occupied various sections of the canyon at the same time. Anasazi village ruins have been noted on the north and south rims and in the depths of the canyon. South of the canyon two aspects of the widely dispersed Hakataya culture, Cohonina and Cerbat, have been identified. The Grand Canyon Anasazi possessed characteristic southwestern culture, but the Hakataya were marginal groups. They integrated enough traits, such as house types, pottery, and elementary farming, to acquire a similarity to Anasazi lifestyle. Determining the cultural continuum between specific Hakataya groups and historic tribes of the Colorado River is another significant aspect of Grand Canyon prehistory.

Explorations and Investigations

Indians are not usually the primary interest of visitors to Grand Canyon National Park. Most come to see the stupendous, multihued chasm that has been deeply scoured into the Colorado Plateau by eons of uplift and the unceasing charge of the Colorado River. Nevertheless, the canyon and its environs contain many signs of prehistoric inhabitants, and several tribes still live there.

The first Europeans to gaze into the shadowy depths of the Grand Canyon were members of the 1540 Coronado expedition. At the Hopi villages they learned of a great river farther west. A secondary force, commanded by García López de Cárdenas, promptly was ordered to locate and explore it. Securing Hopi guides, Cárdenas and his men traveled twenty days before reaching the brink of the Grand Canyon late in September. The Cárdenas party worked along the south rim of the canyon for some distance, estimated its width to be eight to ten miles, but failed to find a route to the river. The men deduced correctly that the river was the Colorado, known then as the Tizón, or Firebrand.

In the first half of the eighteenth century the Spanish militia made sporadic attempts to bring the Hopi and recalcitrant Rio Grande Pueblos back into their fold. None succeeded. In 1776 Fray Francisco Tomás Garcés, a Franciscan missionary who had explored the Colorado River, was rejected by the Hopi. However, Garcés found the Hualapai, in the western section of the Grand Canyon, and the Havasupai, of Cataract or Havasu Creek, much more hospitable. They served him as guides, provided him with food and shelter, and otherwise contributed to a successful trip that generated a second eyewitness description of the Grand Canyon.

A few months later while returning from an unsuccessful attempt to find a route from Santa Fe to California, Fray Silvestre Vélez de Escalante met a group of Southern Paiute Indians north of the canyon. As a consequence, he compiled the first account of these hunters and gatherers who roamed the plateaus along the north rim.

Although surveys were made of the Grand Canyon region following American

Archaic: Pinto
Anasazi: Pueblo I, II, III
In-betweens and Outliers:
Hakataya culture
(Cohonina, Cerbat)
All-Southwest: Villages,
plateau zone, western
periphery

acquisiton of Arizona, it was not until John Wesley Powell and his crew made two exploratory boat trips down the Colorado River, first in 1869 and again in 1871–72, that archeological materials were reported there. Powell recorded eight small canyon-bottom ruins, of which only foundations and a tumble of building stones remained.

During the 1870s Powell and his associates in the newly formed Geographical and Geological Survey of the Rocky Mountain Region continued explorations and geological investigations in the Colorado River basin. More attention was given to the conditions, customs, languages, and history of the Indians of the region, prompting the founding in 1879 of the Smithsonian Institution's Bureau of Ethnology dedicated to studying all facets of American Indian culture. Powell was named the first director, and a few years later he also assumed leadership of the new U.S. Geological Survey.

After Powell had demonstrated that the river was navigable, others worked their way through the canyon, finding limited evidence of prehistoric occupation in the inner canyon and on the north and south plateaus. In 1882 Frank Cushing visited the Havasupai, whom he found to occupy and farm Havasu Canyon only in the summer, spending their winters hunting and gathering on the plateau.

During the first half of the twentieth century, systematic description of archeological remains in Grand Canyon National Park and the gathering of more ethnological information about the four native groups who utilized the region—the Havasupai, Southern Paiute, Hopi, and Navajo—began to fill out the previously sketchy picture of regional cultural history. With a program that got under way in 1915, Neil M. Judd, then of the Bureau of American Ethnology, was the first professional archeologist to work within the present boundaries of the park. After several years of survey and excavations north of the Colorado River, he suggested that the sites there were related to those of the prehistoric Pueblo culture, reiterating an idea that Powell put forth fifty years earlier. Both men had no clear perception of the age of the remains.

The necessary ordering of Grand Canyon archeology within a time frame and a better comprehension of its ties to other Puebloan centers came about in the 1930s. Tusayan Ruin on the south rim was studied by Emil Haury, then of the Gila Pueblo, and Walhalla Glades on the north rim was surveyed by E.T. Hall, Jr. The Judd and Hall surveys disclosed nearly five hundred sites, from single-room houses to complicated multiroomed units, and a number of check dams and terraces associated with agricultural plots. Utilizing tree-ring dating and rapidly accumulating information about prehistoric pottery types, these surveys suggested two sources of Puebloan culture in the Grand Canyon. One was the San Juan country to the east, and the other was the Virgin River region to the north and west. An occupation from about A.D. 500 to 1200 was postulated.

Additional archeological investigations were conducted in ruins along the south rim and toward the San Francisco Peaks, primarily by Harold S. Colton and Lyndon L. Hargrave of the Museum of Northern Arizona. These revealed such a distinctive set of architectural styles, pottery, and stone artifact types that a second prehistoric culture, called the Cohonina and believed to have been to some extent contemporaneous with the Anasazi, was suggested. Although there is no evidence of conflict between these two peoples, some constructions of dry-laid masonry on free-standing pinnacles or isolated cliff projections suggest defensive needs.

After excavation of another sixteen sites south of the Grand Canyon by John C. McGregor of the University of Illinois, and further analyses of artifacts, the Cohonina people were judged to be part of a larger cultural component, the Hakataya. They were thought to have occupied an expansive range on both sides of the Colorado River as far north as the Grand Canyon. Although recognized as having an identifiable culture, the Cohoninas adopted many traits of others with whom they came in contact. Some see the Cohoninas as ancestral to the Havasupai. Others disagree, pointing out that they disappear from the cultural record about A.D. 1150. Perhaps it was still another group, the Cerbat, that drifted into the territory from the west after A.D. 1300 and slowly evolved into the modern Havasupai and probably the Hualapai. Meanwhile, Southern Paiute bands claimed the north rim.

Accumulating details about prehistoric use of the inner recesses of the canyon have been contributed by several archeologists, most importantly Douglas W. Schwartz of the School of American Research and Robert C. Euler, formerly of the National Park Service. They have made painstaking surveys of portions of the canyon bottom, some of the river terraces, and many overhangs and caves in the canyon walls to find hundreds of small dwellings and granaries tucked onto ledges, large pits where mescal was roasted, and numerous trails crisscrossing the cliff escarpments. Excavations have been conducted in house and village ruins on Unkar Delta and elsewhere. To date, some fifteen hundred sites have been recorded, with peak occupation in the century between A.D. 1050 and 1150. These projects have convincingly demonstrated that the inner recesses of the canyon offered the Anasazi advantages in the way of wild plants and animals and a floodwater farming opportunity not available on the rims. Seasonal use of lower and higher elevations is likely. Schwartz also has researched Havasupai prehistory and has located and cleared many ancient habitations on Walhalla Glades.

One of the most fascinating developments in Grand Canyon archeology goes back to 1933 when three members of a Civilian Conservation Corps crew found three miniature animal effigies in a cave in the canyon. Each figurine had been made by bending and folding a single split-willow twig. They were thought possibly to have been fashioned by Indians and hence were placed in the collections of the park. More than three hundred similar specimens made of willow and cottonwood have since been collected from several almost inaccessible caves in the Grand Canyon. Additional examples are known from other localities in Arizona, Utah, Nevada, and California. These cleverly contrived representations of deer and desert bighorn sheep, possibly of elk and antelope, have become known as split-twig figurines and are believed to have been created by ancient hunters as magic or religious objects. The caves in which they were placed were shrines for imitative magic rites to assure success in the hunt. Split-twig figurines from the Grand Canyon have been meticulously studied and dated by radiocarbon means at three thousand to four thousand years old. These, some unusual rock art, and Pinto complex projectile points are interpreted as Archaic.

Split-twig figurine, four-thousand-year-old remnant of early Grand Canyon hunters.
COURTESY GRAND CANYON NATURAL HISTORY ASSOCIATION.

Studies are under way to determine the erosional effects on canyon-bottom sites of regulated water release from the Glen Canyon Dam. The Western Archeological and Conservation Center in Tucson is the repository for the large array of specimens resulting from the excavations and surveys by both the School of American Research and the National Park Service. ◢◣

ADDITIONAL READINGS, Grand Canyon National Park
Euler, Robert C.
   1967   The Canyon Dwellers. *The American West*, Vol. 4, No. 2. Palo Alto, California:
          American West Publishing Company. 22–27, 67–71.
   1988   Demography and Cultural Dynamics on the Colorado Plateau. In *The Anasazi in
          a Changing Environment*, edited by George J. Gumerman. Cambridge:
          Cambridge University Press. 198–200.
Fowler, Don D., Robert C. Euler, and Catherine S. Fowler
   1969   *John Wesley Powell and the Anthropology of the Canyon Country.* Geological
          Survey Professional Paper, No. 670. Washington, D.C.: U.S. Geological Survey.
Hughes, J. Donald
   1978   *In the House of Stone and Light, A Human History of the Grand Canyon.* Grand
          Canyon, Arizona: Grand Canyon Natural History Association.
Jones, Anne T., and Robert C. Euler
   1979   *A Sketch of Grand Canyon Prehistory.* Grand Canyon, Arizona: Grand Canyon
          Natural History Association.
Schwartz, Douglas W., Michael Marshall, and Jane Kepp
   1979   *Archaeology of the Grand Canyon: The Bright Angel Site.* Santa Fe, New
          Mexico: School of American Research Press.
Schwartz, Douglas W., Richard C. Chapman, and Jane Kepp
   1980   *Archaeology of the Grand Canyon: Unkar Delta.* Santa Fe, New Mexico: School
          of American Research Press.
   1981   *Archaeology of the Grand Canyon: The Walhalla Plateau.* Santa Fe, New
          Mexico: School of American Research Press.

GREAT SAND DUNES NATIONAL MONUMENT, COLORADO

Cultural Significance and Archeological Classification

Paleo-Indian: *Clovis, Folsom, Cody*
Archaic: *Oshara*

The San Luis valley of southern Colorado is a broad, flat expanse that periodically was wet and grassy. Along its eastern flank are approximately fifty-five square miles of the tallest sand dunes in North America. The valley was an especially favorable, discretely defined environment for Paleo-Indian and Archaic populations. During sufficiently mesic periods, at least three distinct, successive groupings of the former were present in some numbers. Although not yet studied in depth, the latter are thought to have found the valley satisfactory for their hunting and gathering mode of life.

Explorations and Investigations

Their unusual geological history in a mountain-valley setting and their grandeur were the reasons for declaring the Great Sand Dunes a national monument in 1932. There was no thought given to their possible role in southwestern prehistory. The explorers, trappers, soldiers, miners, and engineers who trudged by them in the course of several centuries were unconcerned about what might have transpired there in former times. All these observers knew was that in their time the dunes and the valley beyond was Ute territory, and the Utes were not always friendly. Nor were the dunes.

Only when American homesteaders and cattlemen began inching their way over the surrounding mountain passes and spreading out into the basin below did an awareness begin to grow of former occupation. Collecting a variety of archeological debris became a local pastime. Some of the material was recovered during development of farms, some from open ranges, and some from dunes banked against the base of the Sangre de Cristo Mountains, where shifting sands had a tantalizing way of revealing and then concealing artifacts. Since there were no surface ruins in the valley to suggest settled farmers, this physical evidence of man's passage was variously attributed by the collectors to some amorphous ancient band of wanderers or perhaps to Pueblo or Plains Indians. They did not contemplate any connection between those transients and the dunes.

Until recently, professional interest in the prehistory of the valley has been sporadic and relatively unproductive. E. B. Renaud, professor at the University of Denver, visited the region in the 1930s without doing more than viewing private collections. Just before World War II, C. T. Hurst of Western State College at Gunnison, Colorado, engaged in a small excavation on a ranch near Great Sand Dunes which produced some fossil bison bones and the characteristically channel-fluted Folsom points. Similar finds at another site in the vicinity were made in the 1950s by Adams State University teacher F. C. V. Worman. Also in that decade Frank Swancara, a student at the University of Colorado, conducted a brief reconnaissance of the monument on behalf of the National Park Service.

Finally, in 1977 a team from the Smithsonian Institution, under leadership of Dennis Stanford, launched a long-term ongoing project in the northern end of the valley not far from the monument boundaries. To date this project has examined four Paleo-Indian sites with significant results concerning a Folsom occupation. Three of the sites are near shallow ponds or bogs thought to have been more numerous throughout the valley in the past. One is in a blowout on a ranch just to the south of the monument, where subsurface deposits have been partially exposed by wind deflation. Two related activity areas are apparent at these sites. One is where Folsom hunters actually killed both extinct bison and modern species such as antelope, wolves, and rabbits. The other is where they camped nearby just long enough to butcher and process the meat, crack bones for marrow, cure hides, and retouch or make new weapons or implements. Almost two thousand chipped stone artifacts came from one camp. These include fifty-five fluted and unfluted Folsom points, scrapers, flake knives, and discarded stone left from making these objects. Cobbles used as hammerstones, anvils, and abraders for pulverizing pigments round out the recovered tool inventory. The stone resources seem to have originated in a number of sources, some hundreds of miles distant. Bone projectile points, needles, and beads also have been found. There is evidence at the camps for hearths but no shelters.

Although all the studied sites are in the open, the researchers theorize that in the moist conditions believed to have prevailed in the San Luis valley during the Folsom period, estimated to have ended there about 8500 B.C., some ponds of water probably were trapped among the dunes. Men could have hidden in the security of the dunes to ambush animals coming to drink. The heavy bones left from butchering and stone spear points would have sunk into the sand in a short time and now would be exposed only at a chance blowout. The dunes also could have afforded some protection from inclement weather and been used as seasonal campsites.

From observations made of numerous private collections gathered in the valley over years of searching, Stanford believes Clovis hunters wandered the region for several millennia before the Folsom, only to be driven away by drought that affected vegetation and the mammoths that fed upon it. One site yielding mammoth bones but no in situ points has been tested. Folsom bands also eventually were forced to leave the area because of another climatic shift toward aridity. When that xeric cycle ended about 7000 B.C., a new breed of hunters called the Cody moved in. Like their predecessors, they had to leave when the water sources once again dried up. Around 4000 B.C. the pendulum moved back toward a wetter climate. Then the Archaic foragers found the valley a good place to stay during warmer months.

Although the Rio Grande lifeline begins in the San Juan Mountains to the east and flows through the southern portion of the basin, thus far there is no evidence for any Pueblo residence in the San Luis valley. If the San Luis Archaic groups slowly disappeared into the Anasazi mainstream, they did so in some other place. It appears the valley was essentially uninhabited except by occasional Pueblo hunting parties coming north from New Mexico until about the 1600s, when the Moache Utes laid more formal claim to it as their traditional territory.

Specimens recovered from the Smithsonian Institution excavations are at that facility in Washington. Those from the monument are held by the National Park Service. ▲

ADDITIONAL READINGS, Great Sand Dunes National Monument
Hurst, C. T.
    1943 A Folsom Site in a Mountain Valley of Colorado. *American Antiquity*, Vol. 8,
            No. 3. Menasha, Wisconsin: Society for American Archaeology. 250–253.
Jodry, M. A.
    1987 Stewart's Cattle Guard Site: a Folsom Site in Southern Colorado. A Report of the
            1981 and 1983 Field Seasons. Master of Arts Thesis, Department of
            Anthropology. Austin: University of Texas.
Stanford, Dennis J.
    1990 A History of Archaeological Research in the San Luis Valley, Colorado. In *Great*
            Sand Dunes National Monument, Stories of the Past. Alamosa, Colorado: San
            Luis Valley Historical Society. 33–39.
Standord, Dennis J., and Jane S. Day, Editors
    1992 *Ice Age Hunters of the Rockies*. Niwot, Colorado: Denver Museum of Natural
            History and University Press of Colorado.
Swancara, Frank
    1955 The Archaeology of the Great Sand Dunes National Monument, a Preliminary
            Survey. *Southwestern Lore*, Vol. 20, No. 4. Boulder: Colorado Archaeological
            Society. 53–58.

Cliff Palace, Mesa Verde National Park. GEORGE A. GRANT, NATIONAL PARK SERVICE, 1929.

MESA VERDE NATIONAL PARK, COLORADO/HOVENWEEP NATIONAL MONUMENT, COLORADO-UTAH

Cultural Significance and Archeological Classification

Its long, rich record of occupation, striking natural setting, and well-developed visitor facilities and interpretive programs make Mesa Verde National Park the nation's most outstanding preserve devoted to the works of ancient man. Its unique cultural value was recognized by the United Nations Educational, Scientific, and Cultural Organization, which in 1978 chose it and Yellowstone National Park as the first American designees for its prestigious World Heritage List.

Discovery and exploration of the Mesa Verde cliff dwellings played a significant part in promoting early scholarly interest in southwestern prehistory. Its presence was also instrumental in the establishment of federal regulations and reserves to protect these and other antiquities. Many of the material aspects of the evolution of Anasazi culture are present. They illustrate man's adaptability to and modification of the environment and ultimately the disastrous consequences of overpopulation and overutilization of available resources. Mesa Verde culture existed well beyond the limits of the Mesa Verde plateau, for example, the complex of pueblos and towers at Hovenweep where the ancient farmers grouped at strategic points near permanent sources of water.

Explorations and Investigations

Mesa Verde is an expansive, elevated, verdant tableland that from a distance suggests a towering green table, hence its Spanish name. The mesa tilts gently southward, cut into ribbons by a labyrinth of deep canyons. Because of its ruggedness, dense vegetation, and distance from areas early settled by whites, it was a region bypassed in the opening of the Southwest. Between 1765 and 1848 Spanish and Mexican explorers and travelers acknowledged it as a landmark on a route running west from the Rio Grande valley that became known as the Old Spanish Trail; they skirted its perimeters but felt no need to penetrate its interior. Finally, in 1859 the first published record of a visit to the heart of the region came when J. S. Newberry, a geologist accompanying an American party trying to chart feasible wagon and rail routes across northern New Mexico and southern Colorado, wrote that he had clambered to the top of the mesa to enjoy the spectacular panoramic view. Little did he realize the quiet testimony to the past concealed all about him.

William H. Jackson, head of the Photographic Division of the U.S. Geological and Geographical Survey of the Territories, usually is credited with being the first person to photograph and describe in print a Mesa Verde cliff dwelling. It was a relatively insignificant structure, not accessible to the modern tourist, that Jackson named Two Story House. He encountered it during the summer of 1874 when his seven-man party was surveying and photographing mountains in southwest Colorado. While he was camped

Anasazi: *Basket Maker III; Pueblo I, II, III (Mesa Verde); Pueblo III (Hovenweep, Yucca House)* All-Southwest: *Hamlets, Villages, Towns (Mesa Verde); Towns (Hovenweep, Yucca House), plateau zone*

Anasazi, Pueblo II, black-on-white dipper. ROBERT H. LISTER.

near Silverton, local folks told Jackson of the Mesa Verde and the Indian ruins rumored to fill some caves there. He promptly secured the guide services of Captain John Moss, a miner working in the La Platas who was familiar with the area and friendly with the local Ute Indians. In early September the group packed into Mancos Canyon, just east of the Mesa Verde, and started its journey through the defile. Almost immediately one of the cliffside houses was spotted. Jackson's official report, with a description and picture of the site, appeared in 1876. Another man in the party, Ernest Ingersoll, actually scooped Jackson's description by two years, when his letter narrating the discovery of Two Story House was published in the *New York Tribune* on November 3, 1874.

In the next few years William H. Holmes, also of the Survey of the Territories, and a few others worked around the craggy flanks of the Mesa Verde. It was the Wetherill family of nearby Mancos who found the antiquities that would make the peaceful plateau into a world-famous archeological zone. With permission from the Utes, whose traditional lands encompassed the Mesa Verde, Benjamin K. Wetherill and his sons ranged their stock there in the 1880s. While riding the promontory looking for water holes and stray cattle, Richard Wetherill and his brother-in-law, Charlie Mason, emerged from the pinyons and cedars covering a mesa top to find themselves staring down the opposite cliff face upon a great masonry shell of an empty house that had once surely quartered many families.

Thrilling though this chance discovery was, it came as no great surprise. Signs of earlier occupation were common throughout the region, and the Wetherills had poked into many of them, randomly searching for artifacts. But the size of this particular ruin, its configuration to the rocky overhang, its degree of preservation, and the promise of discarded materials made it special. Richard grandly named it Cliff Palace. Richard's brother, Al, actually had viewed the site from a distance some time earlier but had not climbed into it because he was too tired.

On the first entry Cliff Palace seemed a house temporarily empty while the residents were away on an errand. Complete clay pots and stone tools sat where last used. But the ashes in ancient fire pits were very cold, and roofs had rotted and collapsed.

By 1890 the Wetherills and their associates had examined 180 Pueblo dwellings perched on the walls of Mesa Verde's canyons, giving the most prominent ones names that are still used. They dug in many of them and accumulated three major collections of specimens and some pertinent data. The artifacts were exhibited at fairs, then sold to private collectors and scientific institutions far from their original sources. Richard sought in vain to interest the Smithsonian Institution and Peabody Museum of Harvard in sponsoring further explorations. Even so, the Wetherill brothers continued their association with Mesa Verde, since scientists and laymen needed guides to the legendary ruins. The Wetherill Alamo Ranch became their headquarters.

One who sought field assistance from the Wetherills was Gustaf Nordenskiöld, a young man from a distinguished Swedish family. With their help in 1891 he excavated in Kodak House, Long House, and Step House on one of the fingerlike projections of Mesa Verde which came to bear the Wetherill family name. He also probed further in Cliff Palace and Spruce Tree House, situated below the rim rock of Chapin Mesa. Nordenskiöld's collection was small, however, because fill in all the sites previously had been turned over by cowboys trying to duplicate the Wetherill haul. The collection was shipped to an unlikely home in the National Museum in Helsinki, Finland. After Nordenskiöld's fieldwork, he wrote the first scientific descriptions of the ancient remains.

Meanwhile, people shocked by what they regarded as blantant vandalism at Mesa Verde began agitating vigorously to have the ruins immediately placed under government custody. Led by archeologists such as Edgar L. Hewett, citizen activists like Virginia McClurg of Colorado Springs, and members of the Colorado State Federation of Women's Clubs and the Colorado Cliff Dwellings Association, their untiring efforts finally succeeded on two fronts in 1906. The Federal Antiquities Act protecting archeological resources on government lands became law that year, and Mesa Verde National Park was established.

Earnest scientific work began at Mesa Verde in 1908 and continues. Intermittently between 1908 and 1922, Jesse Walter Fewkes, of the Smithsonian Bureau of American Ethnology, excavated in Spruce Tree House and fifteen other dwellings on the mesa and in the cliffs. His work included the intriguing Sun Temple structure and a group of ruins at Far View, where some stabilization was undertaken.

Although the first park administrators were necessarily occupied with building roads, developing facilities, and establishing means to display and guard the ruins, Superintendent Jesse L. Nusbaum found time in 1910 to clear and stabilize Balcony House, which represents the classic period of Mesa Verde culture. In the 1920s he cleared several pithouses, including those in Step House. How these sites fit in the local chronology still was based primarily upon the types of artifacts recovered.

During the late 1920s and early 1930s well-preserved timbers in Mesa Verde houses proved important in an electrifying new approach to one of archeology's key questions: when was a given site in use?

University of Arizona astronomer A. E. Douglass theorized that by charting the pattern of annual growth rings in a tree's cross-section, the date at which it was felled could be determined. From a long series of such cross-sections, it might be possible to work out a calendric chart, progressing from the present back in time as far as that particular wood or charcoal had endured. Using hundreds of wood samples from ruins throughout the Colorado Plateau, including those at Mesa Verde, his theory was proved so dramatically that numerous villages are now firmly dated. Cliff Palace, for example, was found to have been occupied between the late twelfth and late thirteenth centuries. The Step House pithouses appeared about the beginning of the seventh century.

Although by 1935 considerable information had been collected about the cliff dwellers, little was known about earlier human occupation of these caves or the mesa tops. To attempt to gauge the size and scope of this horizon, a systematic survey of the park's prehistoric resources was initiated. Locating and recording sites was tedious, and the project extended over forty years. By then, National Park Service and University of Colorado archeologists had found some four thousand sites within Mesa Verde National Park.

Needing more information about Mesa Verde culture before the cliff-dweller period, a

Jesse W. Fewkes conducted research in Mesa Verde for the Smithsonian Institution from 1908 to 1922. NATIONAL PARK SERVICE.

series of excavations in mesa-top and talus-slope village sites was accomplished between 1941 and 1955 by Gila Pueblo, the University of Colorado, and the National Park Service.

Concurrent with accelerated archeological research were activities to preserve additional important Mesa Verde ruins. In 1934 Earl Morris completed repairs and stabilization work at Cliff Palace, Spruce Tree House, Balcony House, and Far View. He was assisted by Al Lancaster, who later managed a maintenance plan for many of the cliff dwellings and more important ruins on the open mesas. This program continues to assure that future generations will see the outstanding accomplishments of the Mesa Verdeans.

By the 1950s the annual number of visitors to Mesa Verde had grown to such proportions that the available ruins were seriously overcrowded and threatened. To alleviate the congestion, the National Park Service decided to prepare for public visitation a series of sites comparable to the Chapin Mesa landmarks of Cliff Palace, Spruce Tree House, and Balcony House. Of equal concern was the desire to conduct a multidisciplinary research program while preparing new exhibits-in-place, to expand those facets of Mesa Verde culture that previously had been only superficially developed, and to pass that information on to scientists and the public. A team of National Park Service archeologists and laboratory specialists, led by Douglas Osborne, was assembled to execute the program.

The area selected for work was Wetherill Mesa, a long narrow tongue of land along the park's western boundary. Sheltered along its cliffs on both sides were several interesting cave sites. Numerous lesser villages were scattered over the top of the mesa. When the Wetherill Mesa Project got under way in 1958, a thorough survey of all archeological remains of the mesa was begun by Alden C. Hayes. Once completed, the survey's findings made it possible to select a representative sequence of sites on the mesa for excavation, stabilization, and display. Three important cliff dwellings to be cleared and prepared for inclusion in the park's interpretive program were Long House by George S. Cattanach, Mug House by Arthur H. Rohn, and Step House by Robert Nichols. Early in the effort the National Geographic Society made possible many auxiliary studies in paleoecology, human osteology and pathology, ethnography among contemporary Pueblo Indians, and analyses of collections of artifacts removed from Mesa Verde during the period of discovery and early exploration.

As anticipated, the Wetherill Mesa Project appreciably added to knowledge of Mesa Verde prehistory. Particularly significant was paleoecological research which, when coupled with archeological findings, provides a more complete perception of prehistoric subsistence techniques, settlement patterns, and living conditions. Dietary habits of the Mesa Verdeans, their illnesses and injuries and likely causes, and certain vital statistics were revealed with analyses of human remains by physical anthropologists. Social organization, internal and external relationships, and ceremonialism were more fully explained after consideration of material attributes, architectural complexes, burial customs, affinity between settlements, and practices of historic Pueblo Indians. And, for the first time, what is left of some of the Mesa Verde cliff dwellings was scientifically excavated and studied. Previously, it had been ranchers and other untrained individuals who had removed most of the artifacts from the caves, generally with total disregard for vital information about origin, condition, or context.

Archeological research at Mesa Verde continued after the Wetherill Mesa Project concluded. Through an agreement with the U.S. Department of the Interior, the University of Colorado established an archeological research center in the park. Working from facilities provided by the National Park Service, students from the university engaged in various studies, directed first by Robert H. Lister and then by David A. Breternitz, for well over a decade. Their activities were not limited to the park but were extended to surrounding areas where Mesa Verde culture also appears. This group completed the archeological survey of Mesa Verde proper and expanded the inventory to include sizable regions adjacent to the park. Numerous sites marked for destruction by road construction, reclamation demands, and other development were salvaged, especially on Wetherill Mesa while it was being prepared for visitor use. In lower Morefield Canyon, a complex of Great Kivas, associated villages, and a water collecting system and reservoir were dug, as was an isolated, above-ground kiva and another village near the Morefield campground. A thirty-five-room mesa-top pueblo, Mummy Lake, and irrigation ditches were cleared in the Far View group. Another extensive survey led by Jack E. Smith during summers 1971–77 covered lands within the park boundaries where no previous work had been done. An additional eighteen hundred prehistoric sites were tabulated, which indicated shifting settlement patterns through time and space. Mesa Verde's Division of Research and Cultural Resource Management continues studies and maintenance of ruins as part of overall park administration.

Beyond the western boundaries of Mesa Verde sprawls the expansive Montezuma valley, which in various sectors experienced a dense Anasazi occupation for at least six centuries. Jackson and Holmes, both of whom traversed the area on their trips during the 1870s, wrote brief accounts of the ruins in McElmo and Yellowjacket canyons. Jackson was the first to apply the Ute word Hovenweep, meaning deserted valley, to the region. Starting about 1890, the Wetherills guided some of their more interested and ambitious visitors to the impressive group of sites in Ruin Canyon. T. Mitchell Prudden accomplished a long reconnaissance and excavation program in parts of this area in the early 1900s. In the same period two young, inexperienced Harvard graduate students, Alfred V. Kidder and Sylvanus G. Morley, struggled through their first archeological survey among sites scattered in the sage plain on the region's western periphery. In succeeding years Kidder and Morley returned as professionals to the region—Kidder to survey and evaluate the principal sites of the Four Corners, including those on Mesa Verde, and Morley to dig in the Cannonball Ruin. To this date that site is the only canyonhead village-tower complex to be excavated.

During the fourteen years that Jesse W. Fewkes worked at Mesa Verde, he periodically diverted his attention to other areas. In 1917 and 1918 he visited, mapped, studied, and named most of the large ruins of the Cajon Mesa. He concluded that the canyonhead towns were contemporaneous with the Mesa Verde cliff dwellings and recommended that they be protected as a national monument. Already the ravages of relic hunters were

Mug House, before excavation and stabilization, Mesa Verde National Park. GEORGE A. GRANT, NATIONAL PARK SERVICE, 1929.

threatening partial elimination of the ruins.

Hovenweep National Monument, under the administration of Mesa Verde National Park, finally was established in 1923 to incorporate six units of the most visible structures on western flanks of the territory. The Cajon Ruin group and the Square Tower Ruin group are in Utah. The Holly, Hackberry, Cutthroat Castle, and Goodman Point ruins groups are in Colorado. Present in these complexes are many-roomed pueblos in the open or clustered around canyon heads, tiny cliff houses, and an unusually large number of well-preserved masonry towers. The towers may have had some purpose in making astronomical observations essential for establishing a calendar by which agricultural routines could be maintained.

Goodman Point Ruin is the only settlement in Hovenweep National Monument not in the Upper Sonoran Desert but instead is at a higher elevation and is surrounded by modern farmlands. It is one of the largest Anasazi communities north of the San Juan River, perhaps as much as twice the size of Cliff Palace at Mesa Verde. In addition to many room blocks and plazas, there are an estimated one hundred ceremonial chambers including two Great Kivas. In recognition of its potential importance, the Public Land Office already had withdrawn the site from homesteading in 1889. Still unexcavated, the pueblo will have value in future research dealing with the final stages of Anasazi presence on the northern Colorado Plateau.

National Park Service experts have strengthened the high-standing walls typical of many Hovenweep ruins. Thorough surveys of the monument and surrounding lands have been performed by government archeologists and university groups from the University of Colorado, Brigham Young University, and San Jose State University. No major excavations have taken place in the monument.

A second detached ruin administered by Mesa Verde National Park is Yucca House, situated near the active Aztec Springs at the base of Sleeping Ute Mountain. Still in mounded condition, it nevertheless is an imposing pair of multistoried house blocks by a courtyard containing a Great Kiva and is one of at least four Chaco outliers in the Montezuma valley environs. A prehistoric road connecting the settlements of the valley to those south of the San Juan likely passed nearby.

During their explorations in the late 1800s Jackson and Holmes visited the site and included descriptions in their reports. It remained for Fewkes to persuade the site's owner, Henry Van Kleeck, to donate the nearly ten acres it covered to the government. Van Kleeck did this with the assurance the ruin would be excavated. However, although Yucca House became a national monument in 1919, no money for its development was appropriated and no public access to it was provided.

Yucca House remains an essentially untapped, relatively pristine archeological reserve. Only limited trenching was done by National Park Service personnel in 1964 in order to better define the structures and obtain wood samples for tree-ring dating. A classic Pueblo period of construction and occupation was confirmed.

Since the 1970s, a burst of archeological activity has gone on in the general Mesa Verde district as a result of possible damaging impact on the antiquities due to exploitation

Anasazi corrugated jar. FRED MANG, JR., NATIONAL PARK SERVICE.

A responsibility of specialized Mesa Verde personnel is to protect and preserve the many habitation remains scattered over the park. Some of the more significant ruins accessible to visitors have been excavated and stabilized. Thus, their features have been exposed, and weakened portions of the structures strengthened.

National Park Service policy is not to rebuild the ruins, but to stabilize them as they are found. Architectural features are secured by reapplying mortar to wall joints, replacing missing or unsteady stone and wooden construction elements, repairing foundations, and protecting the ruins from water.

Cliff Palace was the first ruin to receive such attention. Views on this page show its condition prior to excavation in 1908 and its appearance in 1946 after several preservation programs had been completed.

Photographs on the opposite page illustrate how stabilization was accomplished concurrent with the 1958–1962 excavations at Long House. One view shows the cliff dwelling during the work. Note the hose that brought water from above for the preparation of mortar, the piles of rubble from the ruins from which stones were selected to repair poorly preserved or leaning walls, and the scaffolding erected to facilitate repairs. The other two photographs depict Long House after stabilization and details of its Great Kiva.

PHOTOGRAPHS FROM THE MESA VERDE NATIONAL PARK COLLECTION.

of natural resources and the initiation of long-term educational and research programs. In 1989 several government agencies evaluated proposals for establishment of an Anasazi National Monument in southwestern Colorado. Such a facility would function as an umbrella organization for management of twenty-one major archeological resources with nationally significant attributes. Yucca House and the Goodman Point Ruin were among those considered. No plan of this sort has yet been implemented.

Early commerical exploitation of articles taken from Mesa Verde cliff dwellings led to wide dispersal of a great number of specimens. Fortunately, four Wetherill collections found their way to public institutions. The first was acquired by the State Historical and Natural History Society in Denver. The second eventually was donated to the University of Pennsylvania Museum. The third, the Nordenskiöld Collection, was taken to Sweden and later moved to the National Museum of Finland in Helsinki. The fourth was joined with the first and placed in the Colorado State Museum. The Mesa Verde Museum and Research Center display extensive assortments of artifacts and records from Mesa Verde and Hovenweep, including those from the Wetherill Mesa Project. Housed in the museum are some of the finer specimens from the Mesa Verde and adjacent localities. Also featured in the museum are the excellently crafted dioramas that faithfully reconstruct stages in the evolutionary process of cultural development in and adjacent to Mesa Verde. ⬛

ADDITIONAL READINGS, Mesa Verde National Park/Hovenweep National Monument
Arrhenius, Olof W.
    1984 *Stones Speak and Waters Sing, the Life and Works of Gustaf Nordenskiöld.* Edited and annotated by Robert H. Lister and Florence C. Lister. Mesa Verde, Colorado: Mesa Verde Museum Association.
Breternitz, David A., and Jack E. Smith
    1972 Mesa Verde, "The Green Table," *National Parkways*, Vols. 3/4. Casper, Wyoming: World-Wide Research and Publishing Co. 49–88.
Hayes, Alden C.
    1964 *The Archeological Survey of Wetherill Mesa.* Archeological Research Series, No. 7A. Washington, D.C.: National Park Service.
Lister, Robert H., and Florence C. Lister
    1987 *Mesa Verde National Park, Preserving the Past.* Santa Barbara, California: ARA Mesa Verde Company, Sequoia Communications.
McNitt, Frank
    1966 *Richard Wetherill: Anasazi.* Reprint of 1957. Albuquerque: University of New Mexico Press.
Noble, David G.
    1985 *Understanding the Anasazi of Mesa Verde and Hovenweep.* Santa Fe, New Mexico: Exploration, Annual Bulletin of the School of American Research.
Nordenskiöld, Gustaf
    1979 *The Cliff Dwellers of the Mesa Verde, Southwestern Colorado, Their Pottery and Implements.* Reprint of 1893. Glorieta, New Mexico: Rio Grande Press.

Smith, Jack E.
    1987 *Mesas, Cliffs, and Canyons, The University of Colorado Survey of Mesa Verde National Park, 1971–1977.* Mesa Verde Research Series, Paper No. 3. Mesa Verde National Park, Colorado: Mesa Verde Museum Association.

Thompson, Ian
    1993 *The Towers of Hovenweep.* Mesa Verde National Park, Colorado: Mesa Verde Museum Association.

Wetherill, Benjamin A.
    1977 *The Wetherills of the Mesa Verde, Autobiography of Benjamin Alfred Wetherill,* edited by Maurine S. Fletcher. Cranbury, New Jersey: Associated University Presses.

Williamson, Ray A.
    1984 *Living the Sky, the Cosmos of the American Indian.* Norman, Oklahoma: University of Oklahoma Press.

Montezuma Castle, Montezuma Castle National Monument. GEORGE A. GRANT, NATIONAL PARK SERVICE, 1929.

MONTEZUMA CASTLE NATIONAL MONUMENT/ TUZIGOOT NATIONAL MONUMENT, ARIZONA

Cultural Significance and Archeological Classification

The Verde valley in central Arizona provided a natural corridor between the desert dwellers to the south and plateau people to the north, and both groups occupied the valley at different periods. One semi-subterranean dwelling that was part of a small community at Montezuma Well is the only typical Hohokam house on display in the National Park Service system. It apparently was used when desert colonists were migrating northward through the valley to settle in the Flagstaff region. Later, after a cultural fusion from all three core areas had taken place about Flagstaff, people from the north and south moved into the upper Verde valley. Although they built plateaulike villages and towns, their diverse ancestry showed in other material traits. The imposing structures of Montezuma Castle and Tuzigoot stem from this occupation, assigned to the Sinagua version of Hakataya culture.

Hohokam: *Colonial (Montezuma Well)*
In-betweens and Outliers: *Hakataya (Sinagua culture)*
All-Southwest: *Villages, Towns, intermediate between desert, plateau, and mountain-valley zones*

Explorations and Investigations

Montezuma Castle and Tuzigoot national monuments, twenty-five miles apart in the Verde River basin in central Arizona, contain the most extensive archeological remains of one phase of what appears to have been a longer, complicated prehistoric evolution elsewhere in the region. Though these sites and many smaller villages spread across the middle Verde valley have been known for years, relatively little scientific notice has been given them.

A Spaniard, Antonio de Espejo, journeying from Santa Fe to Acoma, Zuni, the Hopi towns, and farther west to investigate reports of rich mines, seems to have been the first white man to have reached the Verde valley and mention its antiquities. Mexican and American trappers and traders followed, who probably saw the stones from old houses or the walls of rooms sheltered by rocky cliffs but who typically kept no written accounts. In the mid-1800s a railroad survey party reconnoitering the area specifically noted abandoned Indian villages on the Verde, which pioneer farmers already were taking for granted. Finally, in 1884 an initial exploration of some of these remains was made by Edgar A. Mearns, a doctor at Fort Verde. Mearns succeeded in mapping and digging pits in several sites, including Montezuma Castle.

Scientific studies of Verde valley antiquities were initiated in 1892 when Cosmos Mindeleff, of the Bureau of American Ethnology, conducted a survey of the entire valley. He made notes, maps, and photographs of the most obvious ruins. Comparing the ancient remains there to those of the plateau and the Salt River valley, he concluded that the old cultural ties had been northerly. Mindeleff further noted the presence of prehistoric irrigation ditches near some ruins. Fortunately his records survive, because most of the aboriginal attempts at water control were destroyed by later land uses.

Three years later another Bureau of American Ethnology scientist, Jesse W. Fewkes, made his way to the Verde valley. He had become an authority on the Hopi Indians of northern Arizona and, like other colleagues, used mythology and so-called migration legends as a basis for formulating ideas about societies and their origins. The purpose of Fewkes's sojourn in the upper and middle Verde basin was to gather archeological data pertinent to Hopi traditions and, coincidentally, to collect specimens for the U.S. National Museum. Specifically, he was seeking data to support the claim of some Hopi that the ancestors of a particular clan came from an area far to the south. Fewkes thought the locale referred to might be the Verde valley and tried to prove his point by systematically comparing the architectural styles of the two regions. To asemble his data for the Verde, he took photographs and drew schematic plans of the more notable pueblos and cliff dwellings. Although Fewkes found the Verde ruins similar to some near the Hopi villages, he was not completely convinced that this resemblance supported the Hopi origin myth. Unsatisfied, he returned to the Verde in 1906 but still reached no conclusions. After that time scientists ignored the area for almost a quarter of a century.

The Verde valley and the surrounding mountainous terrain were part of the Gila Pueblo Foundation's thorough survey of the Southwest. By 1930, 185 sites had been identified. Pottery analysis indicated that in addition to a Pueblo occupation, responsible for many of the multiroomed masonry communities erected in the open and in cliff alcoves, at least three other groups of people had entered the basin, settled, and inevitably interacted. To the Gila Pueblo researchers, the Verde valley represented an aboriginal melting pot.

During the 1920s and 1930s uncontrolled pothunting, which damaged or destroyed much archeological evidence in the middle Verde valley, roused a few professionals to take to the field to recover materials and background information for scientific interpretation before they fell to the picks and shovels of untrained collectors. A leader among them was Byron Cummings. He and his University of Arizona students searched the Verde for ruins and trenched some of them, including Tuzigoot pueblo and a few pithouse structures, which yielded artifacts similar to those found in sites to the south on the middle Gila.

Since the 1940s a number of investigators have spent short periods of time in the Verde valley doing surveys, test excavations, a few major digs, and several salvage projects. Surveys filled the gaps between areas previously worked, identified many more prehistoric irrigation works, and designated sites and areas where additional excavations promised a solution to problems of Verde valley prehistory. An underwater exploration of Montezuma Well was done by a team of National Park Service divers but produced few results. Small-scale excavations cleared ballcourts, meager cave deposits, isolated burials, scatters of stone artifacts, and salvaged the remains being destroyed by nature, vandals, or road construction. More substantial excavations in pueblos, pithouse villages, and cave litter attempted to outline and refine the tentative cultural evolution and confirm external connections enjoyed by the region's aborigines.

The research shows that the Verde valley was for a long time a corridor between major cultural developments, a zone where slightly dissimilar groups intermingled. Complete understanding awaits more detailed study of some of the contributors to this cultural blend. Meanwhile, the federal areas preserve and interpret the most outstanding examples of the period of greatest population concentration in the valley.

One of these is Montezuma Castle. Early white settlers named the site, erroneously believing that the Aztec ruler or his people had migrated through the region. Part of the structure, an earthen and stone house seemingly glued to a hollow in the face of a high limestone cliff, was in danger of disintegration when first observed. To prevent collapse, the Arizona Antiquarian Association performed some emergency repairs on a few walls between 1896 and 1900. Little further attention was given the building until President Theodore Roosevelt proclaimed it a national monument in 1906. Although it came under National Park Service jurisdiction ten years later, the first permanent custodian was not named until 1927. Despite earlier preservation efforts, the National Park Service found that ravages of the elements and nearly a century of wanton destruction by treasure seekers necessitated a complete stabilization of the terraced, twenty-room cliff dwelling. Ceilings of the lower front rooms had to be repaired, and the joints of many outer masonry walls had to be retouched with mud. Even with this work, more than 90 percent of the building is original construction, attesting to the dry climate and the builders' skills.

There are no absolute dates for the occupation of Montezuma Castle. The sequence of settlement patterns, types of locally made pottery and tools, dated trade items introduced into the valley, and comparison with dated sites indicate that the habitation gradually evolved to its maximum size, declined, and finally was abandoned between about A.D. 1100 and 1400.

Many habitations and storage units are in caves and on ledges in Beaver Creek Canyon, a tributary of the Verde River. One poorly preserved community, of at least forty rooms originally, had been fashioned in tiers on recesses eroded in the cliff west of Montezuma Castle. Called Castle A, it was cleared in 1933–34 by Earl Jackson, working for the National Park Service with funds provided by the Civil Works Administration. Some rooms were erected in terraces against the cliff face, while others were created by simply walling up the fronts of small natural caves eroded in the soft whitish limestone. A fire razed the entire building, presumably some time after its builders abandoned it. The conflagration caused the upper tiers of rooms to collapse. Only a few floor remnants and the cliff rooms were left at those levels. Of the lower stories, archeologists found only wall fragments and floors of nine rooms built against the cliff or within small cavities in the rock. A limited assortment of artifacts was recovered during the digging. The most important items were textiles removed from the upper chambers. Castle A contained no datable timbers, but archeological evidence indicates that it is the same age as Montezuma Castle.

A few miles northeast of Montezuma Castle in the national monument is Montezuma Well, a large limestone sink partly filled with water from a constantly flowing spring. Water escaping from the well's outlet was used to irrigate the Indians' gardens. It remains

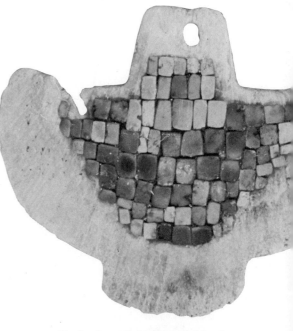

Eagle-shaped shell pendant set with turquoise. SOUTHWEST PARKS AND MONUMENTS ASSOCIATION.

a valuable resource for local farmers. Ruins of a few ancient settlements, including some small masonry houses perched on sheltered outcrops just below the rim of the sinkhole, may be seen. Although none is located in as picturesque a setting as the Castle, as a group they more clearly illustrate various aspects of the cultural history of the Verde valley. Near the well is an excavated pithouse, one of a group cleared by David A. Breternitz in the 1950s for the Museum of Northern Arizona. It represents an early intrusion into the Verde basin of people from the south whose way of life typified those groups dwelling along the middle Gila and Salt rivers of southern Arizona. Closer to the well are the partially cleared remains of two small pueblos more recent than the pithouses, built by people from the north who brought a certain new cultural orientation into the Verde.

A second important aboriginal complex situated in the Verde valley is Tuzigoot. Taking the Apache name for crooked water because of a crescent-shaped lake near the site, this ruin stands on top of a limestone and sandstone ridge that juts above the flood plain on the north side of the Verde River. It is all that remains of one of several early fourteenth-century towns in the vicinity. After white settlement of the region, farmers and ranchers, then prospectors and miners, took to pothunting the site for pleasure. Because Tuzigoot was on land belonging to the United Verde Company, a mining concern, the looting was not as extensive as it might have been.

With local and federal support, the clearing of Tuzigoot was started in 1933 by Louis R. Caywood and Edward H. Spicer, two of Bryon Cummings's graduate students. By 1935 the main block of rooms and four small isolated units had been exposed, amounting to 86 rooms of an estimated 110. Refuse deposits around the main pueblo were tested. Several hundred burials were encountered within the pueblo and in its trash piles. Once the excavations were terminated, floors and masonry walls were preserved and certain rooms of the pueblo were restored for public display. The excavators postulated that originally a few families lived in several small groups of rooms, followed by two periods of growth and expansion that resulted in a pueblo which in its heyday had seventy-seven ground-floor rooms. Several of these had second and possibly third stories. The scientists' deductions were based on superposition of structures, relation of rooms and trash, sizes and types of units, and ceramic analysis. Reliable tree-ring dates were not available at the time the work was done. A museum to house and display the collections from the ruin was built nearby with additional federal relief funds. Finally, through the interest of public-spirited local residents, the entire ridge with the site of Tuzigoot, the museum, and its collections were donated to the federal government. It was proclaimed a national monument in 1939.

A few small archeological investigations have been undertaken at Tuzigoot by National Park Service workers. Some have sought to provide a better chronology and trait list for the site. Others have examined areas before development of monument lands took place. Most significantly, tree-ring dates for the ruin were obtained in 1961, when Caywood submitted some additional wood specimens from the 1933–34 excavations to the Laboratory of Tree-Ring Research. Now, twenty-eight tree-ring dates are available for Tuzigoot. The earliest phase of Caywood and Spicer's architectural history remains undated, but it likely falls in the twelfth century. The two expansion periods of the site occurred about A.D. 1200 and in the late 1300s.

Stabilization and maintenance of the relatively poorly constructed stone and mud walls of the aboriginal building have been a constant problem for the National Park Service.

Most of the collections from Montezuma Castle and Tuzigoot are housed in the National Park Service Western Archeological and Conservation Center in Tucson. Some specimens are displayed or stored in the respective visitor centers. ▲

ADDITIONAL READINGS, Montezuma Castle National Monument/Tuzigoot National Monument

Colton, Harold S.
  1946 *The Sinagua. A Summary of the Archaeology of the Region of Flagstaff, Arizona.* Bulletin, No. 22. Flagstaff: Museum of Northern Arizona.
Fish, Paul R., and Suzanne K. Fish
  1977 *Verde Valley Archaeology: Review and Perspective.* Research Paper, No. 8. Flagstaff: Museum of Northern Arizona.
Hartman, Dana
  1976 *Tuzigoot, An Archeological Overview.* Research Paper, No. 4. Flagstaff: Museum of Northern Arizona.
Jackson, Earl, and Sallie P. Van Valkenburgh
  1954 *Montezuma Castle Archeology, Part I: Excavations.* Technical Series, Vol. 3, No. 1. Globe, Arizona: Southwestern Monuments Association.
Schroeder, Albert H., and Homer F. Hastings
  1958 *Montezuma Castle.* Historical Handbook Series, No. 27. Washington, D.C.: National Park Service.

Keet Seel, Navajo National Monument. GEORGE A. GRANT, NATIONAL PARK SERVICE, 1935.

NAVAJO NATIONAL MONUMENT, ARIZONA

Cultural Significance and Archeological Classification

The three major cliff dwellings of Navajo National Monument are illustrative of that particular time when some Anasazi of the Four Corners preferred to settle in arched caves or on narrow ledges cut into vertical canyon walls. The obvious cost in time and energy to build homes in such unlikely places is made more poignant by their ultimate failure.

Anasazi: *Pueblo I, II, III*
All-Southwest: *Hamlets, Villages, Towns, plateau zone*

Explorations and Investigations

In the winter of 1895 Richard and Al Wetherill and Charlie Mason outfitted themselves in Bluff City, Utah, and for four months packed into Monument Valley, Marsh Pass, and Tsegi Canyon in northeastern Arizona. Many fine ruins were encountered, and quantities of specimens were taken from them. Among them were four hundred pieces of pottery removed from one burial ground, a major Wetherill collection that has not been traced. One site they discovered is the largest cliff dwelling in Arizona. The Wetherills called the 160-room structure Long House, but the Navajo name, Keet Seel, which means broken pottery, became its accepted designation. Although the present building dates to a forty-year period between A.D. 1240 and 1280, excavations in trash deposits suggest utilization of the alcove beginning as early as Pueblo I.

Two years after the discovery of Keet Seel, Richard Wetherill returned to the great ruin in a lofty arched cave worn into a sheer, red sandstone cliff. This time he was guiding an expedition financed by a rich eastern family for their son and his tutor. Richard measured and photographed the cliff house, diagrammed its plan, catalogued everything he found, and kept notes about the site and his diggings. These were practices he followed at all the ruins they examined. After three months of collecting, they loaded pack animals with nearly a ton of specimens to be carried into Bluff City, Utah. From there they were hauled by wagon back to the Wetherill ranch in Colorado. A year later the collection was purchased for the American Museum of Natural History in New York for three thousand dollars.

Betatakin, Navajo for ledge house, was discovered fourteen years later in the summer of 1909. This find was made by Byron Cummings and his party who, with guide-interpreter John Wetherill, were returning from archeological explorations in upper Tsegi Canyon for the University of Utah. The 135-room structure was built on the steep floor of a beautifully vaulted alcove at the head of a forested canyon. It is the only one of the three cliff dwellings in the monument which was not built over remains of an earlier occupation. Cummings worked at Betatakin in the winter of 1909. Neil Judd, a student assistant to Cummings when the site was found, returned there in 1917 to direct a program of preservation and repair. A large portion of the cave roof fell after Betatakin was abandoned by the Anasazi and knocked many room walls into the canyon below.

A few days before Betatakin was discovered, John Wetherill had led the Cummings party to Inscription House, the third important cliff house in the area. Located in a shallow shelter near the base of a sandstone dome in Nitsin Canyon, it contains seventy-four rooms and granaries and one kiva. While the ruin was being examined, the Wetherill and Cummings children found the dim inscription carved in the plaster of a wall. At one time the date accompanying the almost illegible inscription was believed to be 1661 and was thought to have been left by an unknown Spanish traveler. Now most observers agree the date of 1861 may have been scratched into the wall plaster by members of a Mormon party who traversed the region at that time, but no accounts are known of that visit. Cummings returned to Inscription House on several occasions to excavate in the ruin, where blocks of adobe were common building materials. He never reported in any detail upon his findings there or on other investigations at Betatakin.

In 1910 John Wetherill and his partner, Clyde Colville, moved their trading enterprise from Oljeto down the valley some thirty miles to a desert basin in the red sand hills known since as Kayenta. There Wetherill and his wife, Louisa, built a new trading post and a permanent home. For years he and Colville boasted that the store–post office was farther from a railroad than any other in the United States. John was an expert trader to the Navajos, but his love of exploring had never been quelled. While at Kayenta, he became well known as a competent guide, equipper, and expedition organizer for many who came to his part of the Southwest. John Wetherill was also the first custodian of Navajo National Monument, established in 1909 to include Betatakin, Keet Seel, and Inscription House.

Under National Park Service administration, protection and preservation of the ruins has continued. Keet Seel was stabilized in the 1930s by a crew directed by John Wetherill. In the 1970s archeologists from the University of Colorado repaired Inscription House and a nearby nineteen-room cliff village called Snake House.

Archeological research in and around the monument during the last two decades has added to an understanding of the aboriginal cultures. Interest in them was stimulated in the late 1950s and early 1960s by the explorations and research done in connection with the construction of the Glen Canyon Dam. Meticulous studies by the Laboratory of Tree-Ring Research at the University of Arizona of timbers incorporated in the cliff dwellings of the Tsegi Canyon area have provided dates for the sites and demonstrated their relationship with neighboring centers. The Museum of Northern Arizona undertook excavations at Inscription House. Limited archeological materials have been secured from other cliff dwellings concurrent with stabilization. A long-term effort by Southern Illinois University on Black Mesa south of the monument rounded out the regional prehistorical record prior to the time of the cliff dwellings.

Collections from Navajo National Monument are housed at the American Museum of Natural History, New York; Arizona State Museum, Tucson; Museum of Northern Arizona, Flagstaff; Peabody Museum of Archaeology and Ethnology, Harvard University, Cambridge; University of Colorado Museum, Boulder; University of Utah, Salt Lake City; and the Western Archeological and Conservation Center, Tucson. ▲

ADDITIONAL READINGS, Navajo National Monument

Ambler, J. Richard

    1985 *Archeological Assessment, Navajo National Monument.* Southwest Cultural Resources Center, Professional Papers, No. 9. Santa Fe, New Mexico: Southwest Cultural Resources Center, National Park Service.

Judd, Neil M.

    1930 *The Excavation and Repair of Betatakin.* Proceedings, Vol. 77. Washington, D.C.: U.S. National Museum.

    1968 *Men Met Along the Trail, Adventures in Archaeology.* Norman, Oklahoma: University of Oklahoma Press.

McNitt, Frank

    1966 *Richard Wetherill: Anasazi.* Reprint of 1957. Albuquerque: University of New Mexico Press.

Viele, Catherine W.

    1980 *Voices in the Canyon.* Globe, Arizona: Southwest Parks and Monuments Association.

Ward, Albert E.

    1975 *Inscription House.* Technical Series, No. 16. Flagstaff: Museum of Northern Arizona.

Pictographs on the eastern wall of Betatakin, Navajo National Monument (Milton Wetherill in foreground). GEORGE A. GRANT, NATIONAL PARK SERVICE, 1935.

Prehistoric trade routes passed through the Organ Pipe Cactus National Monument area. GEORGE H. H. HUEY.

ORGAN PIPE CACTUS NATIONAL MONUMENT, ARIZONA

Cultural Significance and Archeological Classification

The cactus-studded Papaguería area encompassed within Organ Pipe Cactus National Monument was a prehistoric crossroads for trade or communication routes coming into the desert from all directions. California traditions of the Paleo-Indian and Archaic periods reached their most easterly extent here contemporaneous with local traditions. A later peripheral Hohokam occupation traded with peoples in northern Mexico, the lower Colorado River valley, and the Tonto basin of central Arizona. These Hohokam likely served as middlemen in shell and salt distribution from the Gulf of California to other Hohokam of the Gila and Salt river areas.

Archaic: *Cochise, Amargosa*
Hohokam: *Colonial, Sedentary, Classic*
All-Southwest: *Hamlets, Villages, Towns, desert zone*

Explorations and Investigations

For nearly four centuries Spanish explorers and missionaries, Anglo parties bound for or returning from the California gold fields, Mexican Boundary and Southern Pacific Railroad surveyors, naturalists, prospectors, travel writers, and assorted desert rats made their way along the treacherous Camino del Diablo on the southern periphery of what is now Organ Pipe Cactus National Monument. Except for noting occasional bedrock mortars left by some unknowns, they were oblivious to any antiquities. Ageless geologic upheavals had molded an eerie, forbidding landscape, and the desert flora that sparsely covered it commanded sufficient attention to lead ultimately to the setting aside in 1937 of 516 square miles north of the international border as a natural preserve.

In 1929, as part of a comprehensive archeological survey throughout the Southwest launched by Gila Pueblo, Frank Midvale reconnoitered the Ajo valley in the northern sector of the later monument and recorded a Hohokam village with trash mounds and what appeared to be a diagnostic ballcourt. The same site was visited eight years later by Emil W. Haury following his work at the Gila River Hohokam community of Snaketown. In 1951 on behalf of the National Park Service, Paul Ezell conducted a more wide-ranging reconnaissance of the monument which included this village and a number of others in the vicinity. Although a considerable human presence representing several cultures was indicated, no excavations were done.

In the belief that earlier surveys had been limited, from the 1989 through 1991 seasons a National Park Service archeological team led by Adrianne G. Rankin took to the field. Eight thousand acres were covered to record 188 archeological sites, some of which related to the protohistoric and historic Tohono O'odham (Pima-Papago) and Hia C-ed O'odham (Sand Papago) occupation of the region. No excavations have resulted yet from these preliminaries, but a notable cultural history pointing up needed further research has been outlined.

Beginning in the 1930s a California archeologist, Malcolm Rogers, devoted much of his career to study of the Paleo-Indian period as encountered in the deserts of southern

California, Arizona, and Sonora, Mexico. His student, Julian Hayden, subsequently focused upon the same horizon in the Pinacate Mountains and rocky slopes of the Sonoran Desert to the west of Organ Pipe Cactus National Monument. Sharing data but sometimes disagreeing in interpretation, the men identified two groups of Paleo-Indians who presumably met along both sides of the Mexico–United States border east of the Colorado River. Formerly, the San Dieguito people were thought restricted to the southern California Mohave Desert, while the Cochise territory was the sweep of lands across southern Arizona. The hunters had slightly differing stone-tool technologies, as evidenced by rare scatters of implements and the residue from their manufacture. Elusive traces of rock alignments, still undisturbed on the empty desert floors, perhaps were created by these nomads to serve as windbreaks. Although no specific Paleo-Indian sites have been located within the monument, further investigation likely will show it to have been part of this zone of contact.

The two Paleo-Indian traditions generally are dated from about 10,000 B.C. to 5,000 B.C. Hayden prefers to regard some San Dieguito points bearing coatings of desert varnish as older. His hypothesis of people in the Southwest by 30,000 B.C. may be supported by recent finds near El Paso of points associated with mammals which became extinct many millennia before the mammoth, the usual target of the earliest recognized Paleo-Indian predators.

Using styles of projectile points as a criterion, the same intermixing of western (Amargosa) and eastern (Cochise) Archaic occupations appears to have occurred within the monument. When explored, potentially fruitful open sites and stratified deposits in caves and rock shelters will help define relationships or hybridization of these peoples and their adaptations to a microenvironment that may or may not have been more hospitable than at present.

Most of the sites noted by all surveys within the monument are of Hohokam affiliation. An important concentration of these remains is in the Ajo valley, where loam and ephemeral waters were attractive to farmers. On the basis of surface sherd collections, occupation is thought to have lasted from A.D. 500 to 1450.

Especially worthy of future attention is the large community first documented in the initial 1929 work. Now it is estimated to extend over some two hundred acres. It contains a ballcourt and numerous pithouse and activity clusters, and is densely sprinkled with artifacts such as pottery, shell, and obsidian from a number of far-flung sources. Researchers postulate that this town was on strategic trails running north-south and east-west, and was a major link in an extensive prehistoric trade network that in some cases reached northward into the Anasazi domain. Four small satellite villages, perhaps for seasonal use only, are nearby. A canal segment at one village reveals attempts to capture runoff waters for agricultural purposes.

Organ Pipe Cactus National Monument presently is the only National Park Service facility with an untapped archeological reserve of Hohokam culture extending over at least nine hundred years. Should excavation and study of these remains take place, the importance of this holding will increase enormously.

Artifacts and notes resulting from archeological surveys of Organ Pipe Cactus National Monument are at the Arizona State Museum and the Western Archeological and Conservation Center, both in Tucson. ▲

ADDITIONAL READINGS, Organ Pipe Cactus National Monument
Hartmann, William K.
    1989 *Desert Heart, Chronicles of the Sonoran Desert*. Tucson, Arizona: Fisher Books.
Rankin, Adrianne G.
    1991 *Archeological Survey in Organ Pipe Cactus National Monument: 1991 Progress Report*. Tucson, Arizona: Western Archeological and Conservation Center, National Park Service.

Hohokam petroglyph, Organ Pipe Cactus National Monument.
GEORGE H. H. HUEY.

PECOS NATIONAL HISTORICAL PARK, NEW MEXICO

Anasazi: *Pueblo I, IV, V*
All-Southwest: *Hamlets,*
Villages, Towns, plateau
zone

Cultural Significance and Archeological Classification

The story presented at Pecos National Historical Park encapsulates the human history of this part of the Southwest, encompassing a thousand years that witnessed Indian, Spanish, Mexican, and Anglo-American presence. This chapter focuses upon the two earliest occupations, which, in fact, consumed a giant portion of that time.

Adolph F. Bandelier at Pecos in 1880. GEORGE C. BENNETT, MUSEUM OF NEW MEXICO.

The prehistoric saga began with a few small familial groups of people influenced by the Colorado Plateau Anasazi who occupied simple one-roomed shelters sunk into the ground and ended with two elaborate multistoried, mulitroomed surface structures that accommodated several thousand inhabitants. Particularly well represented at Pecos is the period of turmoil caused by the late prehistoric coalescence along the upper Rio Grande of scores of uprooted Pueblo groups to abandonment of the pueblo in the early nineteenth century. Artifacts and tipi rings confirm extensive contacts between Pecos and Apache and other tribes who roamed the grasslands to the east. A bulky shell of an adobe church and some Europeanization of material culture afford evidence of acculturation during the Spanish colonial period.

Explorations and Investigations

One of the largest and most easterly of the pueblos encountered by sixteenth-century Spanish conquistadors, Pecos was important in the exploration, colonization, and missionization of New Mexico. An archeologically and historically documented story of Pecos and its environs from the middle of the ninth century to the third decade of the nineteenth century has been achieved through a synthesis of data from various sources. Knowledge of the first several centuries of its existence came through the picks and shovels of archeologists. The three hundred years from 1540, when the first Spaniards arrived, to 1838, date of the abandonment of the town, have been fleshed out by accounts written by explorers, missionaries, soldiers, historians, and ethnologists.

Chroniclers of the Coronado expedition of 1540–41 recorded the name of the settlement as Cicuye, which probably was the natives' own designation for their village. Other Pueblo Indians, speaking different languages, called it by a term that Spanish soldiers interpreted as "Pecos."

Pecos was a populous community from the time of first contact with Europeans until the Indians drove the Spaniards from the country during the Pueblo Revolt of 1680. Its inhabitants, who had a reputation for being warlike, are thought to have numbered between one thousand and two thousand. After Santa Fe became the capital of New Spain in 1610, Pecos assumed great importance for the Spanish military, secular, and religious authorities. Strategically located on a natural route from the northern Rio Grande valley around the southern end of the Rockies to the Great Plains, Pecos was seen as a friendly Pueblo community that could provide a buffer against Apache and Comanche raiders. At the same time it could serve as an intermediary in a profitable trade between its inhabitants and the Spaniards.

The Pecos Indians, however, were unpredictable in their attitudes toward the Europeans. At times they actively resisted intrusion by Spanish military and administrative groups and rejected attempts by dedicated friars to convert them to Christianity. On other occasions they acquiesced to the invaders and adopted use of many of their tools, food, and livestock. They accepted the Spanish god and built structures for his worship. They professed allegiance to a distant king and even joined forces with Spaniards against other pueblos and marauding Indians from the plains. Underlying the pattern of wavering alliance between the conquerors and the conquered was a fierce internal church-state struggle among the colonists. Friars and governors, at cross-purposes, created conflicting regulations and policies concerning the Indians, adding little strength to already uneasy relationships.

Fragment of seventeenth-century saucer, found in Pecos Convento.
ROBERT H. LISTER.

Eventually the New Mexico Pueblos had enough of Spanish imposition. Exasperated by unstable affairs, demands for goods and services, and religious persecution, they went to war. During the summer of 1680 Pecos warriors united with those from all the Pueblo villages in a successful revolt, although it is said that a pro-Spanish faction at Pecos warned of the impending rebellion several days before it was launched.

With the Palace of the Governors in Santa Fe under siege for ten days of bloody ambush, raids, and plundering, the Spaniards began their painful withdrawal from New Mexico. Led by Governor Otermín, some one thousand surviving Spaniards and sympathetic Indians made their way south down the Rio Grande to the tenuous security of El Paso. During the hostilities four hundred colonists had been murdered, twenty-one Franciscans martyred, and an unknown number of Indians killed or executed after having been taken prisoner. During and shortly after the uprising, many symbols of Spanish dominance, such as public buildings, homes, farms, and especially religious structures, were put to the torch by the rebels. The church at Pecos did not escape the flames.

In 1692, shortly after he had become governor of the lost province of New Mexico, Captain General Diego de Vargas marched a small army back up the Rio Grande valley. Within four months he had succeeded in a bloodless reconquest of the territory. The village of Santa Fe was re-established as the seat of authority.

When Vargas first approached Pecos, he found the town deserted. Hearing of his coming, the residents had fled. Although the governor contemplated punishing them by burning their homes and cornfields, instead he withdrew from the pueblo and left its fields unharmed. Releasing the few Indians he had captured, he admonished them to tell the others of his kind treatment of them. By these acts of good faith, Vargas hoped to gain the confidence and respect of the Pecos people. In this, he was successful. When he returned several weeks later, Pecos again was thriving, and a welcoming mob awaited him at the entrance to the plaza.

After a rebellious spell in 1696, the Pueblos resigned themselves to dealing with Spanish officials and new residents of the borderlands. Most of their towns, vacated during the rebellion, were eventually reoccupied. Secular officials were selected according to Spanish dictates. A legal code protected the Indians' lands from white encroachment. Inevitably, however, as the Hispanic population expanded the natives were increasingly squeezed into tighter enclaves. In time, the Pecos valley transformed into a predominantly Spanish community. Franciscan padres resumed their duties, which necessitated refurbishing many desecrated missions and building new ones. Old quarrels between the religious and the secular branches were renewed, to the detriment of effective government. Somehow the Indians suffered through these various problems, but they were unprotected against white men's diseases. Smallpox virtually wiped out some villages.

Added to their troubles were mounting incursions by nomadic tribes who, upon acquiring the use of horses, heavily preyed upon them and then galloped to safety. Pecos was particularly vulnerable to such attacks from the Apache and Comanche because of its proximity to the plains where they traditionally roamed. Although small units of Spanish troops sometimes were quartered there to help protect the village and the important communication trail that passed nearby, the constant skirmishes, added to the other difficulties, made inevitable the ultimate abandonment of this easternmost toehold of the Pueblo Indians.

Sixty years after the Vargas re-entry, the once booming town of Pecos had shrunk to half its size. A 1750 census listed only 449 residents, 255 of whom were adults. By 1821, when Mexico became an independent nation with New Mexico its most northern territory, eight or ten Indian families amounting to possibly about fifty people were left. From their crumbling citadel, these doomed survivors glumly witnessed the swell of caravans passing along the Santa Fe Trail to engage in a trade in which they would have no share.

In 1838 the hard decision to move out of Pecos pueblo was made by the last seventeen residents. They packed up their ceremonial gear, gathered their few personal belongings and available crops, arranged with local Spaniards to care for their church, and took the eighty-mile trail northwest to Jemez, the only other pueblo that spoke their language. The people of Jemez had given them permission to come, assisted in the move, and provided houses and fields. But neither the people nor the village of Pecos really died. At Jemez, the Pecos refugees steadfastly clung to their own heritage, although they comfortably settled into their new surroundings. From time to time they made pilgrimages to their ancestral home. Their descendants, who still live in Jemez, retain pride in their old ties to Pecos and annually return in August on the Pecos saint's day for moving services held within the massive adobe ramparts of the church nave.

Pothunters, scavengers, and transients hastened ruination of what had become a lifeless clutter of roofless, cell-like rooms and a wrecked church. Their callous vandalism was softened by a compendium of romantic impressions left by antiquarians, artists, and travelers drawn to the silent site by its enormous size and glowing reputation as one of the most outstanding Rio Grande pueblos.

Sketches in 1846 of both mission church and pueblo ruins by artist John Mix Stanley, who accompanied the Army of the West, depict the pueblo in ruins but still standing, two and three stories in places with a great many beams, lintels, and other wooden elements in place. In these renderings, the church appears relatively intact. By 1858 a painting by German artist Heinrich B. Möllhausen illustrated the rapid deterioration of the town and church, many of whose walls are shown protruding from enveloping masses of rubble and dirt. In 1880 Adolph F. Bandelier began his exhaustive investigations of southwestern Indians by examining the remains of Pecos. He spent a week amid the tumbled walls, photographing them, accumulating artifacts, and interviewing local residents about their recollections of the village and its former occupants. He saw the church gone to ruin because unknown persons had ripped out ornamented beams, scarred the walls, and even disinterred the dead in the cemetery. Bandelier's report on Pecos was the first of a scientific nature and also was the first publication of the Archaeological Institute of America, his sponsor.

It remained for archeologists to pry the truth about Pecos from the blanket of soil and legend which in time surrounded it. Early in the twentieth century Phillips Academy of Andover, Massachusetts, decided to excavate Pecos pueblo. Alfred V. Kidder was placed in charge. Excavations began in 1915 and continued intermittently for ten summer field seasons. The financial crash of 1929 brought an abrupt end to the undertaking, but not before a great volume of data and many artifacts had been gathered.

Kidder's work at Pecos came at a time when southwestern archeology was maturing from the sentimental accumulation of crates of Indian objects for museum display to systematic research, controlled excavations, and detailed analyses. Prior investigations a

Abandoned "Catholic Church," Pecos, 1846. JOHN MIX STANLEY, EMORY, *NOTES.*

short distance to the south conducted by Nels C. Nelson, of the American Museum of Natural History, had proved that stratigraphic excavations of refuse deposits and analytical studies of potsherds from them could produce information about sequences of pottery types. These in turn would permit recognition of contacts and information about occupation of those ruins. This significant step in southwestern archeology set the pattern for later research throughout the area, particularly at Pecos.

Kidder focused on ceramic analysis at Pecos as a means of charting a sequence of pottery types for the entire northern Rio Grande region. The strategic position of Pecos on the main passageway between the interior of the Pueblo domain and the buffalo plains gave hope that excavations would uncover artifacts to link a chronology of local culture with cultures west and east. Wide archeological ties were urgently needed for placing southwestern prehistory in proper perspective. It was hoped that pottery would provide such information. To a considerable extent this expectation was realized.

Situated on a narrow, red stone mesa in the midst of pinyon- and juniper-clad hills, Pecos consisted of two large mounds of house remains, enormous drifts of trash, and the wreckage of its last mission and convent. Aided by a team of highly competent associates, Kidder concentrated on stratigraphic excavations in the trash along the east slope of the mesa and elsewhere. He recovered masses of potsherds, other artifacts, and many burials. Digging into a portion of the north mound, he outlined the final compact, four-sided, multistoried pueblo surrounding a wide plaza, built in the vestiges of an earlier, sprawling one-story community. The south mound was only tested. Uncovering the pueblo ruins proved to be demanding because of the instability of the walls once they were freed from their enveloping dirt and rubble. It became necessary to promptly backfill excavated units to preserve the architecture and avoid danger to the crew and staff.

A notable event took place at the Pecos field camp in August 1927 when, upon an invitation from Kidder, leading regional archeologists met to discuss the status of southwestern archeology and to postulate eight prehistoric periods based on the stratigraphic record. These were Basket Maker I through III and Pueblo I through V.

At the conclusion of his studies Kidder believed that Pecos probably reached its greatest size sometime between A.D. 1500 and 1600, when it had a population of approximately one thousand persons. He thought that the two room blocks, the larger northern four-story unit, and the smaller southern complex likely contained 1,020 rooms. Not all of them were in use contemporaneously. It was obvious that even at its heyday Pecos had continually undergone additions, alterations, and rebuilding. In its later stages, as population declined many sections were deserted, fell into disrepair, and were filled with trash.

While Phillips Academy interested itself in the Pecos ruins, the Museum of New Mexico, under the guidance of Jesse L. Nusbaum, began clearing and repairing the hulking, mud-brick remains of its eighteenth-century church. After Pecos became a New Mexico State Monument, the museum also excavated a portion of the church's convent and a section of the south pueblo. The dilapidated rock walls of the cleared pueblo rooms and the large, adobe religious enclosure were stabilized for display purposes.

For years historians and archivists could not agree on the number and characteristics of the Spanish churches at Pecos. Details given in various eyewitness accounts did not correlate with physical evidence at the site. Following the acquisition of Pecos pueblo as a national monument in 1965, additional digging and stabilization of the last church and convent by a National Park Service archeological team, directed by Jean M. Pinkley, uncovered the buried foundations of an older, much larger church beneath the footings of the one standing at the time. Archeological findings showed that the earlier church had burned and that the existing building had gone up almost entirely within its nave. The edifice that had been consumed by fire turns out to have been the second church at Pecos. Now the evidence in the ground has been neatly meshed with contemporary documents of the seventeenth and eighteenth centuries by Alden C. Hayes to show that Pecos had a succession of four churches, two of which left little trace.

The first was a small isolated church or chapel, erected at the instigation of an unknown friar probably in the late 1590s or early 1600s, several hundred yards northeast of the north quadrangle of the pueblo. It seems to have been in use for only a few years. Between 1622 and 1625 the second house of worship was built by Fray Andrés Juárez at the southern end of the mesa a short distance from the south pueblo. This was a spacious structure embodying three hundred thousand adobe bricks in its eight- to ten-feet-thick walls which enclosed a nave about 40 by 133 feet. There were closely spaced, ground-to-roof buttresses along the exterior walls which may have stood forty-five feet high. Six towers rose above its roof line. Overall, it was the most impressive of the churches erected at the pueblo. A convent with rooms, corrals, and a cloister area was joined to the south wall. It was this edifice which rebellious Indians completely destroyed in 1680.

The third church was little more than a temporary chapel. It was erected after the reconquest in 1694 by Fray Diego de la Casa Zeinas by leveling off the rubble of the south wall of the razed church and building three walls against the north side of the convent wall. A permanent structure placed upon the debris of the pre-revolt church in 1705 by Fray José de Arranegui was the fourth place of Christian worship at Pecos. It was neither as large nor as imposing as the church from whose ruins it grew, but it served until the village was deserted. Today its roofless walls stand as a reminder of the Christianization of Pecos.

Within the past decade, National Park Service archeological survey and testing around the principal settlement have revealed two large partially subterranean pithouses lined with logs which contained a scattering of smashed pottery and other nonperishable specimens attributable to a generalized Pueblo I horizon. Tree rings produced a cutting date of A.D. 850. These are the first such structures found in the upper Pecos area and may have been used only seasonally. At present it appears that the region did not attract many settlers until fourteenth-century population pressures in the Rio Grande valley forced outmigration eastward and were responsible for what became Pecos pueblo. Contemporary small house sites are scattered through the Pecos valley, showing that town and village occupation occurred simultaneously.

In 1990 what had been Pecos National Monument, set aside in 1965 to preserve and interpret for the public the Indian and early Hispanic remains, became Pecos National

Historical Park due to three important additions to the federal holdings that brought the history of the Pecos area up to the twentieth century. One was the 5,500-acre adjacent Forked Lightning Ranch acquired from the estate of Colonel E. E. Fogelson and his widow, Greer Garson Fogelson, long-time benefactors of the monument. Indian and nineteenth-century Hispanic sites on the property offer numerous future research opportunities, as do a riparian environment along the Pecos River and the still-observable ruts of the old Santa Fe Trail that for sixty years in the nineteenth century served as a lifeline between the central United States and this remote corner of the continent. However, historical and ecological value does not stop there.

On August 17, 1846, American forces under orders from President James Polk and led by Brigadier General Stephen Watts Kearny camped near Forked Lightning Ranch lands or Pecos pueblo on their way to seize California. The next day, after Mexicans who were to halt their progress at the narrow defile of Apache Canyon to the west, had fled, Kearny triumphantly raised the Stars and Stripes over the plaza in Santa Fe. Much of the Southwest thereafter belonged to the United States.

A few years later, eccentric Captain Napoleon Kozlowski, a Polish immigrant who had served in Kearny's Army of the West, built a stagecoach stop on what became part of the modern ranch using handy materials salvaged from Pecos pueblo and its mission. This structure later was incorporated into the Forked Lightning Ranch house.

Two other detached parcels of land added to former Pecos National Monument, each in excess of three hundred acres, were where decisive battles of the Civil War took place. One is the former Johnson's Ranch at the west entrance to Apache Canyon. There on March 26, 1862, a Confederate army contingent known as the Texas Rangers and its supply train were routed by Union troops. Although the site itself is historically significant, little other than some ceiling beams still remains of the original ranch buildings.

Two days later a second Civil War engagement was fought at Pigeon's Ranch, located six miles to the east on the old Santa Fe Trail between Apache Canyon and Pecos pueblo. It now also is included in the Pecos National Historical Park. A stage stop at this locality was converted into a hospital for wounded on both sides of the battle that was fought across the surrounding valley. During the 1980s the remains of thirty-one Confederate soldiers were uncovered on these grounds during construction of a residence, three of which were later identified either by uniforms or diaries. The First Colorado Volunteers, the New Mexico Volunteers, and regular army units made up the victorious Grand Army of the Republic, which for a time used the springs behind the Forked Lightning Ranch buildings as its headquarters. The Battle of Glorieta culminating at Pigeon's Ranch effectively ended Southern dreams of creating a new nation reaching from Dixie to the Pacific.

Most of the specimens, photographs, and notes resulting from Kidder's many years of work at Pecos pueblo now are housed at the monument visitor center. Others are in the custody of Phillips Academy. Recovered aboriginal skeletal remains and records derived from their study by E. A. Hooton are curated at the Peabody Museum, Harvard University. The Museum of New Mexico cares for the recently discovered unclaimed remains of some of those who fell at the Battle of Glorieta.

ADDITIONAL READINGS, Pecos National Historical Park

Bezy, John V., and Joseph P. Sanchez, Editors
   1988   *Pecos, Gateway to Pueblos and Plains, The Anthology.* Tucson, Arizona:
            Southwest Parks and Monuments Association.

Hayes, Alden C.
   1974   *The Four Churches of Pecos.* Albuquerque: University of New Mexico Press.

Kessell, John L.
   1979   *Kiva, Cross, and Crown: The Pecos Indians and New Mexico, 1540–1840.*
            Washington, D.C.: National Park Service.

Kidder, Alfred V.
   1932   *The Artifacts of Pecos.* New Haven, Connecticut: Yale University Press.
   1958   *Pecos, New Mexico: Archaeological Notes.* Andover, Massachusetts: Phillips
            Academy.
   1962   *An Introduction to the Study of Southwestern Archaeology with a Preliminary
            Account of the Excavations at Pecos.* Revised edition of 1924. New Haven,
            Connecticut: Yale University Press.

Noble, David G., Editor
   1981   *Pecos Ruins: Geology, Archaeology, History, Prehistory.* Santa Fe, New Mexico:
            Exploration, Annual Bulletin of the School of American Research.

Whitford, William C.
   1989   *Colorado Volunteers in the Civil War, the New Mexico Campaign of 1862.*
            Reprint of 1906 edition. Glorieta, New Mexico: Rio Grande Press.

Jean Pinkley overseeing National Park Service excavations at Pecos Mission. NATIONAL PARK SERVICE.

Puerco Ruins, Petrified Forest National Park, Arizona. FRED HIRSCHMANN.

PETRIFIED FOREST NATIONAL PARK, ARIZONA

Cultural Significance and Archeological Classification

The archeological sequence in Petrified Forest National Park encompasses a cultural continuum extending from an ephemeral Paleo-Indian presence to that of the Pueblo Indians living during the latter half of the fourteenth century. Situated between the Anasazi plateau and Mogollon mountain and valley core areas and bordering the Hakataya territory, the region was subject to different sets of influences from surrounding cultures. The southern impact appeared early in the transitional period between the nomadic Archaic and semi-nomadic Basket Maker II periods, dated here between A.D. 1 and 200, when a brown pottery made by the paddle and anvil method appeared. It is the oldest ceramic material known in the Little Colorado River area. At the final occupation as represented by the Puerco Ruin (A.D. 1250–1380), trade from Zuni to the east and Hopi and Homol'ovi to the northwest is evident. Rock art of this period reflects the introduction from the Jornada Mogollon of the kachina cult. Surprisingly, although petrified wood was used locally for lithics, no substantial trade in this abundant natural resource seems to have occurred.

Archaic: *Oshara*
Anasazi: *Basket Maker II, III; Pueblo I, II, III, IV*
Mogollon: *1, 2, 3*
In-betweens and Outliers: *Hakataya (Sinagua culture)*
All-Southwest: *Hamlets, Villages, Towns, intermediate between plateau and mountain-valley zones*

Explorations and Investigations

Some archeological reconnaisssance had been undertaken in the region of Petrified Forest National Park prior to 1906 when it was set aside as an area of outstanding geological importance by President Theodore Roosevelt. At the end of the nineteenth century Jesse W. Fewkes, of the Bureau of American Ethnology, and Walter Hough, of the U.S. National Museum, located and partially exposed many of the larger ruins in the vicinity and collected more than five thousand specimens. The two also attempted to correlate archeological data with ethnological information to substantiate oral traditions of early Hopi migrations. Hough dug in several ruins now included in the park, some of which have been further cleared.

Harry P. Mera and C. B. Cosgrove, from the Laboratory of Anthropology in Santa Fe, headed a Civil Works Administration archeological project in the 1930s that conducted the first systematic archeological survey of part of the park and probed some of the ruins. One hundred nine ancient features were recorded within and immediately adjacent to the park. An eight-room pueblo, known as Agate House because it was constructed of chunks of colorful agatized wood, was cleared and partially restored. Several rooms were opened in the Puerco Ruin, a 125-room pueblo site on a bluff near the Puerco River, which was added to the federal holding in 1930. Two units of the Flattop Site, a pithouse village, were cleaned out. Mera worked out a chronology of regional pottery development which is used to the present time. National Park Service personnel expanded the survey of the park in 1941 and 1942, bringing the total number of recorded sites to 339. Following World War II Fred Wendorf excavated eight of twenty-five pithouses at the Flattop Site and two others at

Mountain lion petroglyph, Petrified Forest National Park.
GEORGE A. GRANT, NATIONAL PARK SERVICE, 1934.

Twin Buttes Site.

The most comprehensive examination of the antiquities of Petrified Forest National Park occurred during the late 1980s. At that time National Park Service researchers and volunteers undertook an archeological survey along the park boundary, recorded rock art at Mountain Lion Mesa, cleared additional parts of Puerco Ruin, tested an adjacent lithic scatter, and mapped and partially excavated the Basket Maker II hamlet of Sivu'ovi.

Collections and notes from the various enterprises in Petrified Forest are to be found at the Museum of Northern Arizona in Flagstaff, the Smithsonian Institution in Washington, at the National Park Service Western Archeological and Conservation Center in Tucson, and in the park's visitor center. ⌂

ADDITIONAL READINGS, Petrified Forest National Park
Burton, Jeffery F.
    1990 *Archeological Investigations at Puerco Ruin, Petrified Forest National Park, Arizona*. Publications in Anthropology, No. 54. Tucson, Arizona: Western Archeological and Conservation Center, National Park Service.
    1991 *The Archeology of Sivu'ovi, the Archaic to Basketmaker Transition at Petrified Forest National Park*. Publications in Anthropology, No. 55. Tucson, Arizona: Western Archeological and Conservation Center, National Park Service.
Schroeder, Albert H.
    1961 Puerco Ruins Excavations, Petrified Forest National Monument, Arizona. *Plateau*, Vol. 33, No. 4. Flagstaff: Museum of Northern Arizona.
Stewart, Yvonne G.
    1980 *An Archeological Overview of Petrified Forest National Park*. Publications in Anthropology, No. 10. Tucson, Arizona: Western Archeological Center, National Park Service.
Wells, Susan J.
    1989 *Petrified Forest National Park Boundary Survey, 1988: The Final Season*. Publications in Anthropology, No. 51. Tucson, Arizona: Western Archeological and Conservation Center, National Park Service.
Wendorf, Fred
    1953 *Archaeological Studies in the Petrified Forest National Monument*. Bulletin, No. 27. Flagstaff: Museum of Northern Arizona.

Different pottery styles found in Petrified Forest attest to its trade route status. Clockwise from top, Tularosa black-on-white, Walnut black-on-white, St. Johns polychrome. GEORGE H. H. HUEY.

PETROGLYPH NATIONAL MONUMENT, NEW MEXICO

Cultural Significance and Archeological Classification

Archaic: *Oshara*
Anasazi: *Basket Maker II; Pueblo IV, V*
All-Southwest: *Towns, plateau zone*

This alfresco art gallery, seventeen miles long and shaped like a shoelace along the west side of the valley in which Albuquerque is situated, contains the most extensive display of prehistoric iconography in the United States. Although some representations pecked into the face and fallen blocks of an ancient lava flow may date to a millennium before Christ and others seem to have been made in the early Christian Era when hunters and gatherers were being transformed into sedentary farmers, the majority of the figures were executed over a 350-year period (A.D. 1300–1650) centered on the opening of the historic era in New Mexico. Their style reflects an important cultural elaboration probably resulting from pervasive influence from the south and an intensification of religious biases attributable to stresses stemming from the abandonment of the Colorado Plateau by the end of the thirteenth century. Some of the visible manifestations of the ideology continue to the present. Nearby is the sole remaining, relatively untouched Pueblo IV–Pueblo V community in this part of the Rio Grande drainage which, if excavated, would provide invaluable insight into the world view of the society responsible for the rock art.

Explorations and Investigations

Geologists estimate that about 190,000 years ago a thin, flat sheet of molten lava poured eastward from a weak spot in the earth's crust and spread across a tableland lying between the drainages of the Rio Puerco and the Rio Grande in what is now the heart of New Mexico. The last phase of this vulcanism saw the formation of five low cinder cones along a north-south fissure, today still visible on Albuquerque's west horizon. The lava stream either stopped abruptly several miles before pouring into the Rio Grande channel or subsequently has been eroded back to form a low, but comparatively abrupt, cliff face on the west flank of the river valley from which thousands of blocky chunks have cascaded downward. This cliff face and its detritus afforded native peoples inviting surfaces for artistic and religious expression.

Archeological surveys and limited excavations in lands to the west of the escarpment and down into the Rio Grande flood plain have revealed an extensive prehistoric occupation covering an estimated twelve thousand years. The beginning and end of this impressive record of human activity are most strongly represented in microenvironments within the tract suitable to the particular subsistence economies practiced at the time.

Judging from scattered finds of stone projectile points which archeologists place into a half-dozen temporal categories, Paleo-Indians stalked large game animals as they came to drink in ponds existing in Pleistocene times in what now are dry basins and arroyos in the western portion of the monument and broken terrain approaching the Rio Puerco. They were succeeded by Archaic hunters and foragers of the Oshara development stage, who adapted to changed ecological circumstances by seeking smaller modern species of

Petroglyphs in Rinconada Canyon, Petroglyph National Monument. GEORGE H. H. HUEY.

animals and processing a variety of vegetal materials. They also congregated near the Rio Puerco until drier weather and an increasing reliance upon horticulture forced movement elsewhere.

One spot that housed those who were making the slow transition to agriculturally based sedentism, defined in southwestern archeological terms as the Basket Makers, was Boca Negra Cave on the side of Bond Volcano.

Although few, if any, of the early groups who were in the general region up to about A.D. 400 or 500 are known to have lived in the immediate proximity of the basalt precipice forming the east face of the West Mesa, stylistic analyses of the petroglyphs placed there suggest that Archaic or Basket Maker bands left behind such pecked motifs as circles, meandering lines, rakes, outlined crosses, sandal tracks, handprints, human stick figures, lizards, and squirrels. Rock art specialist Polly Schaafsma, in relating some of the petroglyph designs to those appearing on pottery, considers them to be Pueblo I in age. However, little evidence of Pueblo I through Pueblo II occupation has yet been noted in this portion of the middle Rio Grande.

About A.D. 1300, or Pueblo IV, throngs of eastern Anasazi migrated into the Rio Grande tributary system because of perennial water, fertile soil, and a reasonably favorable climate for horticulture. They merged with a resident population into large communities on both sides of the main stem of the river. Bottomlands were farmed, but numerous constructions along the base or top of the sinuous petroglyph escarpment show that it too was used. These were lines of rocks set up to form terraces for gardening, others placed to divert runoff waters onto such plots, temporary shelters or windbreaks of stones, and worn rock surfaces where seeds or corn kernels were ground with hand stones.

The regrouping of a large part of the eastern Pueblo population in what seems to have been a more benign environment, and perhaps some influences from the south, brought about a cultural rejuvenation that was expressed in a notable social and artistic enrichment. Much of the West Mesa rock art represents a decided break from the past, both in style and content, due to an infusion of new ideas. One of these appears to have been the kachina cult. Kachinas are interpreted as the physical embodiments of certain deities. They must have been a significant religious expression among the Tiwa of the middle Rio Grande. Many of the human and animal masked figures displayed in West Mesa petroglyphs can be identified with known figures. However, many other representations cannot be placed so definitely in the Pueblo pantheon. These are large animals, reptiles, birds, human hands, star faces, stepped clouds, and kokopellis. Although their symbolic meanings are not totally understood, they confirm a basic cultural continuity dating back to the earliest Anasazi. Perhaps when the thousand-room adobe pueblo of Piedras Marcadas (marked rocks) in a detached area just a mile east of the escarpment is cleared, it will be found to contain a kiva with painted wall murals such as in several other Pueblo IV ruins in the vicinity. Then the underlying symbolism of the petroglyphs executed by the same artisan base will be more fully comprehended.

There is no indication that there was common knowledge among Europeans of the Indian rock art along the West Mesa bluffs until the early eighteenth century. Even though the very first Spanish entrada into the central Rio Grande valley in 1540 must have passed nearby, surviving records fail to note it. Scribes indicated seventeen to twenty native towns along that stretch of the river, two of which the Spaniards destroyed and one in which they wintered. But if the figures pecked into rocks were observed, they were not considered important enough to mention. Nor were the motifs worked into stone documented during the entire seventeenth century, a time when the associated indigenous towns were threatened with extinction because of Spanish oppression, raiding by nomadic Indians, disease, and disillusionment. Those settlements that were not temporarily vacated during the years of the Pueblo Revolt (1680–1692) were emptied soon thereafter and left to melt down into mounds of hardened mud.

In the next century as the Indians moved out, Hispanics moved in. The Villa of Albuquerque was established in 1706 on lowlands east of the Rio Grande, and a number of neighboring haciendas on both sides of the river followed. Sheepherders at the Atrisco Land Grant, encompassing the southern end of the petroglyph panel, grazed their flocks in the protection of the western lava cliffs and the volcanoes. Probably for the first time they became aware of the jumble of strange designs pecked into the patina-blackened stones, and, being superstitious, they hammered Christian crosses alongside some of the them to ward off what they considered evil pagan spirits. Meantime, two pueblos, Sandia to the north and Isleta to the south, were reoccupied. Apparently through the ensuing years, little other attention was given by any group to the aboriginal etched symbols blistering on the bleak terraces west of settlement.

Two hundred years later, after World War II, Albuquerque real estate developers cast covetous eyes on the benches lining the west bank of the Rio Grande. Inevitably, vandalism of the age-old resource resulted. Recognizing the rock art's intrinsic value in understanding the socio-esoteric aspects of the native cultures and its irreplaceable nature, concerned citizens were instrumental in getting the state to take part of the lands on which the petroglyphs are present into its park network. The entire escarpment, designated Las Imagenes National Archeological District, was accepted for a place on the National Register of Historic Places. Later efforts on a higher level resulted in the setting aside in 1990 of 7,060 acres of the West Mesa as Petroglyph National Monument. It is the only such facility in the federal system focused exclusively upon aboriginal artistic works applied to rocks. In addition to the decorated cliff face, the five volcanoes and two geomorphic features called windows were included. The monument is administered by the National Park Service, the state of New Mexico, and the city of Albuquerque. Interpretations and developments designed to enhance tourism are just under way at this writing.

In connection with the founding of Petroglyph National Monument, Congress also authorized a Rock Art Research Center to undertake studies of the Rio Grande and other styles of work within the monument and in more removed sectors of the northern Southwest. Scholarly publications, as well as dissemination of less technical information, will add to the public appreciation of this unique patrimony.

ADDITIONAL READINGS, Petroglyph National Monument
Ireland, Arthur K.
  1987 *The Cultural Resources of the West Mesa Petroglyphs Study Area and Immediate Environs.* Santa Fe, New Mexico: Southwest Cultural Resources Center, National Park Service.
Irwin-Williams, Cynthia
  1973 *The Oshara Tradition: Origins of Anasazi Culture.* Contributions in Anthropology, Vol. 5, No. 1. Portales: Eastern New Mexico University.
Schaafsma, Polly
  1980 *Indian Rock Art of the Southwest.* School of American Research, Southwest Indian Arts Series. Albuquerque: University of New Mexico Press.
  1992 *Rock Art in New Mexico.* Santa Fe: Museum of New Mexico Press.
Schmader, Matthew F.
  1987 *The Archeology of the West Mesa Area, a Summary.* Santa Fe, New Mexico: Southwest Regional Office, National Park Service.
Weaver, Donald E.
  1984 Images on Stone: The Prehistoric Rock Art of the Colorado Plateau. *Plateau.* Vol. 55, No. 2. Flagstaff: Museum of Northern Arizona.

Star Being petroglyph, Petroglyph National Monument.
GEORGE H. H. HUEY.

SAGUARO NATIONAL MONUMENT, ARIZONA

Archaic: *Cochise*
Hohokam: *Sedentary, early Classic*
All-Southwest: *Hamlets, desert zone*

Cultural Significance and Archeological Classification

Although a secondary resource of Saguaro National Monument, the prehistoric remains cover a long period of time. They represent certain Archaic and Hohokam culture phases and their basic adaptation to the harsh realities of the Tucson basin. Bordered by lands where farming, urban sprawl, and industrial development are rapidly destroying evidences of the past, the monument holds a valuable future reserve of archeological material and data.

Explorations and Investigations

In 1933 Saguaro National Monument was established as an outstanding saguaro cactus ecological zone. Before that time limited archeological surveys and two minor excavations had been conducted in the area by Byron Cummings and Emil Haury. Their projects permitted tentative identification of the local cultural sequence and an idea of how it fit into the prehistory of the larger Tucson basin.

Several kinds of prehistoric sites have been recognized in the two sections of the monument, which are located east and west of Tucson. Temporary campsites where food was gathered and processed are located near arroyos where water would have been available periodically. Bedrock mortars, hearths, scatters of stone chips, and an occasional stone cutting or scraping tool are found at such places. In temporary shelters in shallow dry caves or under rock overhangs can be found preserved cordage, wooden items, and plant materials. Habitation sites, concentrated in the eastern section of the monument, tend to be small, meager remnants of a few brush and mud dwellings. Some larger accumulations of similar houses are situated near major washes where more water allowed larger groups of people to live. The nonperishable discards of village life, such as potsherds, ash, broken stone and bone implements, and the debris from making such artifacts, are scattered over the surface of the dwelling sites. Panels of easily identifiable rock art can be seen at several places.

In both sections of the monument most campsites were left by Archaic foragers, who for thousands of years visited the region in seasons when edible materials were available. Most of the cave and shelter sites and the habitation remains were left by later Hohokam farmers during their Sedentary and early Classic stages from about A.D. 900 to 1300. The rock art seems to have been made during this occupation.

The monument also contains evidence of some historic camps that the Papago Indians used while gathering saguaro cactus fruit.

Outside the monument three main sites excavated by University of Arizona students have confirmed the findings within the monument. These are the Hodges Site on the Santa Cruz River northwest of Tucson, the Tanque Verde Ruin near the headquarters section, and the University Indian Ruin west of the headquarters section.

Small collections of artifacts from Saguaro National Monument are deposited in the park and in the Arizona State Museum, University of Arizona. ▲

ADDITIONAL READINGS, Saguaro National Monument
Gregonis, Linda M., and Karl J. Reinhard
    1979 *The Hohokam Indians of the Tucson Basin.* Tucson: University of Arizona
          Press.
Stacy, V. K. Pheriba, and Julian Hayden
    1975 *Saguaro National Monument, An Archeological Overview.* Tucson: Arizona
          Archeological Center, National Park Service.

Petroglyphs, Saguaro National Monument (west section).
KENNETH ROZEN.

Gran Quivira, Salinas Pueblo Missions National Monument. CHARLES F. LUMMIS, 1894. SOUTHWEST MUSEUM COLLECTION.

SALINAS PUEBLO MISSIONS NATIONAL MONUMENT, NEW MEXICO

Cultural Significance and Archeological Classification

The three large groups of ruins at Gran Quivira, Abó, and Quarai were populous communities at the time of the Spanish entrada and soon came under the powerful influences of European military, secular, and religious pressures. They did not survive foreign dominance for long, and all had entered the realm of archeology before the Pueblos revolted against the Spanish in 1680. As a part of the population expansion in northern New Mexico during Pueblo IV, these many-roomed, several-storied towns thrived in a marginal area for Pueblo farmers. The ability of Spanish priests to draw on the skills of native craftsmen in building missions in which the newly implanted doctrine was practiced is evidence of the zeal of the Spaniards, many of whom suffered martyrdom in pursuit of their duties.

Explorations and Investigations

Salinas National Monument was established on December 19, 1980, when President Jimmy Carter signed a bill abolishing Gran Quivira National Monument, which had been a National Park Service area since 1909. Subsequently the facility was renamed Salinas Pueblo Missions National Monument. Gran Quivira was combined administratively with the New Mexico state monuments of Abó and Quarai after their formal transfer to the federal government. Now all three sites, including their Indian ruins and impressive remnants of seventeenth-century Franciscan missions, are included in the new installation with headquarters in Mountainair, New Mexico. Salinas is a Spanish word meaning saline or salt lagoons. It is the former name of the Estancia valley, a narrow, interior drainage basin in central New Mexico where the runoff flows into several desolate playas, which are ephemeral lakes ringed with salt, alkali, and other mineral deposits.

The Salinas country supported a large Pueblo Indian population at the time of Francisco Vásquez de Coronado's first exploring party into New Mexico in 1540–41. Though its members managed to visit most other settlements in the Southwest, it is doubtful that they entered the Salinas basin. Forty years later in 1581 and 1583 the expeditions under command of Francisco Chamuscado and Antonio Espejo did visit some of these Indian towns, but the first significant contact between Europeans and Salinas natives came with actual Spanish settlement in the province of New Spain at the end of the sixteenth century. At the urging of the first governor, Juan de Oñate, several hundred Salinas Indians voluntarily took oaths of allegiance to the Spanish crown, although they undoubtedly did not understand the meaning of becoming royal subjects. Within a few months they belligerently rebuffed an attempt by one of Oñate's agents to collect tribute of blankets and provisions. Oñate personally returned to punish the recalcitrants but only

Anasazi: Pueblo IV, V
All-Southwest: Towns, plateau zone

succeeded in triggering confrontations in which villages were burned and Indians and soldiers were killed.

By 1600 exchange between natives of Salinas Province and Spanish authorities had formed a pattern that was to cause the indigenes many hardships. In order to exist, the early Spaniards imposed countless levies of food and clothing against all the Pueblos. Those demands were particularly deleterious to the Salinas people because theirs was an unusually harsh land, where survival was difficult even under the best circumstances. Spanish requirements, added to recurring droughts, crop failures, and epidemics, contributed more to population reduction than did the sword. Within three-quarters of a century, they had abandoned their homes and scattered to other parts.

The Spaniards, finding New Mexico less wealthy and productive than they had anticipated, decided to change the nature of their venture there. The abundance of Pueblo souls available for conversion from heathenism kindled the missionary zeal. With greater support from the royal treasury, the church grew in power and number of clergymen. Conflicts with civil governors, *encomenderos* (citizen-soldiers), and private landholders intensified, while all parties vied for control of the Indians, who provided most of the food, clothing, and labor necessary for survival.

Accelerated missionary activities in the Salinas Province began with a 1609 order from the viceroy to concentrate the Indian population into fewer settlements to facilitate their administration. Under the guidance of resident Franciscan friars, by 1630 missions had been erected in six of the larger towns, among them Abó, Quarai, and Gran Quivira. Indian laborers were directed in cutting timbers, quarrying rock, making adobe bricks, carrying water for construction materials, and actually erecting the buildings. A memorial delivered to the Pope at that time related that about ten thousand Indians of the region had been converted to Christianity, most of them having been baptized.

Once established, the missions were virtually self supporting and drew upon their parishioners for help in preparing and tending gardens, maintaining buildings and grounds, tending livestock, and otherwise serving the priests. To varying degrees, priests carried out an edict to eliminate all traces of native religion. Some went so far as to destroy ceremonial paraphernalia and buildings. In many instances those measures caused aboriginal rites to become secretive, evidence that most Pueblos tolerated but did not fully accept Christianity.

Civil authorities and encomenderos, who had been granted land near pueblos and who were allowed to collect tribute, increasingly exploited the Indians for personal gain. Their labor and products, such as corn, beans, pinyon nuts, cotton and woolen cloth, dressed deer and buffalo skins, firewood, jackets, skirts, stockings, and salt, were demanded by government officials. Encomenderos expected labor for operating their ranches and a portion of the food produced by Indians living on their granted lands.

Before Spanish occupation, the Salinas pueblos had a friendly trading relationship with Apache Indians to the south; but when Spanish militia and encomenderos began trading Apache slaves, peace between the two Indian groups broke down. From the 1630s onward, Apaches, made extremely mobile by acquisition of the horse, turned to bloody

Tabira black-on-white pottery canteen, Gran Quivira, Salinas Pueblo Missions National Monument. GEORGE H. H. HUEY.

retaliation against all settlements, Spanish and Christian Indian alike.

The deepening problems faced by the Pueblo residents of the land of the salt lakes took their toll. Several years before the general uprising of all the Pueblos, the southeastern border of Pueblo territory already had been depopulated. The survivors moved west and south, some to join their kin in towns along the Rio Grande in central New Mexico, others to mingle with compatible groups around El Paso.

Though each of the three sections of Salinas Pueblo Missions National Monument is dominated by a large, decayed church complex, all have ruins of former habitations that extend far backwards in time before Europeans entered the scene. It was, after all, the populous communities that had attracted the missionaries.

Several early writers of modern times made references to the antiquities of the Salinas basin. Although Josiah Gregg in his 1844 *Commerce of the Prairies* described Gran Quivira, it is doubtful that he had ever seen it. Major James H. Carleton and his command marched by the ruins during a blizzard in December 1853. Even under such adverse conditions, his descriptions and measurements were accurate, first-hand reporting. Two well-known students of the Southwest, Charles F. Lummis and Adolph Bandelier, provided accounts of Quarai, Abó, and Gran Quivira after each had visited them in the late 1800s. Lummis called the old Salinas towns "The Cities that Were Forgotten," saying that if the mission of Quarai had been on the Rhine, it would be famous, and that Quarai, Abó, and Gran Quivira were smaller versions of Montezuma's capital. Bandelier wrote more from a scientist's point of view. His academic writings did not reach as wide an audience as those of Lummis, but they more often separated truth from fiction.

The main Indian ruins at Quarai are adjacent to the high, reddish stone walls of the church. The oval mound and outlying segments of the former pueblo were partially trenched in 1913 and 1920 by the School of American Archaeology while more extensive excavations were under way at the church and convent. No reports of the work are available, but it is known that the excavators recovered a number of fine pottery vessels and artifacts indicating a long pre-Hispanic occupation. It was believed that the community house had risen in tiers back from the central plazas into which kivas were sunk, to a height of at least three stories, and that a protective wall had surrounded the buildings. The School of American Research completed clearing and repair of the mission units in the 1930s. Wesley R. Hurt directed a Works Projects Administration program in 1939–40, which further excavated the convent, outlined walls of the cemetery in front of the church, and traced the outside walls of the nearby pueblo mounds. After becoming a state monument, the buildings were further stabilized by the Museum of New Mexico.

The conversion of the residents of Quarai and erection of the church of La Purísima Concepción are ascribed to Fray Estévan de Perea about 1628, but earlier missionary efforts are suggested by the presence of ruins of a smaller, earlier chapel that may have preceded the church by several years.

At Abó, the unexcavated Indian ruins and remarkably intact walls of the mission are located on a hill near a steadily flowing spring. The Indian stone houses there had once been three stories high. Erection of the church of San Gregorio de Abó and its attached convent probably began about 1626.

Gran Quivira was the largest pueblo in the Salinas Province. A Spanish chronicler of 1627 estimated that it housed three thousand Indians. Of the Salinas ruins it is the one most frequently studied archeologically and historically. Gran Quivira has come to be the widely used term for the site, though its pre-Spanish name is recorded as Cueloze. After Oñate's era, it was known as Zumanas, Jumanos, or Humanas. During the colonial period until its abandonment, Las Humanas seems to have been the common name, by which it is still known to some scholars. How the place came to be identified as Gran Quivira is not completely clear. Some attribute it to an erroneous association of the site with Quivira, a fabled city of gold and riches which Coronado sought in 1541 during a trek to present Kansas. Others believe it evolved out of persistent rumors that the Spaniards buried valuable bells or a treasure there. Over the years these tales lured a small army of treasure seekers to dig many unproductive shafts throughout the pueblo and mission remains. The last was sunk in 1933.

Archeological excavations at Gran Quivira, with its seventeen significant house mounds and vestiges of two missions, were concentrated first on the only structure whose walls stood well above the ground. That was the large church and convent of San Buenaventura which was cleared by a team from the Museum of New Mexico and the School of American Research, directed by Edgar L. Hewett, from 1923 to 1925. In addition, some digging was done in a burial zone and in rooms and kivas fronting a plaza of the pueblo.

The National Park Service has sponsored two excavation and stabilization efforts at Gran Quivira. The first, led by Gordon Vivian in 1951, exposed thirty-seven rooms of a pueblo unit known as Mound 10, uncovered a kiva, and cleaned out the badly vandalized remains of the small mission of San Isidro, which was filled with the detritus of treasure hunting operations. The second was in the field during the summers from 1965 to 1968. Directed by Alden C. Hayes, it excavated Mound 7, a high, rubble-covered hummock.

Hayes uncovered three superimposed structures in Mound 7. Earliest was a circular, single-story community, whose 150 to 200 rooms were arranged in concentric arcs around a small plaza with one kiva. It is believed to have been occupied from about A.D. 1300 to 1400. Next, a small linear block of rooms and three kivas, in use from approximately A.D. 1400 to the early 1500s, were attached to the original complex. During that time many unoccupied rooms of the first unit were partially razed for building materials needed elsewhere in the village and used as dumping places. For a brief period the entire structure was almost totally abandoned. During that time additional destruction and filling of rooms with rubbish took place. Finally, about 1545, construction of a linear, one-story house block was started on top of the earlier, somewhat demolished, trash-covered habitations. By 1600 the edifice had grown to some two hundred rooms arranged in an F-shape with five associated kivas. This is one of the buildings that was left standing when Gran Quivira was deserted in 1672.

The mission chapel of San Isidro was erected in 1629 by Fray Juan Letrado to minister to Gran Quivira and two other towns in the neighborhood. The first missionary effort did

Mission church at Quarai, Salinas Pueblo Missions National Monument. GEORGE H. H. HUEY.

not last long. Within two decades the building was vacated and possibly wrecked by Apache raiders. When missionary activities were resumed, a new, much larger church with an attached convent was built in 1659. It was dedicated to San Buenaventura by Fray Diego de Santander.

Cultivation of the usual southwestern crops, combined with considerable gathering of wild plants and with hunting, was how most of the region's people lived. The absence of running water at Gran Quivira may have made farming more difficult than at the other Salinas villages. It is possible the Quivirans may have exploited their strategic position between the Pueblos along the Rio Grande and the Apaches to the east and south to act as middlemen in trade of hides and meat from the plains, corn and cotton from the riverine villages, and salt and pinyon nuts from local sources. Domestic water for the town seems to have been supplied by wells and cisterns.

Included among finds at Mound 7 were portions of murals painted on plastered room walls, a collection of faunal remains, and many human skeletons. Artifacts from all three sites included Spanish metal tools and tin-glazed, wheel-turned ceramics. Further Spanish influence on native culture was apparent in vessel forms and burial practices.

Most of the collections resulting from the National Park Service investigations are stored at the Western Archeological and Conservation Center in Tucson. The Laboratory of Anthropology in Santa Fe curates specimens resulting from the Museum of New Mexico work. A small display of artifacts can be seen at the monument visitor center. ▲

ADDITIONAL READINGS, Salinas Pueblo Missions National Monument
Hayes, Alden C., Jon N. Young, and A. H. Warren
   1981 *Excavation of Mound 7, Gran Quivira National Monument, New Mexico.*
         Publications in Archeology, No. 16. Washington, D.C.: National Park Service.
Hayes, Alden C., et al.
   1981 *Contributions to Gran Quivira Archeology, Gran Quivira National Monument,
         New Mexico.* Publications in Archeology, No. 17. Washington, D.C.: National
         Park Service.
Hewett, Edgar L., and Reginald G. Fisher
   1943 *Mission Monuments of New Mexico.* Albuquerque: School of American
         Research and University of New Mexico Press.
Hurt, Wesley R.
   1990 *The 1939–1940 Excavation Project at Quarai Pueblo and Mission Building,
         Salinas Pueblo Missions National Monument, New Mexico.* Professional Paper,
         No. 29. Santa Fe, New Mexico: Southwest Cultural Resources Center, National
         Park Service.
Kubler, George
   1972 *The Religious Architecture of New Mexico in the Colonial Period and Since the
         American Occupation,* 4th edition. Albuquerque: University of New Mexico
         Press.

Murphy, Dan
    1993 *Salinas Pueblo Missions National Monument.* Tucson, Arizona: Southwest
        Parks and Monuments Association.
Noble, David G., Editor
    1982 *Salinas National Monument, Archaeology, History, Prehistory.* Santa Fe, New
        Mexico: Exploration, Annual Bulletin of the School of American Research.
Toulouse, Joseph H., Jr.
    1949 *The Mission of San Gregorio de Abó.* Monograph, No. 13. Santa Fe, New
        Mexico: School of American Research.
Vivian, Gordon
    1964 *Excavations in a 17th Century Jumano Pueblo, Gran Quivira.* Publications in
        Archeology, No. 8. Washington, D.C.: National Park Service.
Wilson, John P.
    1977 *Quarai State Monument.* Santa Fe: Museum of New Mexico Press.

Lower Ruin, Tonto National Monument. GORDON VIVIAN, NATIONAL PARK SERVICE, 1957.

TONTO NATIONAL MONUMENT, ARIZONA

Cultural Significance and Archeological Classification

This amalgam of cultures is another that sprang up in central Arizona due to the overlapping of materials and influences from at least two core areas. Pueblolike habitations and pottery bearing black-and-white designs on a red base were characteristic of the Salado, which gave them an Anasazi resemblance, but canal irrigation farming and earthen platform mounds were borrowed Hohokam traits. Toward the end of their known cultural history, the Salado relocated among the Hohokam. From there, the telltale track of their distinctive pottery indicates that they pushed on to the southeast. Raising and weaving cotton were specialties of the Salado.

Explorations and Investigations

The Tonto basin of central Arizona derived its name from a band of Apache who once ranged there, though in the nineteenth century the term Tonto was loosely applied to many other Apache and some Yavapai Indians living west of the White Mountains. The cliff dwellings situated in caves high above the Salt River valley were identified by the same name by the first whites to observe them. Most likely these were members of military or other parties passing through the region during the 1870s. Certainly the ruins were familiar to the ranchers who moved in during the next decade, who commonly distinguished two separate remains as the Lower and Upper Ruins. These names have continued in use.

The earliest known description of the ruins was that of Adolph Bandelier, who arrived on May 24, 1883. He observed old dwellings in two caves, one at the base of a cliff and the other higher up and more difficult to reach. They were constructed of large, irregularly broken stones set in a gravel mortar. Many roof beams and the cactus ribs, reeds, and mud that topped them were still in place. Local whites told him that Apaches had burned out both houses. Bandelier found a sandal, fragments of basketry, rope and twine, many corncobs, some cane arrow shafts, and several types of potsherds.

In 1907 the ruins and a small amount of land around them were designated Tonto National Monument to protect them from increased visitation and vandalism stimulated by the construction of Roosevelt Dam nearby, at the confluence of the Salt River and Tonto Creek. The installation remained under Forest Service control until 1933, when it was transferred to the National Park Service. Like most other accessible, easily seen ruins in the Southwest, the Tonto cliff dwellings suffered from many years of illicit digging by treasure seekers and collectors of Indian relics until the National Park Service finally could guard them full-time. One of the first orders of business was to stabilize the major ruins, the lower one in 1937 and the upper in 1940.

Concurrent with stabilization of the Upper Ruin, some excavation was necessary to expose portions of walls that required strengthening. Seven rooms were completely

In-betweens and Outliers: *Salado culture*
All-Southwest: *Towns, intermediate between plateau and mountain-valley zones*

cleared. National Park Service archeologist Charlie Steen, the excavator, estimated that the dwelling originally had about forty rooms, whose walls had been poorly fashioned of native rock set in mud mortar. Thirty ground-floor rooms were outlined, and eight or ten second-story chambers were believed to have existed. Even though the ruins had been subjected to many years of pothunting, archeologists were fortunate to recover a few artifacts of wood, fiber, pottery, stone, bone, antler, shell, plant material, and one burial. Most important was an assortment of well-preserved cotton textiles that furnished information about the processing of fibers, weaving techniques, and types of clothing worn by those who lived in the cave during the fourteenth century.

Because it was more reachable than the Upper Ruin, the Lower Ruin endured greater plundering. At the time of its stabilization in 1937, it was reported that all rooms except one had been gutted. Debris that had been sifted through by pothunters was scattered and heaped in most of the chambers. While cleaning the rooms, the preservation crew found some objects overlooked by those who had thoughtlessly damaged the building and its contents. Retaining walls and sections of rooms were rebuilt and some of the roofs were strengthened. After being opened to the public, the Lower Ruin became the featured attraction of the monument and drew heavy visitation. In 1950 it was further excavated. An adjacent smaller house, called the Lower Ruin Annex, was dug simultaneously. This project tested subfloor deposits of the principal structure and removed the fill from the poorly preserved rooms of the annex. The former had consisted of sixteen ground-floor rooms and a few second-story units built like those of the Upper Ruin. Stubs of twelve rooms were outlined in the annex. Three burials were exhumed in the two caves.

Many perishable items that had been protected by the caves' dry environment are of special interest. The preserved plant material allowed Vorsila L. Bohrer to accurately identify cultivated and wild plants used for food, medicine, clothing, tools, weapons, containers, and religious objects. Kate P. Kent studied the cotton textiles, many having been worked into items of clothing, such as aprons, wrap-around dresses, shoulder blankets, and belts for females; and breechclouts, kilts, shirts, shoulder blankets, and belts for males.

An intensive archeological project, being carried out by Arizona State University on lands to be flooded by raising the water level behind the Roosevelt Dam on the Salt River, is expected to provide much new information about the Salado culture, of which the Tonto cliff dwellings were a late manifestation.

Most items recovered from National Park Service investigations at Tonto National Monument are stored at the Western Archeological and Conservation Center in Tucson. ◤

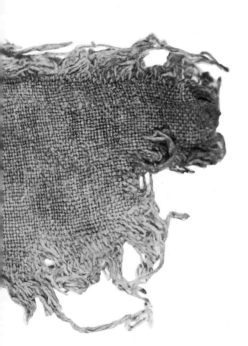

Many cotton textiles were found in the dry caves at Tonto.
SOUTHWEST PARKS AND MONUMENTS ASSOCIATION.

ADDITIONAL READINGS, Tonto National Monument
Steen, Charlie R., Lloyd M. Pierson, Vorsila L. Bohrer, and Kate P. Kent
  1962 *Archeological Studies at Tonto National Monument, Arizona.* Technical Series, Vol. 2. Globe, Arizona: Southwestern Monuments Association.

WALNUT CANYON NATIONAL MONUMENT, ARIZONA

Cultural Significance and Archeological Classification

Among the sheltered ledges of Walnut Canyon are many evidences of tiny cliff houses built by the Sinagua, a Hakataya group that once spread extensively over western Arizona. The archeological remains in the monument were a result of the intermingling in central Arizona of people from all southwestern culture centers and the turmoil and population movements that followed the eleventh-century eruption of Sunset Crater. A strong influx of Anasazi traits from the north is evident.

In-betweens and Outliers: *Hakataya (Sinagua culture)* All-Southwest: *Villages, intermediate between desert, plateau, and mountain-valley zones*

Explorations and Investigations

The antiquities of Walnut Canyon, named for the stand of Arizona walnut trees that grow in the canyon bottom, have been known since the 1880s when Smithsonian Institution expeditions combed the area about Flagstaff. James Stephenson was the first to carefully examine the Walnut Canyon cliff dwellings and to collect objects from them to take back to the Smithsonian. At the turn of the century Jesse W. Fewkes searched for archeological evidence throughout the region.

These expeditions had two purposes. One was to record the sites in maps, photographs, and written notes. The other was to gather artifacts for museum display. Their work recognized regional cultural distinctions and exchange between cultures. Although recent research has changed their basic conclusions only slightly, modern advances in theory and methods have made possible more detailed, accurate observations.

Unfortunately, soon after the ruins of Walnut Canyon became public knowledge, they were disturbed or destroyed for personal or commercial reasons. This continued until the area was placed under National Park Service care in 1933. So much of the material left by the Indians was removed, and the dwellings themselves so defaced or damaged, that our perception of what took place at Walnut Canyon has been derived almost entirely from work at other sites in the vicinity.

Harold S. Colton commenced serious archeological studies in the canyon in 1921, when he surveyed its steep slopes and rims. He devoted most of his time to the large, more obvious sites, recording 120 occupation areas. These included pueblos of one to five rooms, cliff dwellings, "forts," and several pithouses. His description of the cliff dwellings was the first of scientific value.

Colton had begun visiting northeastern Arizona in 1910. In the following years he and his wife, Mary Russell F. Colton, crisscrossed the Navajo and Hopi country on foot and by horseback, wagon, and Model T Ford. Greatly impressed by what they saw, both desired to delve more deeply into the natural and cultural history of the region. In 1926 Colton left the University of Pennsylvania, where he was a professor of zoology, and moved permanently to Flagstaff. His personal interest was archeology; those of his wife were ethnology and art.

Stimulated by Colton's enthusiasm, an organizing committee founded the Northern Arizona Society of Science and Art in 1929, setting up a small museum at the local women's club. Within a year the Museum of Northern Arizona was in operation with Colton as its director. In 1934 the museum began to build permanent storage units, exhibition halls, a library, and research laboratories on land three miles north of town. From these attractive, well-equipped facilities the museum has continued research and educational programs in geology, biology, anthropology, and art of the Colorado Plateau.

Colton is best known for his analytical studies of ancient potsherds, identifying types, their relationships, and distribution. His scheme of pottery classification proved useful when combined with other archeological evidence. Utilizing such ceramic information and other data gleaned by a team of experts, Colton's reconstruction of aboriginal life in the Flagstaff area affords a broad understanding of remains at Walnut Canyon, Wupatki, Tuzigoot, and Montezuma Castle national monuments. Colton died in 1970, leaving the Museum of Northern Arizona as a permanent memorial.

Lyndon Hargrave, a Museum of Northern Arizona staff member, was the first archeologist to dig in the cliff dwellings of Walnut Canyon. In 1932 he cleared part of a nine-room unit beneath a rock overhang on what is now the Island Trail and later stabilized it. Since then, archeology within the monument has been performed by National Park Service personnel in conjunction with programs to care for the cliff dwellings.

Aside from those on Island Trail, approximately thirty other small cliff dwellings in the monument have been stabilized. In the process of the preservation work, some artifacts have been recovered from sites that had not been completely gutted by pothunters. A few whole pottery vessels, several thousand potsherds, fragments of textiles, basketry, sandals, and cordage, as well as tools of stone, bone, and wood, were reclaimed. Also recovered were remnants of vegetable and animal foodstuffs. One cave, thought to have been used for ceremonial purposes, yielded wooden prayer sticks similar to those used in the rituals of modern Pueblo Indians. These prayer sticks (pahos) probably will be deposited with the Hopi and the cave closed to the public.

On the north and south rims a 1985 survey identified 241 sites, including small pueblos, boulder outlines that may be remains of farming plots or terraces, and rock shelters. Examination and evaluation of known sites in Walnut Canyon National Monument for inclusion on the List of Classified Structures resulted in the listing of fifty-six sites in the monument, all but two of which are cliff dwellings. The list is an inventory of the nation's historic or prehistoric structures considered important enough for permanent preservation by the federal government. Expansion that would double the present size of the monument has been proposed.

Archeological specimens collected from Walnut Canyon after the era of pothunting are stored in several locations. These include the Western Archeological and Conservation Center, Tucson; the Museum of Northern Arizona and Northern Arizona University, Flagstaff; the U.S. National Museum, Washington, D.C.; and Walnut Canyon National Monument. ◢◣

ADDITIONAL READINGS, Walnut Canyon National Monument

Baldwin, Anne R., and J. Michael Bremer
  1986 *Walnut Canyon National Monument: An Archeological Survey.* Publications in Anthropology, No. 39. Tucson, Arizona: Western Archeological and Conservation Center, National Park Service.

Colton, Harold S.
  1946 *The Sinagua: A Summary of the Archaeology of the Region of Flagstaff, Arizona.* Bulletin, No. 22. Flagstaff: Museum of Northern Arizona.
  1960 *Black Sand: Prehistory in Northern Arizona.* Albuquerque: University of New Mexico Press.

Gilman, Patricia A.
  1976 *Walnut Canyon National Monument: An Archeological Overview.* Tucson, Arizona: Western Archeological Center, National Park Service.

Schroeder, Albert H.
  1977 *Of Men and Volcanoes: The Sinagua of Northern Arizona.* Globe, Arizona: Southwest Parks and Monuments Association.

Walnut Canyon cliff dwellings,
Walnut Canyon National Monument.
NATT DODGE, NATIONAL PARK SERVICE.

Wupatki communal house, Wupatki National Monument. GEORGE A. GRANT, NATIONAL PARK SERVICE, 1935.

WUPATKI NATIONAL MONUMENT/SUNSET CRATER VOLCANO NATIONAL MONUMENT, ARIZONA

Cultural Significance and Archeological Classification

This is the northern frontier of the kaleidoscope of cultures that extended down to Flagstaff and south into the upper Verde valley. To the Sinagua base, colonists from the south introduced such Hohokam traits as ballcourts, and Anasazi from the north brought plateau-style houses and pottery. Some Mogollon elements and a few traits from the Cohonina branch of the Hakataya also added flavor. These foreign entities sometimes retained their identity for a while, but almost invariably they were subjected to processes of acculturation.

Wupatki's large ruins date from after the eruption of Sunset Crater, when a large influx of newcomers from all directions settled here. The Wupatki region thus is further evidence of the almost constant shift of populations that stimulated general cultural similarities throughout the Southwest.

In-betweens and Outliers: *Hakataya (Sinagua culture)*
All-Southwest: *Villages, Towns, intermediate between plateau, mountain-valley, and desert zones*

Explorations and Investigations

After the Territory of New Mexico was created in 1850, the American government dispatched military expeditions to map its new acquisition. The discovery of gold in California at about the same time underscored the need for safe overland trails across this largely unknown region.

One such expedition in 1851, commanded by Captain Lorenzo Sitgreaves, produced the first known account of the archeological remains in the vicinity of Wupatki. Leaving Zuni, his party worked along the Little Colorado drainage west to the Colorado River, then followed downriver to Fort Yuma. Relative to the Wupatki country, Sitgreaves's diary mentions only that after leaving the Little Colorado they saw ruins of stone houses of considerable size, some three stories high.

Sitgreaves was followed by other government surveys that poked through some of the ruins. However, for the next three decades no more than casual attention was given them until 1885, when Major John Wesley Powell more thoughtfully examined and wrote of them.

Fifteen more years elapsed before another researcher became interested in the heaps of red stone dwellings along the crests of the barren ridges. This was Jesse W. Fewkes, who shot photographs, mapped most of the ancient habitations in the area, and gathered artifacts. Fewkes visited Wupatki several times. Most of the names now applied to ruins in the vicinity originated with him and his associates; many were derived from the Hopi language and legends.

The establishment of Wupatki National Monument in 1924 was due primarily to the work of Samuel A. Barrett, Director of the Milwaukee Public Museum; Harold S. Colton;

and J. C. Clarke, an amateur archeologist from Flagstaff. Barrett located and described fifty-five sites in the district and did some digging in the ruin for which the monument was named. During the 1930s Colton and his Museum of Northern Arizona staff, with funding from the Civil Works Administration, cleared many of the other villages. Subsequently, some excavations, reconnaissance surveys, and stabilization were done by National Park Service personnel. At that time, they estimated that some eight hundred ruins were within the fifty-six square miles of the monument.

The important communal house of Wupatki, or Tall House, so named because of its three-story unit, was cleared of its fallen and drifted debris. Some of the more than one hundred rooms were then rebuilt. After the National Park Service adopted a policy of preserving rather than restoring archeological remains, the reconstructed portions were removed. A group of ruins in Big Hawk Valley on the western edge of the monument, whose interpretation shed further light on central Arizona prehistory, was dug by Watson Smith. Dale King worked the site of Nalakihu, sections of which were later restored and then dismantled. Several other minor clusters of ruins—Lomaki and Wukaki pueblos and the Heiser pithouse—were opened for interpretive purposes. The so-called Citadel, a fifty-one-room house dominating a concentration of smaller units, remains unexcavated. Of particular significance in clarifying cultural relationships was the exposure in 1965 of the Wupatki ballcourt.

For seven seasons between 1981 and 1987 National Park Service archeologist Bruce A. Anderson directed the first intensive archeological inventory survey of the monument. The results increased the number of known sites to 2,268. These ran the full gamut from scatters of potsherds and stone flakes discarded from tool manufacture to simple shelters near farm plots where caretakers likely stayed seasonally. A few rooms were found huddled in the protection of rocky overhangs. Four hundred fifty panels of rock art were noted on dark escarpments. Surveyors encountered large multiroomed buildings stretched along ridge crests. Correlary studies were undertaken of soil types and prehistoric strategies for exploitation of potentially productive farmlands and of settlement patterns. In order to round out knowledge of the Native American usage of the monument territory, ethnoarcheological examination was made of a limited number of Navajo remains left from the late eighteenth century to the present.

Dramatic geological circumstances make Wupatki and its neighboring settlements especially interesting. They are located in and near a craggy, black volcanic field spreading east from the San Francisco Mountains. The principal cinder cone is Sunset Crater, eighteen miles south of Wupatki. Dates obtained from dwelling timbers dug from volcanic ash indicate that it furiously burst into existence in A.D. 1064, causing what must have been a major calamity for the terrified aborigines. Recent studies suggest that at least five additional eruptive episodes may have continued over a two-hundred-year period.

Close to Sunset Crater the scorched land was left blackened, lifeless, or buried beneath a thick coating of rock. Where the ground was not too deeply mantled with volcanic residue, vegetation shortly reappeared; the thin powder of fine ash and cinders proved beneficial to plant growth by absorbing and holding moisture and shading the surface. More water could soak into the ground, and additional supplies of surface water also were created by the interruption of drainages and increase in ground water.

As archeology progressed in the region, it was realized that before the eleventh-century vulcanism only a relatively small population had managed to eke out an existence in this marginal agricultural zone. Within the boundaries of the modern monument, there was no important pre-eruption occupation. Although some use areas still may be buried beneath the ash fall, to date a mere ten sites seem to represent human life around the red rocks of Wupatki prior to the dramatic appearance of Sunset Crater. Nearby, when homes and farm plots were destroyed, residents bundled up their few bits of worldly goods and moved elsewhere. Exactly where remains a mystery, but it was probably just beyond the ring of devastation.

Within several decades after the initial massive eruption, they and other farmers from several slightly varying cultural backgrounds apparently observed the environmental improvement that had come from what had seemed a disaster. Ceramic evidence is that a major infusion of Kayenta Anasazi, possibly from Black Mesa to the northeast, occurred at this time. Sinagua and Cohonina peoples joined them, enriching the cultural content as the eruption had enriched the soil. This is demonstrated by the presence of a southern ballcourt, a northern Great Kiva, and a mixture of pottery types from various derivations.

During the years between A.D. 1130 and 1160 the greatest population growth occurred, estimated to reach approximately twenty-two hundred persons. Such increase in a demanding environment, gripped at the same time in an epoch of subnormal precipitation, was made possible by intensification of various kinds of field and water management techniques. Success apparently was not enduring, however, because the population gradually concentrated into small villages on the rim and mouth of Antelope Mesa in the central part of the monument. The final tree-ring date at A.D. 1212 indicates that abandonment of the entire region likely had begun. Possibly the ash mulching that had helped retain what limited moisture there was had weathered away, making even limited horticulture impossible.

Archeological specimens and the records from the various projects conducted in Wupatki National Monument are divided among three repositories. The Museum of Northern Arizona has the bulk of the materials taken from Wupatki Ruin in the 1930s and from the 1965 excavation of the ballcourt. The National Park Service Western Archeological and Conservation Center in Tucson curates the collections from several surveys and from numerous prestabilization excavations. The visitor center at the monument retains a small assortment, part of which is displayed, with the remainder in storage. ▲

Sinagua black-on-white bowl.
SOUTHWEST PARKS AND MONUMENTS ASSOCIATION.

ADDITIONAL READINGS, Wupatki National Monument/Sunset Crater Volcano National Monument
Anderson, Bruce A., comp.
1990 *The Wupatki Archeological Inventory Survey Project: Final Report.* Professional Paper, No. 35. Santa Fe, New Mexico: Southwest Cultural

Resources Center, National Park Service.

Colton, Harold S.
  1945 Sunset Crater. *Plateau*. Vol. 18, No. 1. Flagstaff: Museum of Northern Arizona.
        7–14.
  1946 *The Sinagua: A Summary of the Archaeology of the Region of Flagstaff,
        Arizona*. Bulletin, No. 22. Flagstaff: Museum of Northern Arizona.
  1960 *Black Sand: Prehistory in Northern Arizona*. Albuquerque: University of New
        Mexico Press.

Davin, Eric, and Gabrielle Dolphin
  1973 Petroglyphs of Wupatki. *Southwestern Lore*. Vol. 39, No. 1. Boulder: Colorado
        Archaeological Society. 1–8.

Hartman, Dana, and Arthur H. Wolf
  1977 *Archeological Assessment of Wupatki National Monument*. Flagstaff: Museum
        of Northern Arizona.

King, Dale S.
  1949 *Nalakihu: Excavations at a Pueblo III Site on Wupatki National Monument,
        Arizona*. Bulletin, No. 23. Flagstaff: Museum of Northern Arizona.

Schaafsma, Polly
  1987 Rock Art at Wupatki: Pots, Textiles, Glyphs. Santa Fe, New Mexico: Exploration,
        Annual Report of School of American Research. 20–27.

Schroeder, Albert H.
  1977 *Of Men and Volcanoes: The Sinagua of Northern Arizona*. Globe, Arizona:
        Southwest Parks and Monuments Association.

Smith, Watson
  1952 *Excavations in Big Hawk Valley, Wupatki National Monument, Arizona*.
        Bulletin, No. 24. Flagstaff: Museum of Northern Arizona.

Ward, Albert E.
  1978 Sinagua Farmers Before the "Black Sand" Fell: An Example from Wupatki
        National Monument. *Limited Activity and Occupation Sites: A Collection of
        Conference Papers*. Edited by Albert E. Ward. Contributions to Anthropological
        Studies, No. 1. Albuquerque, New Mexico: Center for Anthropological Studies.
        135–46.

Some pre-eruption sites have been found in lava flows at Sunset Crater Volcano National Monument, Arizona. GEORGE H. H. HUEY

Anasazi granary, Zion National Park. GEORGE H. H. HUEY.

ZION NATIONAL PARK/BRYCE CANYON NATIONAL PARK, UTAH

Cultural Significance and Archeological Classification

Although no Paleo-Indian or Archaic materials have yet been identified within the park boundaries, scattered finds across southern Utah confirm human presence during those periods. As native peoples adopted a more sedentary mode of life partially sustained by horticulture, they settled in the canyon bottomlands of what is now Zion National Park and exploited nearby high country for game and raw materials. Their numbers never were large, and their cultural advancement from Basket Maker through Pueblo III retained a provincialism considered diagnostic of the Virgin Branch of the Anasazi.

The high Paunsaugunt Plateau of Bryce Canyon National Park was primarily a resource area for local Kayenta or Virgin Anasazi and Fremont groups with few or no permanent structures.

After A.D. 1300 both park areas were visited periodically by Southern Paiutes who remained in the vicinity until driven out by Mormon settlers at the end of the nineteenth century.

Anasazi: *Virgin Branch; Basket Maker III; Pueblo I, II, III, IV*
In-betweens and Outliers: *Fremont (San Rafael, Parowan)*
All-Southwest: *Hamlets, peripheral plateau zone*

Explorations and Investigations

In 1858 Nephi Johnson, a Mormon missionary to the Paiutes, was the first white man to explore the upper Virgin River and Zion Canyon. Soon the village of Springdale was established near the canyon's mouth. A few years later one of the settlers, Isaac Behuin, began farming land near where the present park lodge is situated. He was followed by a succession of homesteaders.

A 1908 government survey was so compelling in its description of the scenic and geologic wonders of the canyons and associated highlands that the next year President William Howard Taft issued a proclamation establishing Mukuntuweap National Monument. The name later was changed to Zion and in 1919 its status was upgraded to a national park.

Meanwhile, in the 1860s another Mormon thrust from the Salt Lake valley brought settlers to within a few miles of Bryce Canyon. They were driven back by warring Ute, Paiute, and Navajo bands determined to hold back the encroaching tide of white men. A Mormon militia dispatched for service in the resulting Black Hawk War is credited with first exploring portions of the Bryce-Paria region. Once that conflict ended in Indian defeat and the concurrent national Civil War concluded, government surveyors such as Powell, Thompson, Dutton, and Wheeler took to the field. In their wake came white colonists, who opened farmlands at the eastern foot of the park. One of them was Ebenezer Bryce.

It was not until 1923 that the fantastically eroded limestone escarpment and the evergreen Paunsaugunt Plateau were set aside as Bryce Canyon National Monument. Five years later it was made a national park.

The relative remoteness of these two facilities, their location on the northernmost periphery of the Anasazi domain, and the lack of large surface ruins meant that archeological research was slow in taking place. The first such survey in Zion National Park occurred in 1933–34 when Ben Wetherill, working then under a Civil Works Administration project, and of the family known for having brought the cliff dwellings of Mesa Verde to public attention forty-five years earlier, recorded nineteen prehistoric sites within the park boundaries. Eight were excavated. For comparative purposes Wetherill also documented a considerable number of sites just outside the park proper. However, little came of this effort because most of Weatherill's notes were lost in a fire. Not until 1955 in an overview of his work did National Park Service archeologist Albert Schroeder expand upon Wetherill's survey and analyze extant artifact collections.

Since that initial work, further research at Zion National Park has emphasized management developments, ruins stabilization, and possible visitation impacts on archeological resources in Zion, Parunuweap, and Kolob canyons. Nevertheless, more traditional, small-scale studies have been carried out by staffs and students from the University of Utah, University of California at Los Angeles, and the College of Southern Utah.

Similarly, between 1974 and 1990 only brief archeological reconnaissances and preconstruction surveys have been undertaken in Bryce Canyon National Park by government personnel or through contracts with private companies. Forty sites within the park and another 109 sites on adjoining Paunsaugunt Plateau have been recorded, several of which were test excavated.

More than one hundred fifty sites now are known for the Zion precincts. Just one-fifth of these have evidence of structures. These include pithouses, small dry-laid masonry surface rooms sometimes arranged in a semi-circle around pit structures, dry-laid masonry cists, and rock and mud-plastered granaries of a chimney shape. Other sites are overhangs used as shelters, rock art panels, and concentrated scatters of sherds and lithics. Although some rock art appears of a Fremont style, most remains are attributable to Virgin Anasazi. Zion Canyon is thought to have experienced more seasonal occupation than Parunuweap Canyon, with the Kolob heights serving as hunting and gathering grounds. A Pueblo II cultural expression is dominant.

While geographically the area of Bryce Canyon National Park was a potential contact zone between Virgin and Kayenta Anasazi and Parowan and San Rafael Fremont, utilization of the immediate region by all groups was either as occasional or seasonal resource-procurement camps or was represented through trade goods. Excavations are needed to determine positive affiliations. The Bryce highlands, like Zion, were vacated by A.D. 1150–1200, to be sparsely used within a century by wandering Southern Paiute.

Notes and specimens from Zion National Park are housed at the park headquarters, the Laboratory of Tree-Ring Research of the University of Arizona, the Museum of Anthropology at the University of Michigan, and the National Park Service Midwest Archeological Center, Lincoln, Nebraska. ▲

ADDITIONAL READINGS, Zion National Park, Bryce Canyon National Park
Aikens, C. Melvin
    1965 *Excavations in Southwest Utah.* Anthropological Papers, No. 76. Salt Lake City: University of Utah.
    1966 *Virgin-Kayenta Cultural Relationships.* Anthropological Papers, No. 79. Salt Lake City: University of Utah.
Bezy, John
    1980 *Bryce Canyon: the Story Behind the Scenery.* Las Vegas, Nevada: KC Publications.
Connor, Melissa A., and Susan M. Vetter
    1986 *Archeological Investigations at Zion National Park.* Midwest Archeological Center, Occasional Studies in Anthropology, No. 19. Lincoln, Nebraska: Midwest Archeological Center, National Park Service.
Crawford, J. L.
    1988 *Zion National Park, Towers of Stone.* Springdale, Utah: Zion Natural History Association.
Schroeder, Albert H.
    1955 *Archeology of Zion Park.* Anthropological Papers, No. 22. Salt Lake City: University of Utah.

INDEX